LITERARY WASHINGTON

About the Author

David Cutler is a writer, editor, literary agent and publishing consultant. A former vice president of Washington Independent Writers, he is president of *David Cutler & Associates*, a literary services and publishing consulting firm.

Mr. Cutler is also a founding partner of *FeatureMedia Films & Books, Inc.*, a feature film/book production company, and chairman and principal shareholder of *Futurebooks, Inc.*, a company formed to package and develop new kinds of publishing technologies (including CD-ROM, hypermedia, lasercard and CD-Interactive reading systems).

Before starting his own companies, Mr. Cutler was communications manager at the Washington Convention and Visitors Association, where he wrote and produced seventeen tourism publications a year about the Washington, D.C. metropolitan area.

He holds a bachelor's degree (magna cum laude) in English from Carleton College and a master's degree in English literature from the University of Virginia. Mr. Cutler lives in Oakton, Virginia with his wife, Laurie, and daughters Leah and Mariah, to whom this book is dedicated.

LITERARY WASHINGTON

Second Edition

*A Complete Guide to the
Literary Life in the
Nation's Capital*

DAVID CUTLER

MADISON BOOKS
Lanham • New York • London

Published by Madison Books
4720 Boston Way
Lanham, Maryland 20706

3 Henrietta Street
London WC2E 8LU England

Distributed by National Book Network

The paper used in this publication meets the minimum
requirements of American National Standard for
Information Sciences—Permanence of Paper for
Printed Library Materials, ANSI Z39.48–1984. ∞™
Manufactured in the United States of America.

Library of Congress Cataloging-in-Publication Data

Cutler, David, 1956–
Literary Washington : a complete guide to the
literary life in the nation's capital / David
Cutler.—2nd ed.
p.
1. American literature—Washington (D.C.)—Bio-
bibliography.   2. Authors, American—Homes and
haunts—Washington (D.C.)   3. Literary
landmarks—Washington (D.C.)—Guidebooks.
4. Washington (D.C.)—Intellectual life.
5. Washington (D.C.) in literature.   6. Washington
(D.C.)—Directories.   7. Washington (D.C.)—
Tours.   I. Title.
PS144.W18C8   1992
810.9'9753—dc20   92–11144 CIP

ISBN 0–8191–8245–1 (pbk. : alk. paper)

Contents

Preface

This book, now in its second edition, was supposed to be easier to research and write the second time around. At least, that's what I distinctly remember saying to my publisher, Jed Lyons, over breakfast at the American City Diner, when we met to discuss how I might revise *Literary Washington* and bring it up-to-date.

While applying ourselves to the Diner's sizable helpings of french toast, eggs, hash browns, etc., we pondered how to make the book even better. That the first edition of *Literary Washington* had sold well, received favorable endorsements and appeared on a number of local "recommended reading" lists was cause to celebrate. We also agreed it justified a need to keep the book current. We then proceeded to negotiate terms for a second edition over coffee, with the understanding that when the bill for breakfast arrived we would each pay *exactly* half of the total amount.

My job, as I remember describing it that morning, would be to eliminate some outdated or erroneous information in the book, make adjustments in the book's structure and tone and add a complete index for reference purposes. The second edition of *Literary Washington* would come rolling off the presses "in no time," I asserted. Even as we finished our meal and parted company, I had every confidence that this plan would work.

In retrospect, of course, one sees the errors of one's ways. One also realizes that, during these blithe conversations with one's publisher, one should have one's head examined for thinking that a complex reference book like *Literary Washington* can ever be easy to do. It wasn't easy the first time around, it wasn't easy this time around and I don't think it ever will be.

On the other hand, as noted in this preface last time, I believe that every worthwhile book like *Literary Washington* finds its own way of happening. And so, once again, I'm happy to have included so much in this edition about the literary life in the nation's capital, and apologize at the outset if some important or useful information may have been inadvertently omitted.

In this book, I have tried to show how a city's

character is both reflected and shaped by its writers and readers. Perhaps this second edition of *Literary Washington* may inspire you to discover more about the literary life here, past or present. Perhaps it will help you find a new bookstore, or join a local writer's organization or attend a local literary reading or take a local writing course. What you read in these pages may prompt action, thereby enriching the literary life around us.

Should this happen, or if you know of some aspect of the literary life in the Washington area which I've neglected to mention, please send a letter to my attention, c/o Madison Books, 4720 Boston Way, Lanham, MD 20706. I would appreciate hearing from you.

I hope that you enjoy *Literary Washington* and use it often.

—**DAVID CUTLER**
December 1991

About This Book

While scholars, critics and others may debate what is "literary" and what is not, *Webster's Dictionary* is quite clear on the subject. The operational phrases regarding the definition of "literary" in *Webster's* are "a: of, relating to or having the characteristics of humane learning or literature"; "b: bookish"; and "c: of or relating to books." These three notions of the word "literary," *taken together*, inform the choices and selections made in researching and writing this book.

Within this second edition of *Literary Washington*, readers will find a mixture of the popular and the highbrow, the traditional and the contemporary, the classic and the not-so-classic. It has never been, nor will it ever be, the editorial policy of *Literary Washington* to be intentionally exclusionary. If a local person, company or organization is legitimately involved in writing, editing, researching, representing, publishing, publicizing, recognizing or in some other way supporting literary or "bookish" endeavors (as defined above) in any genre, then that person, company or organization can, should and/or will be included in this book.

To this end, every effort has been made to consult all primary and secondary sources available to ensure the accuracy and completeness of *Literary Washington*. The information in this edition was current as of March, 1992. Unfortunately, in a work of this size and scope, errors and omissions do sometimes occur. Should you spot any, please send a letter to the author, c/o Madison Books, 4720 Boston Way, Lanham, MD 20706. Your remarks and assistance will be greatly appreciated.

Having defined "literary" for purposes of this book, it makes sense to also define the second part of the book's title. For purposes of this edition, "Washington" always refers to Washington, D.C. and the suburban areas in Northern Virginia and Maryland which comprise the Washington, D.C. metropolitan area. In addition, this book contains information on literary people, places and activities which may be found in an extended geographic area bounded by Winchester, Virginia on the east, Annapolis, Maryland on the west, just below Baltimore, Maryland to the north and just above Charlottesville, Virginia to the south.

Regrettably, this limitation excludes a number of prominent Baltimore and Charlottesville authors and some prominent regional companies and organizations from the listings herein. However, as I think most readers will agree, the "extended" Washington metropolitan area doesn't reach so far as to include either Baltimore or Charlottesville yet, although both cities have substantial "literary lives" of their own.

Readers of the first edition of *Literary Washington* will note some significant changes in this edition. The "Literary & Tour Maps" section, which folded out of the back covers of copies of the first edition, has been dropped from this edition for two reasons: (1) the rights to reproduce both maps were not readily available before this book went to press and (2) binding the maps into the book would have unnecessarily raised the book's list price.

In place of maps, this edition of *Literary Washington* features a much-needed *Index* instead. The *Index*, which contains all significant proper names mentioned in the book, will help readers more readily find information listed herein.

One final note. As a popular reference book, *Literary Washington* was designed to be used regularly and often. Any suggestions you might have on how it can be enhanced, altered or improved are welcome.

—DAVID CUTLER

Acknowledgments

Once again, I am indebted to my patient, supportive family and to many friends and colleagues for their help in making this edition of *Literary Washington* possible.

For this edition of the book, chief credit for its success goes to Dorian Patchin, who worked tirelessly to check facts, run down leads and type up entries at all hours of the day and night when he wasn't working at *The Washington Post*. Dorian's commitment to *Literary Washington* is a matter of legend among those familiar with this book, and his good humor and friendly disposition were indispensable throughout. He also plays a wicked game of racquetball.

This edition was strengthened by advance information provided by Beth DeFrancis from her excellent book *The Writer's Guide to Metropolitan Washington* (Woodbine House, 1991), an act of supreme literary generosity which will not go unrewarded. Useful suggestions and improvements for this edition were also made to me by Donald Ritchie, Jacklyn Potter, Betty Parry, Paul Dickson, Ruth Kampmann and Michael Schaffner.

The people at Madison Books continue to get high marks for their patience and grace under pressure in dealing with my notorious inability to meet their deadlines. My heartfelt thanks go to Jed Lyons, Jennifer Smith, Lynn Gemmell, Gisèle Byrd and others at Madison who manage to put up with me. For the first edition of *Literary Washington*, my thanks go to Chuck Lean (now gone from Madison) who first championed and acquired this book.

Since its inception, *Literary Washington* has received generous support and encouragement from Washington Independent Writers, the largest regional writer's organization in the country. As an unabashed fan of WIW, as well as a former officer, I'm continually amazed by this dynamic organization and how it continues to improve Washington's literary life.

Regarding the first edition of *Literary Washington*, Zak Mettger and Ed Terrien deserve special mention for their substantial contributions to the research and compilation of the original material used in this book. Their patience, perception and stamina will forever be appreciated.

For reviewing portions of the first edition of *Literary Washington* in 1989 before publication, I'd once again like to thank each member of an Editorial Board assembled at the time for the purpose:

John Y. Cole, director, The Center for the Book, Library of Congress

Doris Grumbach, author and book critic (National Public Radio)

Rudy Maxa, former senior writer, *Washingtonian* Magazine

Diane Rehm, host, The Diane Rehm Show (WAMU-FM Radio)

Colin Walters, book editor, *The Washington Times*

From among the dozens of people who have reviewed sections of this book at one time or another and made helpful suggestions, I'd especially like to thank Gail Ross, Tim Wells, John Greenya, Mark Perry, Marguerite Kelly, Isolde Chapin and Bill Adler, Jr. for their contributions.

To all "friends of the book"—including my partner Jeri Held, my many friends at GTE Spacenet (especially Barbara Foelber and Shari Furst), my longtime friend Mark Hulbert, dozens of helpful research librarians and so many others—a heartfelt thank you. And to my parents, Tina and Bruce, I thank you for giving John and Ann and me the love for reading and writing that animates this book.

Finally, to my wife, Laurie, and my daughters Leah and Mariah—this closing note is to once again inform you that your husband/father is finished with the latest edition of what we affectionately call "the book from hell." I am therefore available for social interaction and family outings again. I love all three of you very much, and rededicate this book to you.

Introduction

Words are all we have.

—SAMUEL BECKETT

Words are so strong, so palpably real, that they can propel us into danger and then miraculously snatch us from destruction. They can soothe, they can woo, they can hurt, they can sing, they can paint pictures or tell stories or be whispered quietly into the night.

This book is about the power of words and the people who write them. It is about a metropolitan area teeming with literary life, a place where more than 350 well-known and lesser-known American book authors presently reside. It is about hundreds of book and audio publishers, literary agents, book producers, organization directors, readings coordinators, teachers, scholars, editors, book fair promoters, librarians, archivists, bookstore owners and private book dealers. Working mostly on their own, these people have paradoxically managed to create one of the most exciting and vibrant literary "communities" in the United States.

This book is even about certain restaurant and saloon owners, who not only allow writers to congregate within the walls of their establishments and imbibe liquids of various kinds, but who actually permit these very same writers to run tabs, consequently helping to contribute, in their own way, to literary achievement throughout the Washington area.

Here in the nation's capital, it was ever thus. On January 21, 1900, *The Washington Post* reported under the headline "A Bright Galaxy of Pensmiths" the following news:

> In the vast concourse of people who pursue their various callings in Washington, no class finds better tools of its craft than the writers of books. These are attracted from larger and more densely populated cities, from old associations, from lifetime friends, to come here and seek among strangers what no other metropolis can give.
>
> Washington is also a city admirably adapted to awaken

in its own growing children whatever germs of talent
await the transfiguring touch of life. There is inspiration
in its very atmosphere and ideas float about like sun-
beams, plentiful, if somewhat elusive to grasp. . . .

Bearing these facts in mind, it is not strange that so
many writers in Washington have wooed and won fame,
and that the city is not behind her competitors in the race
for literary supremacy.

Skipping ahead 34 years, one may also find a similar
(though less flowery) refrain in *The Washington Post*,
this time under the headline "Capital's Famous Authors
Sigh for Bohemia":

Washington has neither a Greenwich Village nor a Latin
Quarter, but it stands out as a literary center which can
boast of more nationally-known authors than any city of
its size in the country.

Scattered from Alexandria to Georgetown are writers
whose names are household words from Maine to California, and yet between them there is practically no
community of interest. In fact, many of them have never
made the acquaintance of their contemporaries who are
producing "best sellers," and know of them only by
reputation.

Finally, if we skip forward in the pages of *The Washington Post* to the recent present, another related observation about Washington's "literary community" by
local poet Anthony Hecht may be found in the July 8,
1990 issue of *Book World*:

I don't think of a literary community as one in which
everybody meets everybody else or even meets one another very frequently. But if you define a literary community as something that makes for a general intellectual
life at a high level, I think that's here in Washington.

Which brings us to the central question of this book:
How and where can "Literary Washington" be found
today? While each chapter in this book makes some
attempt to answer this question, there are some other
revealing insights to consider as well.

According to the latest available statistics, as compiled
from 1987 U.S. Census data and released by the Department of Commerce, the Washington metropolitan area
ranks seventh nationally in bookstore sales per capita.
Boston and Chicago, which placed third and fourth in
the rankings, outsold the Washington area by less than

15 percent. The rankings, which obviously don't reflect the phenomenal growth in numbers of local bookstores during the past two years, may be confirmed by perusing listings for more than 400 bookstores and 30 private book dealers in the chapter entitled *Bookstores & Book Dealers*.

Here's another insight into "Literary Washington." In a story entitled "This Month It's Tolstoy," which appeared in the local magazine *Washingtonian* (April 1990), journalist Leslie Milk identifies a number of enthusiastic book clubs which have sprung up throughout the city and in the suburbs. In describing her own experiences with a book club she helped to start in 1970, Milk visualizes "standing alone on an endless plain . . . a prairie of infinite possibility—wonderful books to be read or reread, stretching as far as the eye can see." Her account in this article of so many serious readers in the Washington area reflects a large and diverse audience which actively supports literary achievement.

Or consider a specific example I mentioned in the introduction of the first edition of this book, published in 1989. At the time, I had recently received a promotional brochure from Book-of-the-Month Club. After taking advantage of their "exceptional offer" and signing up, I sat down to peruse the list of 97 top books they wanted me to choose from. From that list of books, eleven were written by local authors—William Greider, Stanley Karnow, Jane Mayer and Doyle McManus, Pete Earley, Hedrik Smith, Richard Restak, David Brinkley, Daniel Boorstin, Neil Sheehan, David Wise and I. F. Stone (now deceased). Aside from New York and possibly Boston or Los Angeles, I doubt that any other U.S. city could make a similar claim.

Why do some cities have a discernible literary life and others don't? This question is often asked, and yet it is both narrow-minded and unfair. *Every* city has a literary life, if care is taken to find and preserve it. For the most part, however, Americans have been notoriously bad about chronicling and preserving this nation's literary heritage. Many of the fascinating anecdotes contained in the *Historic Authors* chapter of this book were quite difficult to find, and virtually all of the places where these authors once lived and worked have been sadly destroyed.

Since 1801, when the first book was published in George Washington's "new Federal City," literary endeavor has thrived here. Like life itself, as each year passes, the size and scope of *Literary Washington* continues to grow. There are more pages in this edition of *Literary Washington* than in the original edition published in 1989. Each week, I receive a new press release about another book being published or another new bookstore opening its doors or another new publisher soliciting manuscripts.

This is as it should be. For, if we are to believe the demographers, Washington is far and away the most affluent and educated metropolitan area in the United States. Researching and writing books falls to the city's many authors, who are becoming increasingly more numerous and diverse. Editing, researching, representing, publishing, publicizing, recognizing or in some other way supporting literary endeavor in the Washington area falls to the rest of the people, companies and organizations listed in this book. And the nation's capital is still fortunate to have, in Barbara Bush, a First Lady who is committed to improving literacy for all Americans.

Charlton Ogburn, Jr., once described the history of the nation's capital as dividing itself into three periods:

> The first [period], tapering off through the 1830's, was a time in which the American people were very much aware of the world abroad and looked to Washington for leadership: there were strong Presidents and the capital was an exciting place. The same may be said, for the most part, of 20th century Washington, the third period. The middle period was one of national self-absorption when, with the towering exception of the Civil War years, Washington followed rather then led the country.

I hope that the careful reader of *Literary Washington* will see what Ogburn describes reflected in these pages, as it seems this city is poised for even greater things to come.

There abounds more literary life here than any single writer can hope to chronicle, and far more than this slim volume could hold. What books have wrought continues to animate this bureaucratic and sometimes faceless city along the banks of the Potomac, revealing its humanity.

—**DAVID CUTLER**
December, 1991

Historic Authors

> Literature is, primarily, a chain of connections from the
> past to the present. It is not reinvented every morning,
> as some bad writers like to believe.
>
> **—GORE VIDAL**

The nation's capital, steeped in tradition and filled with memorials and monuments to the past, is captivated with news of the moment. Every summer or early fall, another national scandal comes to the fore, disturbing the otherwise serene pace of life here and prompting furious debate. Many local television sets are permanently tuned to Ted Turner's 24–hour Cable News Network (CNN), which is an omnipresent force. And Washington's main streets perennially fill with interest groups of one kind or another, drawn to the nation's capital in hopes of affecting the daily course of events.

Such intense concern for the present, however, has often led to a neglect of the past. The price for this neglect may be seen in many aspects of this city, whether by the swift, sure stroke of a developer's wrecking ball or by the slow water torture of witnessing yet another self-serving committee of inquiry up on Capitol Hill.

Over the years, however, the nation's capital has also suffered equal, quieter losses in the neglect of its own rich literary heritage. While other American cities may be commended for doing a great deal to preserve the landmarks and memory of famous authors who resided there, the same cannot be said for attempts to preserve this city's literary past. And that is a shame, because there are many stories from that past which, if translated to the present, would have people talking.

Imagine, for instance, a modern-day Anne Royall sitting upon the President's clothes while he swims in the Potomac, refusing to move until she is granted an interview. Imagine a modern-day President being verbally assaulted by the likes of Walt Whitman, who once wrote: "The President eats dirt and excrement for his daily meals, likes it and tries to force it on the States." Picture a modern-day Joaquin Miller roaming Pennsylvania Avenue, bedecked in his high-heeled boots, tasseled sombrero, bright bandana and fur coat with gold-nugget buttons, reciting poems at full voice from his *Songs of the Sierras*. Or a modern-day Oscar Wilde, regaling guests at a fancy cocktail party while dressed in his dark waistcoat, knee breeches, silk stockings and patent leather pumps.

This chapter contains many such stories and anecdotes about 39 historic American authors, now deceased, who lived and/or worked in the Washington area for a time. In addition, there are a few entries concerning historic American authors who, after arriving here as corpses, proceeded to take up permanent residency within the Washington area whether they wanted to or not.

It should be noted that some of the authors mentioned in this chapter are not typically associated with the Washington area, including Bret Harte, James Thurber, Paul Lawrence Dunbar, Dashiell Hammett, F. Scott Fitzgerald, Mark Twain and Ezra Pound. For many years, the nation's capital was a less-than-desirable place to live, and people came and went. So if a historic American author voluntarily or involuntarily spent "some" time here for any interesting reason at all, he or she got mentioned below. Those authors who, without choosing, came to be buried here have also received their due.

Some of these authors, wildly successful in their own time, are barely known to us today. Take Emma Dorothy Eliza Nevitt (E.D.E.N.) Southworth, who, during the last fifty years of the nineteenth century, wrote 73 novels, many of which sold more than a million copies each—an astonishing figure for any time. Today, Southworth is virtually unread. Conversely, the public acclaim we now bestow on Walt Whitman was largely absent during the poet's long lifetime.

In some respects, Washington is still a transient city. It is certainly a place of transience for U.S. Presidents, many of whom wrote a great deal while in office. In my opinion, only two U.S. Presidents—Theodore Roosevelt and Woodrow Wilson—merited inclusion in this chapter. This is because each man wrote a copious amount of "pure literature" in addition to the usual quota of state papers, articles, memoirs, personal correspondence, diaries and political tracts one expects most Presidents to write.

While it is true that other Presidents (notably Jefferson, Madison, Lincoln and Kennedy) wrote brilliantly, none in my opinion wrote so much for the popular audience or cultivated the literary life as completely as Roosevelt and Wilson did. In addition, Wilson was the only U.S. President who chose to retire to a house in Washington after his term of office was over. That house, located at 2340 S Street NW, is open to the public today.

There is another group of illustrious historic authors who resided here in Washington and yet, with one exception, aren't listed in this chapter. These are any now-deceased poets who came to Washington to serve as Consultants in Poetry at the Library of Congress. Except for Archibald MacLeish, who resided in the nation's capital for many years, other such poets (including Robert Frost, Robert Lowell, Randall Jarell, Allen Tate and Stephen Spender) spent so little time in town during their appointments at the Library that they might be described more as visitors than residents.

Whenever known, mention is made in this chapter of where a historic author lived in the Washington area. Sadly, nearly all of these residences are now gone. The demands of "development" have consumed them, destroying our tangible links to the past and obliterating any reminders of literature's human dimension. This is abundantly clear after perusing James M. Goode's excellent book, *Capital Losses: A Cultural History of Washington's Destroyed Buildings* (Smithsonian Institution Press, 1979), an invaluable resource used in compiling information for this chapter.

After uncovering a large amount of information while researching this chapter, I should note that the chapter is by no means complete. Frankly, a full-length book on the subject would be a helpful and welcome addition to any reader's collection.

Until that book becomes available, readers of this chapter may find brief sketches of some historic American authors who lived, worked and/or now find themselves buried in the nation's capital. At best, it is a fleeting glimpse into Washington's rich and varied literary past.

Henry Adams   Author, historian, novelist, educator (1838–1918).

The popular fictional genre we now call the "Washington novel" was invented by Adams in 1880, with the publication of his brilliant work *Democracy*. The novel examines the financial and political scandals of the Grant administration, while skillfully capturing the political affairs of Washington in the decade following the Civil War.

In his time, no man better knew the ins and outs of both "political" and "literary" Washington than Henry Adams. The grandson of President John Quincy Adams, he served as private secretary to his father, a Massachusetts Congressman, worked the city as a newspaper correspondent and circulated about town with a keen eye for the latest developments. His vantage point for observation was ideal: he built his home across from the White House, on the present site of the *Hay-Adams Hotel* (at *16th & H Streets NW*).

Perhaps no finer literary salon has ever existed in our nation than in the home of Henry Adams. He and his wife, Marian, served up breakfasts that became a local institution in the late 1880s. They were a witty, urbane pair; she once described her husband as a man "who chews more than he bites off." In time, they came to be regarded as Washington's foremost private citizens.

Even with his consuming social activities and prodigious correspondence, Adams was able to sustain a considerable literary output. Four years following his first novel, he brought out a second, *Esther*, which was less successful with the public but was thought by Adams to be the better work. An accomplished historian, Adams also wrote the nine-volume *History of the United States During the Administration of Jefferson and Madison*. He followed with biographies of Albert Gallatin and John Randolph, two more novels, a study of medievalism and his superb autobiography *The Education of Henry Adams*, which was actually published after his death. It received the Pulitzer Prize in 1919.

The home of Adams was built as an attached dwelling to the home of his friend (and Secretary of State) John Hay by architect Henry Hobson Richardson, who designed a common facade for both structures. Here, as Adams recalls in his autobiography:

> Hay and Adams had the advantage of looking out of their windows on the antiquities of Lafayette Square, with the sense of having all that any one had; all that the world had to offer; all that they wanted in life. . . . Their chief title to consideration was their right to look out of their windows on great men, alive or dead, in Lafayette Square, a privilege which had nothing to do with their writings.

Although the adjoining houses were among the most important private residences ever built in Washington, they were razed in 1927 by builder Harry Wardman to make way for the Hay-Adams Hotel. However, the ground-floor arches of the homes were rescued and reinstalled as main and garage entrances to a Tudor house which currently stands at *2618 31st Street NW*.

Adams is buried in *Rock Creek Cemetery*, off North Capitol Street at *Rock Creek Church Road & Webster Street NW*, in a setting designed by architect Stanford White. The grave of his wife, who committed suicide after her father's death in 1885, is in the same cemetery, and is graced by a famous sculpture by Augustus Saint-Gaudens, the leading American sculptor of the nineteenth century. Both graves are unmarked.

When Mark Twain saw Saint-Gauden's statue, which was called "The Peace of God," it is said that Twain renamed the statue "Grief." Others have called the work "Despair" or "Mourning." Critic Alexander Wolcott called the seated statue "the most beautiful thing ever fashioned by the hand of man on this continent." A replica of the statue also stands in the courtyard of the National Museum of American Art.

Louisa May Alcott   Novelist, memoirist (1832–1888).

Disdaining what she called the "trap" of marriage, Alcott set her sights on a career that might give her family financial support. This she finally achieved with the huge success which accompanied publication of her 1869 novel, *Little Women*.

Embarking on the writing life, Alcott wrote several unproduced plays and dozens of sketches, stories and poems, some of which first appeared in *The Atlantic Monthly*. In 1854, she published her first book, *Flower Fables*, but her writing career was then interrupted by a call to serve as a nurse in Washington during the Civil War.

Reporting to what was then the *Union Hotel*, at *30th & M Streets NW (Northeast Corner)*, Alcott found the establishment converted into a hospital for the treatment of contagious diseases and overflowing with pain and misery. She worked here as a nurse for a time, but being exposed to so much suffering and death overcame her and she experienced a nervous breakdown.

Alcott's vivid letters, describing medical conditions of the time, were later collected in her book *Hospital Sketches*. Today, a gas station sits on the site of the former hotel where Alcott nursed hundreds of Union troops.

Stephen Vincent Benét   Poet, novelist, short-story writer (1898–1943).

Although this Washington-born writer may best be known for his famous short story "The Devil and Daniel Webster" (1937), Benét's true strength was as a folk balladist. Even his folk tale about Webster is really prose in name only.

History, tradition and a deep interest in contemporary national issues served to inform all of Benét's published works. He poured exhaustive period detail into his emotional epic poem *John Brown's Body*, for which he received the Pulitzer Prize for Poetry in 1929. Benét also received a second Pulitzer for his epic poem *Western Star* in 1943.

As a young boy, in 1901, Benét lived with his family just down the block from James Thurber and his family, near *20th & I Streets NW* (now all office buildings). Thurber recalled in a private letter the time when he and Benét worked together during World War I in Washington:

> In 1918, when I was a code clerk in the State Department, Steve Benét was also one, until he went to Ordnance. He sat across the table from me, both of us fresh out of college, Yale and Ohio State respectively, he sporting his Wolf's Head pin, and my vest bespangled with the pins of Phi Psi, Sigma Delta Chi, and Sphinx, Senior Honorary at Ohio State (I was taken into that the same time as Elliot Nugent and Chic Hartley). I lost track of those pins darn near forty years ago.

Benét's brother, poet and novelist William Rose Benét, said that Stephen's "poetry was, from the first, a bright valor in his heart."

Ambrose Bierce   Short-story writer, essayist, journalist (1842–1914).

Having done his part to help William Randolph Hearst defeat the notorious "refunding bill" of 1896, witty, vitriolic Bierce returned to Washington two years later to set up shop as a feature writer for the Hearst chain. "Bitter Bierce" seemed well suited for the job, keeping hypocritical politicians on their toes with his mordant approach to any doings on Capitol Hill. For the next decade, Bierce performed for Hearst in all things, with occasional time off for travel.

The next phase of Bierce's life found him pursuing an independent writing career, building on the successes of his published books *Can Such Things Be?* (1893), *The Devil's Dictionary* (1906) and *In the Midst of Life*. Life did seem to be going well for Bierce, as he prepared for the publication of his *Collected Works* in 1913. He seemed to enjoy hobnobbing with his cronies along "*Newspaper Row*," and serving as cook and host in his living quarters in the *Olympia Apartments* (at *16th & Euclid Streets NW*) for brilliant Sunday breakfasts.

But Bierce was not a happy man. One autumn day in 1913, he wrote to his sister Lora a short letter message:

> I go away tomorrow for a long time, so this is only to say good-bye. I think there is nothing else worth saying; therefore you will naturally expect a long letter. What an intolerable world this would be if we said nothing but what is worth saying! And did nothing foolish—like going to Mexico and South America. . . .
>
> Good-bye—if you hear of my being stood up against a Mexican stone wall and shot to rags please know that I think that a pretty good way to depart this life. It beats old age, disease or falling down the cellar stairs. To be a Gringo in Mexico—ah, that is euthanasia!

The next day, Bierce set out on this mysterious journey, seeking "that good, kind darkness." It is thought he found what he was looking for amidst the turmoil of the Mexican Revolution, for he vanished utterly, never to return to his apartment in the nation's capital.

Sterling Brown   Poet, essayist, critic, lecturer, educator (1901–1989).

It is saddening to realize that Brown is so recently gone from Washington's literary scene. His devotion to his Howard University students, past and present, was legendary, and he willingly sacrificed time from his own writing to invest in the future of promising young talent.

Discussing his role as professor, Brown once told a newspaper reporter: "We give extra. I have given extra. That's the reason I am not a writer of more books, because I gave my creative energy to the classroom, and to the conferences and to people coming to this house and sitting down."

His home in the *Brookland* section of upper *Northeast Washington* was always bubbling with activity. According to *Washington Post* columnist William Raspberry, "the most incredible assortment of people would show up. The group could include a stiff professor or two, people from SNCC [the Student Nonviolent Coordinating Committee], white English teachers from the suburbs, usually a reporter or two. It was just fun. He would talk about other writers, kick their butts sometimes or say how great they were. He would give value to the thoughts of the people around him in the room. It made you feel included in this grand salon, not simply to show up, but to be treated like what you thought had merit."

Brown's collection of poems entitled *Southern Road* was published in 1932. Critics and readers alike were impressed with his ear for music in language and his capacity for humor. Brown was one of the first intellectual writers to appropriate folk material for purposes of crafting serious-minded poetry. On the heels of *Southern Road*, Brown brought out several important works of literary criticism. Some of his other books are *The Last Ride of Wild Bill* and *Eleven Narrative Poems*. His *Collected Poems* was published in 1980.

Born in Washington and educated at Dunbar High School, Brown went on to earn a master's degree from Harvard in 1923. In 1929 he joined the faculty at Howard University and taught there full-time into the mid–1970s, then on and off after that. Of Brown, Howard University vice president Michael Winston said, "He was one of the great professors of his time—of this country."

Frances Eliza Hodgson Burnett   Novelist, famous hostess (1849–1924).

Nicknamed "Fluffy" by those who knew her well, the author of *Little Lord Fauntleroy* and *The Secret Garden* was also a legendary hostess of Washington parties and social events. Tough and demanding when she wanted to be, Burnett was born in England and raised in Tennessee after her family came to the United States to escape poverty. Burnett began writing, achieved success, migrated to Washington, left her first husband and then created a spectacular salon at *1219 I Street NW* (the house in which she wrote *Fauntleroy*, now a parking lot).

Here, at one afternoon reception, guests were amazed at the memorable entrance of Oscar Wilde, who was on the road performing his American lecture tour of 1882.

There stood Wilde, arrayed in "black silk clawhammer coat, fancily flowered dark waistcoat, knee breeches, silk stockings and patent leather pumps with broad buckles," and all of Washington gasped at the outrageous genius in his eccentric attire.

From 1886 to 1890, Burnett held court at *1730 K Street NW* (now an office building). Then, drawing from the tremendous success of *Fauntleroy*'s success as both a book and a play, she and her second husband, the famous oculist Dr. Swann Burnett, commissioned the construction of a grand new home at *1770 Massachusetts Avenue NW*. It was here that Burnett eventually wrote more than 50 books, until her death in 1924.

Rachel Carson   Zoologist, author (1907–1964).

A brilliant interpreter of science for the general public, Carson published her first book in 1941, entitled *Under the Sea Wind*. Ten years later she followed with a national best-seller, *The Sea Around Us*, and a sequel, *The Edge of the Sea*. But it was her famous book *Silent Spring* (1963) that shook the nation and catapulted her into the national spotlight. In this well-received book, Carson was the first author to alert the world to environmental damage caused by insecticides.

When Carson won the National Book Award for *The Sea Around Us* in 1952, she had an answer for those who wondered about the undisputed popularity of her books:

> Many people have commented with surprise on the fact that a work of science should have a large popular sale. But this notion that "science" is something that belongs in a separate compartment of its own, apart from everyday life, is one that I should like to challenge. . . . The aim of science is to discover and illuminate truth. And that, I take it, is the aim of literature, whether biography or history or fiction. It seems to me, then, that there can be no separate literature of science.

Carson lived at *204 Williamsburg Drive* in Silver Spring, Maryland from 1949 to 1957. The following year, she built her final home at *11701 Berwick Road*, also in Silver Spring. She had the second house constructed on a one-acre lot, preserving half the land in its natural state to serve as a wildlife habitat.

Bruce Catton   Author, journalist, historian (1899–1978).

Although he originally moved to Washington to work as a journalist, Catton wound up working for the government instead. In 1942, he became director of information for the War Production Board, and later worked at the Departments of Commerce and Interior. He eventually managed to realize his first career dream by becoming a Washington columnist and book reviewer for *The Nation*, followed by a stint as editor of *American Heritage*.

Drawing on his experience at the War Production Board, Catton published *The War Lords of Washington* in 1948. Following the publication of that book, Catton developed a keen and abiding interest in the Civil War. This interest led to many extraordinary books, most significantly his trilogy on the Army of the Potomac: *Mr. Lincoln's Army* (1951), *Glory Road* (1952) and *A Stillness at Appomattox* (1953). This last book, perhaps Catton's best, earned him a Pulitzer Prize for History in 1954.

Scholar David K. Adams commented that Catton's "view of history as a crusade of ideas (rather than as a matter of economic factors and power conflicts) . . . represents popular history at a very high level of achievement."

Elmer Davis Novelist, short-story writer, essayist, journalist, broadcaster (1890–1958).

Davis achieved fame during the early years of World War II for his news reports and analyses on CBS Radio (1939–42). In 1942, he agreed to interrupt his broadcasting career to head the Office of War Information, which he did until the war's close in 1945. When Davis resumed radio work, he started working for ABC, where he stayed for years. Prior to his radio experience, Davis worked as a political commentator for *The New York Times* from 1914 to 1924.

A man with a strong sense of duty and moral conscience, Davis took up serious writing when he wasn't working on the radio, achieving superior results. In 1954, his book *But We Were Born Free*, an attack on McCarthy and other political witch-hunters, became a national best-seller. This was followed by *Two Minutes Till Midnight*, which addressed nuclear weapons and peace, and other titles.

James Thurber was a good friend of Davis, recalling in a 1958 private letter that "Washington was also the home of my favorite American of this century, the late

Elmer Davis, to whom I dedicated my last book of fables." And Thurber's fellow *New Yorker* writer E. B. White said of Davis that "he got up in the morning to work in defense of freedom as methodically as most of us get up and brush our teeth."

Frederick Douglass Author, editor, diplomat, orator (1817–1895).

The son of a Maryland plantation owner who owned his mother, Douglass was able to escape slavery by disguising himself as a sailor and fleeing to New England in 1863. A fiery speaker, Douglass began describing his experiences as a slave and denouncing slavery at abolitionist rallies throughout New England, gaining applause and recognition wherever he went.

Douglass was so effective and articulate that some people began expressing doubt that he had ever been a slave or struggled to educate himself. These suspicions led Douglass to write his first book, *Narrative of the Life of Frederick Douglass, An American Slave* (1845), now recognized as an important American work. The book proved so popular that Douglass, fearing he might suffer recapture by his "legal" masters, fled to England. There he also enjoyed wide acclaim, and was able to earn enough money to purchase his freedom.

Returning to the United States, Douglass founded an influential antislavery weekly, *The North Star*, in New York (later renamed *Frederick Douglass's Paper*). In 1855, he came out with his best-known work, *My Bondage & My Freedom*.

After the Civil War, Douglass moved to Washington and held a number of government positions, including U.S. marshal of the District of Columbia, recorder of deeds for the District and minister and counsel general to Haiti. In 1881, he wrote a second autobiography, *The Life & Times of Frederick Douglass*, which is a classic of American literature. Douglass, who found genuine acceptance in Washington as a free man, was widely admired throughout the city as a writer and orator. In 1877, he said of Washington: "Wherever the American citizen may be a stranger, he is at home here."

During his early years in Washington, Douglass lived with his family in a large Victorian house near the U.S. Capitol, at *316 A Street NE*. For years after Douglass's death, this house was known as the "Frederick Douglass Town House" and then became the first site of the

Smithsonian's Museum of African Art. Today it houses private offices.

In 1877, while serving as U.S. marshal for the District of Columbia, Douglass decided to purchase *Cedar Hill*, a fourteen-room house on fifteen acres high above the Anacostia River in southeast Washington. To do so, Douglass helped to break a longstanding covenant in that area which restricted property sales to whites only. Now open to the public as a historic home, Cedar Hill (located at *1411 W Street SE*) is an elegant white house filled with Douglass's original furnishings and memorabilia. Of special note is the library, which contains Douglass's original desk, walking canes and other effects.

Listed in the National Register of Historic Places, Cedar Hill is open to the public daily from 9 am to 5 pm (Apr-Oct) and 9 am to 4 pm (Nov-March). It offers a lovely view of Washington, and has a Visitor's Center with gifts, souvenirs and copies of Douglass's books for sale.

Paul Laurence Dunbar   Poet, novelist (1872–1906).

Born of former slaves in Ohio, Dunbar was a prominent poet and novelist of the "Harlem Renaissance" movement who became one of the leading authors of his day. He is best known for his novel *The Sport of the Gods*, which was published in 1902, four years before his death.

In high school, Dunbar showed a great deal of promise, not only serving as president of the literary society and as editor of the student monthly magazine but also composing the class song. Dunbar's second book of poems, *Major and Minors*, received a glowing one-page review in *Harper's Weekly* by William Dean Howells, and other praise soon followed.

Dunbar's *Lyrics of a Lowly Life*, published in 1896, established the young man as the first African-American poet of national reputation since the Colonial era's Phyllis Wheatley. Following the publication of *Lyrics*, Dunbar moved to Washington in 1897 and worked for the next fifteen months at the Library of Congress.

Dunbar might have remained in Washington at the Library had he not been forced to quit because of tuberculosis. Ironically, like Wheatley, Dunbar was ravaged by the disease during much of his lifetime, which hampered his productivity and eventually took his life at the age of thirty-four.

F. Scott Fitzgerald Novelist, short-story writer, screen-writer (1896–1940).

Fitzgerald's mother was immensely proud of marrying into a prominent Maryland family that could claim lineage (however remote) to Francis Scott Key. She therefore named her son Francis Scott, boasting that her husband's great-great grandfather had been the brother of Francis Scott Key's grandfather. F. Scott's mother also put great stock in being Catholic, a path that her son did not follow.

By the time F. Scott died, it was widely known that he had strayed far off the path of Catholicism. Therefore, despite F. Scott's wish to be buried next to other family members in the Fitzgerald family plot at St. Mary's Cemetery in Rockville, Maryland, the Catholic Church declined.

Instead, when F. Scott's body arrived in Washington in 1940, the author was interred in Rockville Cemetery nearby. And when Fitzgerald's famous wife, Zelda, died by fire in a local nursing home disaster eight years later, she was buried next to her husband.

This might have been the end to the tale, except that F. Scott and Zelda's daughter, Scottie, was not content to let her father's original wishes regarding burial go unfulfilled. After applying pressure on local and national Catholic Church officials, Scottie succeeded in 1975 in getting both of her parents' remains disinterred and belatedly buried in St. Mary's small church graveyard (located at *600 Viers Mill Road* in *Rockville, Maryland*).

On the headstone marking F. Scott and Zelda's grave is the last, haunting line of *The Great Gatsby*: "So we beat on, boats against the current, borne back ceaselessly into the past."

Edward Everett Hale Novelist, short-story writer, critic, memoirist, Senate Chaplain (1822–1909).

Hale, an ordained chaplain, was a distinguished man of letters in his time. He was the first literary critic who gave warm approval to Walt Whitman's *Leaves of Grass*. His most famous short story, *The Man Without a Country*, was first published in 1863 in *The Atlantic Monthly* and was later collected with other stories in *If, Yes and Perhaps* (1868). As a scholar, his best-known work is *Franklin in France*, a fascinating look at Benjamin Franklin's years as an ambassador in Paris.

In a pair of memoirs, *A New England Boyhood* and *Memories of a Hundred Years*, Hale chronicled his remarkable career as a clergyman, philanthropist, popular author and government servant. For years, he lived at *1741 N Street NW* in downtown Washington near Dupont Circle. Hale's small townhouse, along with two others, now comprise today's *Hotel Tabard Inn*.

While serving as chaplain of the U.S. Senate (1903–1909), Hale was asked: "Dr. Hale, do you pray for the Senate?" "No," Hale replied, "I look at the Senators and pray for the people."

Edith Hamilton   Translator, classical scholar, essayist, educator (1867–1963).

The founder of Bryn Mawr School, Hamilton gained national prominence in 1930 when, at the age of 63, she sat down and wrote a book entitled *The Greek Way*. A formidable educator, Hamilton had a gift for making history come to life. Her book brilliantly captured the spirit and achievements of the ancient Greeks, and it was followed during the next 30 years by other popular interpretations of classic civilizations.

Today, many college and university graduates are familiar with such Hamilton classics as *The Roman Way* (1932), *Mythology* (1940) and *The Echo of Greece* (1957). These works simultaneously drew praise from scholars for Hamilton's depth of understanding while being embraced by the general public. In 1957, six years before her death, Hamilton was made an honorary citizen of Athens.

During the last twenty years of her life, Hamilton lived at *2448 Massachusetts Avenue NW*, in a lovely house backing onto Rock Creek Park. The house is not open to the public.

Dashiell Hammett   Novelist, short-story writer, screenwriter (1894–1961).

Born in St. Mary's County, Maryland, Hammett became well known as an author after he created the character Sam Spade and wrote *The Adventures of Sam Spade* and *The Maltese Falcon* (both popularized as successful Hollywood films). Hammett also lived in Hollywood for awhile and wrote scripts for the movies, including *The Glass Key*, *The Thin Man* and *Watch On The Rhine*.

As a writer of hard-boiled fiction, Hammett saw his books banned from many library shelves during the 1950s. Yet, despite his radical politics, Hammett asked to have his remains buried with those of other men who had fought or died for the United States. Having served as a sergeant in the U.S. Army's Motor Ambulance Corps in World War I, Hammett also served with the U.S. Army Signal Corps from 1942 through 1945 during World War II. The Army approved Hammett's request shortly before his death.

Today, Hammett is buried under a simple gravestone in Arlington National Cemetery which commemorates the famous writer's volunteer service during both World Wars: "Samuel D. Hammett, Maryland, Tec5 HO CO, Alaskan Department, World War I & II, May 27, 1894– January 10, 1961."

Bret Harte   Short-story writer, poet, novelist, playwright, critic, journalist (1836–1902).

Harte's popular short stories of life on the American frontier were instrumental in shaping the mythology of the West. With the publication of *The Luck of Roaring Camp and Other Sketches* in 1870, worldwide fame and fortune descended upon the struggling young writer. Harte immediately resigned from a teaching position in California to travel East, where he began writing for *The Atlantic Monthly*. However, his subsequent stories never achieved the quality and success of his early work.

In 1877, Harte jumped at an offer by Ohio poet John James Piatt to move to Washington and edit a new literary periodical, to be called *The Capital*. Lured by the promise of a heady annual salary of $5,000, Harte moved to the nation's capital and spent several anxious months living at the old Riggs House at *1617 I Street NW* (now an office building) while waiting for Piatt to raise the remainder of the magazine's financing.

When Piatt's plans finally collapsed and forced him into bankruptcy, Harte found himself stranded in the nation's capital. But Harte's political friends came to the rescue, securing for him the job of U.S. consul to Germany and later Scotland. Harte spent the remaining years of his life in London, never venturing back to the United States.

Francis Scott Key   Poet, lawyer (1779–1843).

A successful lawyer throughout his life, Key served as the U.S. Attorney for the District of Columbia from 1833 to 1841. A devout Episcopalian, he started out with his political allegiance committed to the Federalists, but in time he became a Democrat and a close friend of

President Andrew Jackson. A man of many interests, Key also wrote numerous poems for his own enjoyment.

It is for just one of these poems that Key is remembered today. In 1814, Key was asked to journey to Baltimore Harbor to negotiate the release of a friend who was being held captive on a British ship. Key was successful, but he and his friend were prevented from leaving the harbor when the British launched a full-scale attack on Fort McHenry.

Key and his friend watched with others as Fort McHenry suffered a tremendous all-night bombardment from the British. Throughout the ordeal, Key's friend, who had lost his eyeglasses during his capture, asked Key repeatedly if the American flag could be seen during the bombardment.

When the bombing finally stopped, Key joined with others in cheering the still-waving American flag above the fort's walls. The exuberance of the moment inspired Key to write a poem, which then began to take on a life of its own.

Soon the poem was being sung to the British drinking song "Anacreon in Heaven," and many people became familiar with the words. But Key never lived to see his poem immortalized as America's national anthem—that happened by presidential proclamation in 1931, nearly a century after he died. And, like many other poets, Key's famous poem wasn't published along with his other work until fourteen years after his death, under the title *Poems of the Late Francis S. Key, Esq*.

For twenty-five years during his early career, from 1805 to 1830, Key lived in a house located at *3518 M Street NW* (the structure was torn down in 1948 to accommodate construction of Key Bridge). Key then purchased *The Maples*, at *630 South Carolina Avenue SE*, and lived there briefly. Today it is *The Friendship House*, with its entrance at *619 D Street SE*. The public can visit the house during the day; the phone is (202) 695-9050.

Key's final residence was at *308 C Street NW* (now gone), which he purchased in 1833 and where he lived until his death at sixty-four years of age.

Margaret Leech   Novelist, biographer, historian (1893–1974).

Leech's most important and widely read book, *Reveille in Washington*, tells what happened in the nation's capital during the Civil War. Written in a lively style and meticulously researched, it won the Pulitzer Prize for History in 1942.

Historian David McCullough, writing in the May 1986 issue of *American Heritage*, says, "If asked to name my favorite book about the city, I would have to pick Margaret Leech's Pulitzer Prize history, *Reveille in Washington*, first published in 1941, one of my all-time favorite books of any kind, which I have read and reread and pushed on friends for years."

Walter Lippmann   Journalist, author, editor, public official (1889–1974).

While serving as an assistant to Woodrow Wilson, Lippmann is said to have wielded strong influence on Wilson's thinking regarding preparations for peace and the formulation of policy on world issues. After leaving government, Lippmann then took editorial positions with *The New Republic* and *The New York World*, before joining *The New York Herald Tribune* as a columnist in 1931.

After joining the *Tribune*, Lippmann began writing a column called "Today & Tomorrow" that was quickly picked up by other newspapers across the country. He eventually became an extremely powerful journalist, one whose words could affect votes and shift public opinion. Lippmann won two Pulitzer Prizes—the first for International Reporting (1962) and the second as a Special Citation for "wisdom, perception and a high sense of responsibility in writing about national and international affairs" in 1958. Lippmann's widely read books include *A Preface To Politics* (1913), *The Stakes of Diplomacy* (1915), *The New Imperative* (1935) and *The Good Society* (1937).

Practically from the moment he arrived in Washington, Lippmann found himself among the city's powerful elite. His first home after getting married was the former bachelor quarters of Supreme Court Justice Felix Frankfurter, located at *1727 19th Street NW*. He and his wife then moved into a house at *3434 Volta Place NW* in 1938, a residence in which Alexander Graham Bell's parents once lived. His final move came in 1964, when he took up digs at the former quarters of the dean of *The Washington Cathedral*, at *3525 Woodley Road NW*.

Henry Cabot Lodge   Biographer, essayist, historian, editor, elected official (1850–1924).

A close friend of Henry Adams, under whom Lodge

studied political science at Harvard, this perennial senator from Massachusetts insisted on living somewhere off
the avenue bearing the name of his native state. The
Lodge house, located at *1765 Massachusetts Avenue
NW*, served as a social, political and literary salon
during most of the two decades preceding the Coolidge
era.

Lodge's published works include: *A Short History of
the English Colonies in America* (1881), *Alexander
Hamilton* (1882), *Daniel Webster* (1883) and a two-
volume study in 1888 entitled *George Washington*.
Lodge turned to a public examination of his own life
with the publication of *Early Memories* in 1913.

Clare Boothe Luce   Playwright, author, novelist, diplomat (1903–1987).

Principally a playwright of biting, sarcastic wit, Luce
married mega-publisher Henry Luce and instantane-
ously became a very wealthy woman. Her plays include
The Women (1936), which satirized wealthy U.S.
women, *Kiss the Boys Goodbye* (1938), which ridiculed
Hollywood's star system and warned of approaching
fascism and *Margin for Error* (1940), a mystery melo-
drama portraying a Nazi consul's murder. Her nonfiction book *Europe in the Spring* (1940) gave a report of
her travels through volatile Europe and urged an American crusade for democracy the world over.

Luce entered public service when she was elected as a
U.S. Congresswoman from Connecticut in 1943. She
also served as U.S. ambassador to Italy from 1953 to
1956.

Luce's will made provision for millions of dollars to
be donated to a number of educational and charitable
interests. Among these is the *Clare Boothe Luce Fund*,
which is used to help provide financial support to
women students and teachers.

Archibald MacLeish   Poet, playwright, essayist, critic,
memoirist, public official (1892–1982).

A man of letters who enjoyed a diverse career, Mac-
Leish's literary reputation was firmly established with
the publication of his long narrative poem *Conquistador*
in 1932. A description of Mexico's conquest, the poem
won the Pulitzer Prize for Poetry in 1933. As a cultural
adviser to President Roosevelt, MacLeish was appointed
Librarian of Congress in 1939, a position he held until
1944.

Along with his job as Librarian of Congress, Mac-Leish organized and served as the head of a new government agency called the U.S. Office of Facts and Figures (1941–42). He was the assistant director of the Office of War Information (1942–43), and served as assistant Secretary of State from 1944–45.

No stranger to the machinations of power, MacLeish knew how to lyrically protect the administration he served, as in this passage from "A Poet Speaks From The Visitor's Gallery":

"History's not written in the kind of ink
The richest man of most ambitious mind
Who hates a president enough to print
A daily paper can afford or find.

Gentlemen have power now and know it,
But even the greatest and most famous kings
Feared and with reason to offend the poets
Whose songs are marble and whose marble sings."

After the war, MacLeish represented the United States in UNESCO. In 1953, his *Collected Poems* brought him a second Pulitzer Prize and a National Book Award. Later, in 1958, the verse drama *JB*, based on the life of the biblical prophet Job, earned the poet yet another Pulitzer Prize.

In accepting his National Book Award in 1953, Mac-Leish had some remarks on what the country's novelists and poets should be permitted to do in the face of McCarthyism:

Their function, their obligation as artists, is to live at the frontiers of the experiences of their time—at the passage of the present toward the future. Unless they are free to report the experience as they live it—unless they are free to present the forms and shapes of meaning as those shapes and forms appear—not they alone but the whole society will suffer.

A country in which agencies of government, party functionaries or inquisitorial committees can dictate or influence the writer's work, or determine the conditions of its publication, is a country which has rejected freedom, and turned its face towards conformity and ignorance and death.

First and foremost a poet, MacLeish was intrigued about writing drama for radio, describing the airwaves as a theater of "the word-excited imagination." So when

Orson Welles wanted to direct a production of Mac-Leish's *The Fall of the City*, MacLeish was extremely interested in the project and helped Welles write and rewrite the script before the program aired. In commenting about his enthusiasm for the radio, MacLeish said: "Only the ear is engaged and the ear is already half-poet. It believes at once: creates and believes."

Joaquin Miller   Poet (1841–1913).

Called "the poet of the Sierras," Miller moved to Washington in 1883 to seek refuge from New York, to recover the "Muse" and to pursue his political ambitions.

Four years earlier, Miller had married Abigail Leland, a hotel heiress and socialite. In 1882, Miller's first wife, poet and writer Minnie Myrtle, paid her husband a visit in New York because she was destitute and dying. Miller did what he could to make Minnie's death less painful, thereby causing a scandal in New York society and infuriating Abigail. Miller also tried unsuccessfully to make amends with his children from the marriage to Minnie, especially his two sons.

After Minnie's death, Abigail insisted that she and Miller flee New York and move down to Washington. In 1883, the Millers took an apartment in the *Florence Court Apartments* on *California Street NW*, not far from Dupont Circle.

But Miller hated the fancy apartment, preferring something more rustic. After only a few weeks, he purchased several acres of land in the *Arlington Heights* section of Washington at *16th Street & Crescent Place NW* (now *Meridian Hill Park*), hired a couple of laborers to chop down some trees and built a two-room log cabin with a loft and fireplace. The cabin, which faced down 16th Street toward the White House, was sparsely furnished and plain. Upon the cabin's completion, Miller told journalist Frank G. Carpenter: "The President's house is at one end of Sixteenth Street . . . and mine is at the other. But while I own a cabin, the President only has his cabin-et." Anything but amused at what her husband had done, Abigail left Joaquin and returned to New York.

A westerner who had already wandered through a myriad of jobs and off-beat experiences, Miller began canvassing anyone he could find for a political office in Chester Arthur's administration. Considering Miller's appearance, however, it appears unlikely he could have ever achieved his goal.

During the day, Miller went about the conservative capital clad in a frock coat and corduroy trousers tucked into high-heeled boots, a huge tasseled sombrero jauntily clamped above his long blond hair and bushy mustachios bristling above his lip. These oddities of appearance, coupled with Miller's rustic abode, did not propel him to the top of the social register.

Unfazed by adversity, Miller then began plying his natural trade about town—the writing and reading of poetry. Confronted with lukewarm public reaction, he decided to sail for England, decked out in his jack boots, trusty sombrero, flashy bandana and a fur coat with gold-nugget buttons. As he boastfully explained: "It helps sell the poems, boys, and tickles the duchesses!"

It seems as though the gold-nugget buttons were unnecessary, because the English Pre-Raphaelites loved Miller's book *Songs of the Sierras* for its sonorous verse and brilliant imagery. Returning to the west coast, the aging bohemian, ever ahead of his time, retired to the hills overlooking Oakland, California to practice and preach a simple life of free love. It is interesting to contemplate what influence Miller might have wielded upon conservative Washington had he been granted the government job he so desperately wanted.

In 1912, Miller's famous log cabin was moved from Meridian Hill Park to *Rock Creek Park* (at *Beach & Military Drives*), where it is now the home of a popular summer poetry reading series.

Edward R. Murrow   Broadcaster, author, government official (1908–1965).

As chief correspondent for CBS Radio's European Bureau during World War II, Murrow captivated Americans with his riveting dispatches describing the Battle of Britain. His radio scripts from this period were collected to form his first book, *This is London* (1941). As Murrow then went on to write and host other radio and television programs, scripts from these shows were also collected under such titles as *See It Now*, *Hear It Now*, *This I Believe* and *Person to Person*.

Among the many programs Murrow wrote, produced, edited or directed from 1947 to 1960 was a withering expose of Senator Joe McCarthy. Murrow left his lucrative work in television in 1961 to become director of the U.S. Information Agency until 1963. During this time, he lived at *5171 Manning Place NW* in Washington.

John Howard Payne   Playwright, actor, journalist, diplomat (1791–1852).

Acclaimed as a prodigy, Payne published "The Thespian Mirror," a theatrical review which attracted the attention of New York's literary and theater critics, when he was fourteen years old. Seduced by the promise of the theater, Payne then authored and saw produced his first drama, *Julia, Or The Wanderer*, at age fifteen. At eighteen, he won rave reviews for his acting in a New York production of John Home's popular drama, *Douglas*.

Following these successes, a curious public backlash set in regarding Payne's work, as people reacted against the early acclaim and praise Payne had enjoyed as a youth. Friends of Payne's father collected funds and sent young Payne off to Europe, where he was expected to reclaim his reputation and earn a fortune.

Payne settled in Europe in 1813, and for several years barely eluded bankruptcy as he continued to write and act in plays. In 1821, Payne tried to produce his own melodramas, but they proved so unsuccessful that he landed in debtor's prison. To buy his way out, Payne wrote *Therese, Orphan of Geneva*, which brought in just enough money to purchase his freedom.

Payne then thought he had finally hit upon financial success with the operatic production of his play, *Clari, The Maid of Milan*, mostly because the play contained the immensely popular song, "Home, Sweet Home." But there was one catch: he discovered he had sold the play outright and couldn't collect any royalties on the song.

Payne continued to write and adapt other plays, remaining always poor. In England, he met and fell in love with Mary Shelley, the widow of poet Percy Bysshe Shelley, and courted her fervently. Again, there was one catch: she wanted nothing to do with him.

Returning to America in a state of destitution, Payne came to see his friends in Washington, who arranged benefit performances in one of the city's larger theaters. This brought Payne a sizable windfall. Could his luck finally be turning? His friend Daniel Webster and others lobbied to get Payne a consul post in far off Tunis. Payne went there and, shortly after his arrival, died. The four Sisters of Charity who nursed Payne on his deathbed reported that in his delirium he sang "Home, Sweet Home" over and over, and was the sweetest man they had ever buried in the Tunisian graveyard.

But mere burial didn't end Payne's journey on earth. Thirty-one years following his death, Payne's body was ordered exhumed by wealthy local arts patron William W. Corcoran and brought back to Washington in a lead coffin. Having never forgotten the time as a boy when he had seen Payne act on stage, Corcoran was determined to honor the author of one of the most popular songs of the nineteenth century.

Not unlike today, money talked. Invitations to Payne's reburial were printed with a Matthew Brady daguerreotype of the young poet. Corcoran draped a portrait of Payne with flowers and hung it in the Corcoran Gallery, where it remains today. Corcoran also commissioned a bust of Payne, and hired a hearse with four white horses to carry Payne's coffin to its final resting place.

Payne's funeral procession, from the Corcoran Art Gallery to Georgetown's Oak Hill Cemetery (owned by Corcoran), was led by President Chester Arthur, his entire cabinet, the Supreme Court, members of the House and Senate and other capital notables. The red-uniformed Marine Band, led by John Philip Sousa, played "Home, Sweet Home," and all those present joined in singing the last verse and chorus.

Today, the bust of Payne which Corcoran commissioned rests on a tall pedestal on the grounds of *Oak Hill Cemetery*. Seen from the corner of *30th & R Streets NW*, any passerby might imagine that here lies a conquering hero who amassed fortune and glory in his lifetime. Certainly, Payne now shares an equal footing with Corcoran, who is buried on the other side of the cemetery.

Drew Pearson   Author, columnist, broadcaster (1897–1969).

Pearson's famous style, once described by *Time* as a "brand of ruthlessness, theatrical crusading, high-voltage, hypodermic journalism that has made him the most intensely feared and hated man in Washington," was calculated to stir up controversy. It also guaranteed that Pearson always got read. His columns were eventually compiled into three wildly successful books.

The incomparable muckraker resided in an eighteenth-century structure located at *2820 Dumbarton Av-*

enue NW. From the comfort of his home, and using a bank of telephones and a teletype machine, Pearson would dispatch his column, "Washington Merry-Go-Round" to hundreds of newspapers and other outlets each day. He also tended one of the finest gardens in the nation's capital. His success at gardening perhaps was not so much a green thumb as a nose for shrewd investment in a complementary property, a 450-acre farm overlooking the Potomac River at *13130 River Road*, near the town of *Potomac, Maryland.*

There, Pearson built a stone mansion in 1937, and was in the habit of going out frequently for relaxation. He also went to check on the state of his lucrative dairy herd. After all, Pearson earned up to $150,000 a year from the sale of manure. The bags read "Pearson's Best Manure—Better Than The Column—All Cow, No Bull." Now, that's muckraking.

Katherine Anne Porter   Novelist, short-story writer, essayist (1890–1980).

Regarded as one of America's finest writers of short stories and novellas, Porter was awarded the Pulitzer Prize and National Book Award in 1966 for her *Collected Stories.* From her astonishing debut in 1930 with the short-story collection, *Flowering Judas,* Porter went on to fashion a relatively small but enormously accomplished body of work. Her additional collections, *Noon Wine* (1937) and *Pale Horse, Pale Rider* (1939), solidified her worldwide reputation. But it wasn't until 1962 that she wrote her first and only novel, the commercially and critically successful *Ship of Fools.*

Financial security provided by the novel's success allowed Porter to abandon a demanding routine of delivering guest lectures and moving from one university to another as a visiting instructor. From 1960 to 1975, she resided in a home at *3601 49th Street NW* near American University in upper northwest Washington (still a private residence). She then moved into a condominium in the *Westchester Park Apartments* at *6100 Westchester Park Drive* in *College Park, Maryland.* The final year of her life was spent in the *Carriage Hill Nursing Home* at *9101 2nd Avenue* in *Silver Spring, Maryland.*

In much of her symbol-enriched work, Porter expressed a sense of bewilderment at the strangeness of life's developments. She captured in masterful prose the solid sense and atmosphere of a place, while evoking deep ambivalence about human conduct, particularly people's inclination toward betrayal. Always a passionate writer, she protested the Sacco-Vanzetti case in the 1930s and made that episode the subject of her last book, *The Never Ending Wrong* (1977). In her collected essays, *The Days Before*, Porter wrote: "I am passionately involved with those individuals who populate all these enormous migrations, calamities, who fight wars and furnish life for the future."

The *University of Maryland Library* has set aside a *Katherine Anne Porter Room*, in which are housed the author's works, her personal library, her papers and personal memorabilia.

Ezra Pound   Poet, critic, editor, translator (1885–1972).

A brilliant poet, linguist and critic, Pound commanded the highest respect on the international literary scene during the opening decades of the twentieth century. He crafted poems of great influence, and provided generous assistance to many promising writers, including T.S. Eliot and Ernest Hemingway.

But when World War II ended, Pound was arrested by Italian partisans and held in an outdoor wire cage for several weeks for having made pro-Fascist radio broadcasts in Italy. He was eventually returned to the United States to be charged with treason.

Prior to his trial in Washington, however, the U.S. attorney requested that Pound be declared "mentally unfit" and sent to a mental institution. This was done, and, for the next twelve years, Pound became an unwilling resident in the *Chestnut Ward* of *St. Elizabeth's Hospital*, at *2700 Martin Luther King Avenue SE*. He remained incarcerated until 1958, when the indictment was withdrawn. Pound promptly returned to Italy, declaring that "all of America is an insane asylum."

Among Pound's best-known books are *Provenca* (1910), *Homage to Sextus Propertius* (1918), and his towering epic, *The Cantos* (1917–69).

Jeremiah Eames Rankin   Poet, lyricist, clergyman, educator (1828–1924).

Rankin is best remembered for his hymn, "God Be With You Till We Meet Again." Pastor of the First Congregational Church in Washington, Rankin later became president of Howard University from 1889 to 1903. Possessing a command of the Scots dialect, he loved to write verse in that musical tongue.

His work is collected in *The Auld Scotch Mither &
Other Poems* (1873) and *Ingleside Rhaims* (1887).

Marjorie Kinnan Rawlings Novelist, poet, journalist
(1896–1953).

Best known for her Pulitzer Prize-winning novel, *The
Yearling* (1938), Rawlings began her writing career as a
newspaper reporter but quickly gravitated toward writing short stories and novels. Most of her fiction and
nonfiction examines life in backcountry Florida, including the famous book *Cross Creek* (1942). Rawlings owed
a tremendous debt to her editor Maxwell Perkins for
help and encouragement throughout her career.

Born and raised in the District of Columbia, Rawlings
displayed her talent in writing from the age of six. For
the next decade, she contributed to the children's pages
of the city's local newspapers while attending Western
High School. At age fifteen, she submitted her story,
"The Reincarnation of Miss Hetty," to *McCall*'s Child
Authorship Contest and won a prize. Two years later,
when her father died, she moved with her mother to
Madison, Wisconsin.

In her formative years in Washington, Rawlings lived
in a still-standing house at *1221 Newton Street NE*. The
house is not open to the public.

Mary Roberts Rinehart Novelist, short-story writer,
playwright (1876–1958).

A successful writer of thrillers and comic novels about
the adventures of her spinster sleuth, Tish, Rinehart
lived in a big cream-colored house at *2419 Massachusetts
Avenue NW* from 1922 through the 1930s. She was
conferred a Litt.D. from George Washington University
in 1923. Because her husband was a major in the U.S.
Army, Rinehart was granted her request to be buried in
Arlington Cemetery upon her death at age 82.

According to a *Washington Post* article written about
her in 1934, Rinehart's $100,000 annual income made
her "one of the highest paid writers in the world" at the
time. "This was far cry from the $10 she received for
the first story she ever sold," the article said, "and it
doesn't hint that this early manuscript story was rejected
by no less than 12 magazines before one finally bought
it."

It was the Stock Market Crash in 1903 that prompted
Rinehart to begin a career in writing, in the hopes of
earning some money. In time, she discovered money

and fame through her long and prolific career, and is considered one of the founders of the American mystery and suspense novel. She was also a co-founder of Farrar and Rinehart, Publishers in New York.

While she lived in Washington, Rinehart wrote more than twenty successful novels which were read by hundreds of thousands of devoted fans. Her books *The Circular Staircase* (1908) and *The Man in the Lower Ten* (1909) are considered classics of the detective genre.

The literature department of *George Mason University* presently administers the *Mary Roberts Rinehart Fund*, set up in Rinehart's name to assist deserving writers in pursuing their craft.

Theodore Roosevelt Author, soldier, President of the United States (1858–1919).

The author of many books, Roosevelt used his popularity as a writer to promote his political views. In fact, of all U.S. Presidents, Roosevelt comes the closest to functioning throughout his lifetime as a true professional writer. The four-volume *The Winning of the West*, written and published between 1889 and 1896, is considered his most significant work.

Roosevelt's first book, *The Naval War of 1812* (1882), served to help him land an elected office. Other important works to follow included *American Ideals & Other Essays* (1897), *The Rough Riders* (1899) and *African Game Trails* (1910).

At 31 years old, Roosevelt moved to Washington following his appointment to the Civil Service Commission by President Harrison. He lived at *1215 19th Street NW* from 1889 to 1895, shortly before going to war with Spain in Cuba at the head of his famed Rough Riders. The attending glory during that campaign made Roosevelt famous, and helped to win successively higher political offices until he became President in 1901.

Roosevelt's former house was turned into an office building in 1987, fetching a record $4 million selling price. At the time, the price was thought to be the highest ever paid for finished office space in the Washington area.

Anne Royall Author, journalist, travel writer (1769–1854).

Unfairly branded "the mother of yellow journalism" by her critics, Anne Royall was in fact a champion of the underdog and indefatigable in her crusades against

Washington corruption and political cronyism. Royall's caustic, sensational attacks on politicians and other Washington figures during her lifetime were legendary. The founder of *Paul Pry*, a weekly Washington newspaper, Royall never found herself lacking in weekly targets for her railing editorials.

In her time, Anne Royall was the most famous woman in Washington, widely feared and hated by those who had something to hide. Congressmen would find themselves hopelessly cornered by Royall, who never gave way until she got answers to her questions. "Tact" is not a word that comes to mind in describing Royall's style.

But it was not always so. In her initial visits to Washington in the early 1820s, many people found Royall quaintly charming. And when she settled in the nation's capital in 1828, she arrived triumphantly as the author of four successful books: *Sketches*, *Black Book*, *Mrs. Royall's Pennsylvania* and *Mrs. Royall's Southern Tour*. To the applause of admiring Senators, Royall became the first woman ever allowed on the Senate floor.

But the Senators, and other public figures, quickly changed their minds about Royall after she began relentlessly stalking them and chronicling their questionable behavior. A scourge of religious fanatics, she is the only American citizen (male or female) to have ever been tried and acquitted on the archaic charge of being a "common scold."

But Royall did more than expose and attack hypocrites in the pages of her newspaper. She also championed many social causes, including ecology, municipal planning and justice for American Indians. Throughout her years of capital muckraking, the frumpy, limp-legged Royall never flagged in her crusade to get the goods on all the scoundrels populating Capitol Hill. As she once boasted to P.T. Barnum:

> All the Congressmen call on me. They do not dare do otherwise. Enemies and friends all alike, they have to come to me. And why should they not? I made them— every devil of them. You know how I look, ragged and poor, but thank God I am saucy and independent. The whole government is afraid of me, and well they may be. I know them all, from top to toe—I can fathom their rascality.

Utterly above corruption, Royall's commitment to the truth remained unswerving. She refused to let her writings become mere political mouthpieces and always spoke her mind. When *Paul Pry* folded in 1836, she promptly started up a new weekly named, appropriately, *Huntress*. She died in 1854, mere weeks following the publication of her last editorial.

Upon visiting Washington for the first time in 1824, Royall observed that, "if you are poor, you have no business in Washington." Throughout her long life in the nation's capital, Royall scrambled for any adequate lodging she could afford. She always managed, however, to live within a stone's throw of the U.S. Capitol.

The first place Royall stayed was with the Dorret family on Capitol Hill, where she was given a free room. For a time, the secretary of the Supreme Court arranged for her to stay in the old *Brick Capitol Building*, the makeshift structure erected by Congress following the bombardments of the *War of 1812* (now the site of the *Library of Congress*, at *East Capitol and 1st Streets SE*).

From 1827 to 1833, through the generosity of her patron Daniel Carroll, Royall stayed rent-free in the old *Bank House* on Capitol Hill, formerly headquarters of the Bank of Washington. Located on what was called *Carroll Row* on the east side of *1st Street, between East Capitol and A Streets*, the house was torn down to make way for the Supreme Court Building.

Royall then moved to the corner of *East Capitol and Second Streets*, near the old Hill Market. And, in 1838, she moved again to *North B & Third Streets* (now *Constitution Avenue and Third Street NE*), just down the block from Vice President Richard M. Johnson. Finally, after several more moves, she returned to her favorite house on *B Street between 1st & 2nd Streets SE* (where the Madison Building of the Library of Congress now stands).

Upon her death, Royall was buried in an unmarked grave in *Congressional Cemetery*, at *1801 E Street SE*. Fifty-seven years later, a small monument was placed on the gravesite by "a few men from Philadelphia and Washington" with the simple inscription: "Anne Royall, Pioneer Woman Publicist, 1769–1854, 'I Pray That The Union Of These States May Be Eternal.' "

Although Royall's story today remains largely unknown, her colorful personality has been treated in a handful of works, including *The Life and Times of Anne Royall* (1909) by Sarah Harvey Porter; *Seventy-Five Years of White House Gossip* (1926) by Edna M. Colman; and a two-act play, *Mrs. Anne Royall's Black Book* (1988) by Minnesota poet and playwright Bruce Cutler.

Emma Dorothy Eliza Nevitt Southworth   Novelist, short-story writer, teacher (1819–1899).

History has not been kind to the memory of Washington native Emma Southworth, who published in her lifetime as E.D.E.N. Southworth. In many ways, her astonishing life stands as the antithesis to the ill-fated career of John Howard Payne, whom she knew.

While in her day Southworth towered as one of America's most prolific and widely read novelists, today she is hardly remembered. Yet, while Payne's career was launched amid praise for his promise as a young prodigy, Southworth had to overcome very hard circumstances to forge a literary career.

Reared in her early years in *St. Mary's County, Maryland*—just south of Washington—Southworth moved into the nation's capital when her widowed mother married Joshua Henshaw, who was secretary to Daniel Webster. Henshaw soon established a school for girls in Washington, where Southworth first attended as a pupil and later worked as a teacher.

Emma was eking out a meager existence in a rowhouse apartment on Capitol Hill when she married Frederick Southworth, who took her to live in a log cabin on the Wisconsin frontier. Frederick worked as a miner, and frequently would leave Emma and their two children alone for weeks at a time. Emma wrote later that wolves would circle around the cabin late at night, howling and frightening the children to death.

Finding herself eventually abandoned by her husband, Southworth bravely gathered her children and returned to Washington, some four years after leaving her job. Since teaching didn't pay enough to support her family, Southworth turned to writing at night to supplement her income.

Her first novel, *Retribution*, made literary history in 1849 when it became one of the first novels to be serialized in *The National Era*, Washington's only abolitionist newspaper at the time. The novel was enthusiastically received, and Southworth was sufficiently encouraged to venture on to her next. By the end of her tremendously successful career, Southworth wrote and published 73 novels, many selling well over one million copies each.

During her early years in Washington, Southworth lived in a house at *13th and C Streets NW*, and taught evening school classes to a wide variety of students. This house was torn down in 1932 to make way for the highly unnotable GSA central heating and refrigeration plant.

After her novels began to sell, Southworth then used her earnings to purchase *Prospect Cottage*, located at *36th & Prospect Streets NW (Southwest Corner)*. The "cottage," a fourteen-room Victorian carpenter-gothic house perched on a bluff in Georgetown overlooking the Potomac River, presented a commanding view of Virginia on the other shore. For half a century, Prospect Cottage became a well-known meeting place for the literary community of Washington. It was even turned into a makeshift hospital for wounded soldiers during the Civil War, and President Lincoln slept there three times on his way to and from the battlefields during the height of the war.

When Harriet Beecher Stowe traveled to Washington to arrange for publication of her novel *Uncle Tom's Cabin* in the *National Era*, Southworth befriended Stowe and invited her to stay at Prospect Cottage. The two women became lifelong friends. Later on, during a trip to England to observe the European publication of one of her books, Southworth also befriended Lady Byron and many other famous European intellectuals and authors. It is odd and sad to consider that, while in her lifetime Southworth was celebrated as one of the most successful woman writers in America, virtually nothing she wrote is read today.

Upon Southworth's death in 1899, she was buried in *Oak Hill Cemetery (30th & R Streets NW)*, on the slope of a hill below the Cemetery's Chapel. When Prospect Cottage was purchased by the National League of the American Pen Women, it was slated for demolition by the organization to construct a national headquarters building on the site. The Cottage was temporarily reprieved by the Stock Market Crash in 1903, but was eventually destroyed in 1941.

Today, the spot is occupied by a pair of ordinary brick townhouses, very near a long flight of steps used in a famous scene from the movie *The Exorcist*.

James Thurber Short-story writer, humorist, essayist, cartoonist (1894–1961).

Equally prized for the sophisticated humor of his short fiction and the hilarious simplicity of his line drawings, Thurber was a celebrated writer and illustrator at *The New Yorker* from 1927 until the late–1950s. Thurber's most famous story was *The Secret Life of*

Walter Mitty, which was made into a movie, as were other of his stories. His collected stories include *My Life and Hard Times* (1933) and *The Thurber Carnival* (1945).

While most of Thurber's childhood is usually associated with Columbus, Ohio, he lived for a time as a child in the Washington area. Here is a lengthy portion of one of Thurber's letters to local writer Elizabeth Acosta, as it may be found in the Virginia Room of the Falls Church City Public Library:

I don't think you know about all the houses I lived in, because one of them was a house on Maple Avenue in Falls Church, Virginia. This was fifty-seven years ago, in the summer of 1901, when my father had a job in Washington.

My mother couldn't stand the heat of the city and so we rented this house on Maple Avenue, but I can't remember the number now. It was there that, one Sunday, I was struck by an arrow fired by my older brother. He was seven, and I was six, and Robert was four, and I'm sure we all threw up together.

My father was on a fishing trip, of course, when I got hurt. It is too late now for you to assassinate Dr. Malone, who must have died years ago, and who did not have the left eye removed soon enough. The operation was finally done by the great Dr. Swann Burnett, whose wife, a dozen years earlier, had written *Little Lord Fauntleroy*.

When I was a code clerk in the State Department in 1918 I went back to the house on Maple Avenue, and it seemed pretty much the same. We had a big back yard and an apple orchard, and there were some seckel pear trees. Our best apples were big yellow ones called Sheep's Nose. A quarter of a mile from our house was a big estate with a winding driveway, called the Evergreens, and a family named McSween lived there.

My brother Robert, now 62—William was 65 in October—still has some photos of the Maple Avenue House, I think, and if he has, I'll send them to you. A lot of good things as well as bad happened in that house. Falls Church was a quiet little village then, and I often wonder what it has become.

My wife Helen and I both loved your letter, one of the best and funniest I have ever got, and we have shown it to all our friends. I love your loving me, and I love you too. . . ."

After several more letters between them, Acosta and Thurber figured out that the Thurber family rented what was then known as "the Loving cottage" in the summer of 1901 and 1902 at *319 Maple Avenue* in the City of Falls Church, Virginia. During the winters of those years, the Thurbers lived at *2031 I Street NW*, just one block from "Bill, Steve and Laura Benét." In other letters to Acosta, Thurber recalled working in later years with Stephen Vincent Benét in the code rooms of the State Department, and that "Washington was also the home of my favorite American of this century, the late Elmer Davis, to whom I dedicated my last book of fables."

"I always think fondly of Washington and Falls Church," wrote Thurber to Acosta in 1958, "and have enough memories of both places, most of them fond, to fill a book." Mrs. Acosta was pleased, because the house that the Thurber family rented for two summers was directly next door to hers. She exchanged letters and phone calls with Thurber until his death in 1961.

In 1965, the Thurber family cottage and Mrs. Acosta's house were both demolished to make way for twenty townhomes, and Maple Avenue was renamed on that day by the city to *James Thurber Court*.

Mark Twain Novelist, short-story writer, journalist, humorist (1835–1910).

Twain traveled to Washington in the fall of 1867 at the request of Senator Stewart of Nevada, whom he had gotten to know some years before out West. From the outset, relations between the two men were strained by what could be politely described as a "difference in temperaments."

Matters didn't improve when the Senator observed that Twain was spending more time completing his new book, *The Innocents Abroad*, than on speechwriting. Having just returned from his first journey overseas, Twain was working hard to complete the manuscript for what promised to be his most popular book to date. The Senator's new aide was also devoting a considerable amount of time toward conducting, with William Swinton, what he described as "the first Newspaper Correspondence Syndicate that an unhappy world ever saw." This put Twain and the Senator on a collision course, and they began arguing violently until Twain's departure in 1868.

In his otherwise forgettable autobiography, Senator Stewart recounted these tempestuous months in Washington with Twain. And Twain himself felt compelled to draft a wry account of his wayward time in the nation's capital, under the title *Washington in 1868*.

During his brief stay in Washington, Twain lived in a house located at *F and 14th Streets NW*. In the 1930s, this house was torn down and replaced by Garfinckel's, a well-known department store that went out of business in 1990.

Daniel Webster   Author, orator, arts patron (1782–1852).

A prominent figure on the cultural scene in Washington, Webster was an active patron of the arts and an oratorical firebrand who made a lasting impression on anyone who met him. During the early nineteenth century, many talented writers sought Webster's influential intervention with the government and enjoyed his generous financial assistance. It is striking how often Webster helped to further the literary life in Washington during this period of American history.

Arriving in Washington first as a New England Congressman and then successfully returning as a U.S. Senator, Webster quickly established his fame as a matchless orator. His talents were soon tapped by Presidents Harrison and Tyler, who appointed him Secretary of State. Among Webster's most famous books are *Discourse in Commemoration of Jefferson and Adams* (1826) and the eighteen-volume *Writings and Speeches* (1903).

Novelist Honore Willsie Morrow appropriated Webster's colorful life for his 1931 novel *Black Daniel*, and Stephen Vincent Benét would further immortalize the man in his classic short story "The Devil and Daniel Webster" (1939).

While serving as Secretary of State in the 1840s, Webster resided at the northeast corner of *H Street & Connecticut Avenue NW* (now the offices of the *U.S. Chamber of Commerce*, where Webster's desk still may be seen). Although the house was given to him by his New York and Boston admirers, Webster's extravagant lifestyle forced him to sell the house to banker William Corcoran eight years after moving in. Webster then moved to rented quarters near *Judiciary Square*, where he died in 1852.

A statue of the great orator now stands at *Scott Circle*, where *Massachusetts Avenue, Rhode Island Avenue & N Street NW* intersect. It was created by the sculptor Gaetano Trentanove, and dedicated in 1890.

Walt Whitman   Poet, journalist, editor (1819–1892).

The editor of *The Brooklyn Times* and other newspapers, Whitman was 43 years old when he came down to Washington from New York for the first time.

Not long before his arrival, *Leaves of Grass* had been praised by Ralph Waldo Emerson as "the most extraordinary piece of wit and wisdom that America has yet contributed." Privately, Emerson had also written Whitman a letter saying, "I greet you at the beginning of a great career, which yet must have had a long foreground somewhere, for such a start." *Leaves of Grass* was in its third edition, and readers were alternately shocked by its strong ideas and moved by its lush, powerful lyricism.

There was growing interest in Whitman's writing, but the nation was also deeply divided by the Civil War. Among the casualties was Walt's brother George, who was seriously wounded at the first battle of Fredericksburg on December 13, 1862.

Walt rushed down to his brother's side, and came face-to-face with unimaginable suffering and pain. The field of battle at Fredericksburg was littered with bodies, he later wrote in *Specimen Days*, and "within ten yards of the front of a house, I notice a heap of amputated feet, legs, arms, hands, &c.; a full load for a one-horse cart. Several dead bodies lie near, each cover'd with its brown woolen blanket. In the door-yard, towards the river, are fresh graves, mostly of officers, their names on pieces of barrel-staves or broken boards, stuck in the dirt."

The experience profoundly affected Whitman. He made his way with the wounded from his brother's regiment up to Washington and rented a room in a small boardinghouse at *1407 L Street NW* (now torn down) from William Douglas O'Connor for $7 per month. He found a part-time job as an army paymaster, but only to make ends meet, and began writing occasional dispatches for *The New York Times* about wartime Washington.

From 1862 until the end of the war, however, Whitman's main energies were devoted to comforting wounded soldiers in makeshift hospitals throughout the city. He was a daily visitor to the old *Armory Square Hospital*, once located at *6th Street & Independence Avenue NW*. In *Specimen Days*, he also describes visiting the wounded at "*the Patent-office*" (in what is now the *National Portrait Gallery*), "English street," "H street," "Campbell hospital" and other places around town. And there were other cheap boarding houses where Whitman stayed during this period, including one at *1205 M Street NW* (now the site of the Claridge Towers apartments).

A Washington correspondent for the *New York Herald* gives us this somewhat hyperbolic account of Whitman during this period of his life:

> I saw him, time and again, in the Washington hospitals, or wending his way there with basket or haversack on his arm, and the strength of beneficence suffusing his face. His devotion surpassed the devotion of woman. . . . Never shall I forget one night when I accompanied him on his rounds . . . there was a smile of affection and welcome on every face, however wan, and his presence seemed to light up the place as it might be lighted by the presence of the God of love.
>
> From cot to cot they called him, often in tremulous tones or in whispers. They embraced him; they touched his hand; they gazed at him. To one he gave a few words of cheer; for another he wrote a letter home; to others he gave an orange, a few comfits, a cigar, a pipe and tobacco, a sheet of paper or a postage stamp . . . from another he would receive a dying message for mother, wife or sweetheart. . . . As he took his way toward the door, you could hear the voices of many a stricken hero calling, "Walt, Walt, Walt! Come again! Come again!"

Everywhere he went in the nation's capital, Whitman's presence was known and felt. His friend John Burroughs describes him on the streets of Washington near the end of the Civil War as "a large slow-moving figure clad in gray, with broad-brimmed hat and gray beard. . . . He had a hirsute, kindly look, but far removed from the finely-cut traditional poet's face." Unfortunately, Whitman's meager salary and his long vigils brought on a physical breakdown. In 1864, hospital doctors ordered him back to his home in Brooklyn for six months of rest.

The next year—two months before Lee's surrender at Appomattox—Whitman felt well enough to return to Washington. This time, he landed a job in the Bureau of Indian Affairs at the Interior Department, which had recently been taken over by James Harlan, a devout Methodist from Iowa who instructed his staff to report employees who could be shown to "disregard . . . the rules of decorum and propriety prescribed by a Christian Civilization." It is said that Harlan searched Whitman's desk himself, and found the heavily edited manuscript of *Leaves of Grass*, which Whitman was updating for publication in 1867. According to Harlan, the work failed the morals test, and Whitman was sacked on June 30th.

Whitman's friends were outraged. They found him a job the next day in the Attorney General's Office. Whitman's fellow government official and former landlord (and novelist) William Douglas O'Connor also came to his friend's defense in a pamphlet called *The Good Gray Poet*. The name of the pamphlet stuck to Whitman, and he carried O'Connor's well-meaning sobriquet with him to his grave.

For seven years, Whitman worked and wrote in the nation's capital. His volume of poems, *Drum-Taps* (1865), contained the great odes to Lincoln "When Lilacs Last In The Doorway Bloomed" and "O Captain, My Captain," which were later absorbed into *Leaves of Grass*. A small group of miscellaneous poems, *Passage to India*, came out in pamphlet form. The essay *Democratic Vistas* was published in its entirety in 1871. The prose book *Memoranda During the War*, the journal entries of *Specimen Days* and two volumes of letters (*The Wound Dresser* and *Calamus*) all belong to this period. And, of course, Whitman was intermittently revising, reshaping and rethinking his masterpiece, *Leaves of Grass*.

In 1873, while living in a small attic room in a long-gone house between *E and F Streets NW* across from the Treasury Department, Whitman suffered a massive paralytic stroke during the night. Unable to work in his bureaucratic job any longer, he was taken up to his brother George's house in Camden, New Jersey. From Camden, the "good gray poet" continued writing, lecturing and traveling until his death in 1892.

Woodrow Wilson   Statesman, historian, educator, 28th President of the United States (1856–1925).

Of all our Presidents, Wilson stands out as being perhaps the most scholarly and deeply interested in books. As a writer, Wilson displayed a love of epigrams, a deftness for turning a well-turned phrase and a knack for good storytelling. Altogether, his gifts elevated his prose far above the usual numbing "bureaucratese" which infects most of governmental Washington.

Among Wilson's many books are *The State* (1889), *Division & Reunion* (1893), *An Old Master and Other*

Political Essays (1893) and the five-volume *A History of the American People* (1902). Today, the *Woodrow Wilson Foundation* in Washington serves to further public understanding of international problems and Wilson's ideals of world cooperation.

The only President to have retired to a home in Washington after leaving office, Wilson moved into a red-brick Georgian Revival townhouse located at *2340 S Street NW*, near Dupont Circle in 1921. Wilson even made a speech from the balcony of this house on Armistice Day 1923, three months before his death. Registered as a National Historic Landmark, the house is presently open to the public for tours (10 am to 4 pm, Tues-Sat, March through December). Visitors will find the home and library richly appointed with virtually all of the original furniture, many books and other personal items belonging to Wilson while he was alive.

Upon his death in 1924, Wilson was entombed in the magnificent *Washington National Cathedral* (*Massachusetts & Wisconsin Avenues NW*), the only U.S. President to be buried in the District of Columbia (Taft is buried in Arlington National Cemetery). His marble sarcophagus rests to the right of the Cathedral's main nave, facing the pulpit.

Contemporary Authors

> We are all apprentices in a craft where no one ever becomes a master.
>
> **—ERNEST HEMINGWAY**

> Writers seldom write the things they think. They simply write the things they think other folks think they think.
>
> **—ELBERT HUBBARD**

> I love being a writer. What I can't stand is the paperwork.
>
> **—PETER DEVRIES**

W hile such things are hard to measure, it appears there are more contemporary book authors residing in the Washington area today than in virtually any other region of the country. In a city where the chief product is words, and where reams and reams of paper are sacrificed to this end, thousands of area residents are obviously writing at breakneck speeds each day to satisfy the demands of their jobs.

The difference between "writing to work" and "working to write," however, can be substantial. It can mean the difference between going flat broke or paying the bills, between finding a style or just banging away on a keyboard. And so, not unlike the practitioners of any other profession or trade, local book authors work hard each day to perfect their literary techniques and develop a distinctive style of writing, both to satisfy their publishers and to keep their readers begging for more.

This edition of *Literary Washington* lists more than 350 of these well-known and lesser-known contemporary American book authors, all of whom currently reside in the Washington area and ply their trade as "working writers." While some readers may feel that certain living American authors who have written brilliantly about Washington but live elsewhere—such as Allen Drury (*Advise and Consent*), Gore Vidal (*Lincoln, Washington*), Ward Just (*Jack Gance*), Ross Thomas (*Out on the Rim*) or Garrett Epps (*The Floating Island*,

The Shad Treatment)—belong in this chapter, please note that the chapter chronicles only contemporary American book authors *who presently reside* in the Washington metropolitan area.

Nearly a hundred of the authors listed in this chapter were not listed in the first edition of *Literary Washington* when it was published in 1989. I would say that this quantum increase reflects two things: the tremendous amount of literary activity in this region and the power of the U.S. Mail. Following publication of the first edition of *Literary Washington*, I received dozens of letters from local book authors requesting to be included in this chapter. For the most part, I have accommodated all requests.

Unlike the previous edition of this book, I chose this time to list only "recent books" of the authors mentioned. Readers should note that a recent book in this chapter may be defined as "any book-length fiction or nonfiction work published by the author during the 1980s or 1990s." On a few occasions, books published before 1980 may be listed for certain well-known contemporary authors whose recent literary output has either slowed or stopped altogether.

Publishers and dates for specific books are noted throughout the chapter, reflecting information which was available prior to June 1991. When either a publisher or a publication date was the *only* piece of information available on a particular book, it is so noted.

In looking over this chapter, I am still struck by how many accomplished American novelists and poets reside here, especially in a city so dominated by journalism and facts. Readers will also note that only contemporary American *book* authors are listed, leaving out the huge pool of local magazine writers, journalists and freelance writers whose articles, essays, poems and short stories have yet to be collected into book-length works.

Despite what some local book critics have written, I also steadfastly defend the validity of this chapter and its intended purpose within this book. All too often, authors of books are neglected or ignored during their lifetimes, then appreciated when it's too late.

This chapter is intended to be a present-day celebration of the variety and virtuosity of Washington's contemporary book authors. Developed in good faith and researched to the best of this author's abilities, I believe this chapter represents the most accurate and comprehensive listing of local book authors presently available.

My only desire is to improve and expand this chapter's contents in successive editions of *Literary Washington*, while giving credit to those who so richly deserve to be recognized for their contributions to the literary life here in the nation's capital.

David Aaron   Author, novelist. Former deputy assistant for National Security Affairs (1977–81).
Recent Books: Agent of Influence (Putnam, 1989); State of Scarlet (1988).

Kenneth L. Adelman   Author, journalist. Columnist, *Washingtonian*. Former director, U.S. Arms Control and Disarmament Agency.
Recent Book: The Great Universal Embrace (Simon & Schuster, 1989).

Bill Adler, Jr.   Author, literary agent (Adler & Robin Books, Inc.). Former president, Washington Independent Writers.
Recent Books: How to Profit from Public Auctions (William Morrow, 1989); Smoking Wars: Nonsmokers' Rights in America (William Morrow, 1989); Outwitting Squirrels (Chicago Review Press, 1988); The Student's Memory Book (Doubleday, 1988); The Wit and Wisdom of Wall Street (with Bill Adler, Sr., Dow Jones-Irwin, 1984); The Home Buyer's Guide (Simon & Schuster, 1984).

Jonathan I. Z. Agronsky   Author, journalist.
Recent Book: Marion Barry: The Politics of Race (British American Publishing, 1991).

Vassily Aksyonov   Novelist, teacher. Professor of creative writing, George Mason University. Noted Soviet author who became a U.S. citizen in 1980.
Recent Books: Say Cheese! (Random House, 1989); In Search of Melancholy Baby (Random House, 1987); Our Golden Ironburg (Ardis, 1986); The Burn (Random House, 1984); The Island of Crimea (Random House, 1983).

Thomas B. Allen   Author, novelist, journalist. Former book editor, *National Geographic*.
Recent Books: CNN Reports: War in the Gulf (with F. Clifton Barry & Norman Polmar, Turner Publishing, 1990); Merchants of Treason (with Norman Polmar,

Delacorte Press, 1988); War Games (McGraw-Hill, 1987); Ship of Gold (Macmillan, 1987); Rickover (with Norman Polmar, Simon & Schuster, 1982).

Susan Alsop   Author, biographer.
Recent Books: The Congress Dances (Harper & Row, 1984); Yankees at the Court: The First Americans in Paris (Doubleday, 1982).

Jack Anderson   Author, journalist, novelist, syndicated columnist. Winner of the Pulitzer Prize for National Reporting, 1972.
Recent Books: Control (Windsor, 1990); Fiasco (Times Books, 1983); The Cambodia File (with Bill Pronzini, Doubleday, 1981); Confessions of a Muckraker (Random House, 1979).

Patrick Anderson   Novelist, author, journalist. Former speech writer for Robert F. Kennedy and President Jimmy Carter.
Recent Books: Rich as Sin (1991); The Pleasure Business (Harcourt Brace Jovanovich, 1989); Sinister Forces (Doubleday, 1986); Lords of the Earth (Doubleday, 1984).

Bob Andrews   Author, novelist. Former CIA officer and ex-Green Beret.
Recent Books: Last Spy Out (Bantam Books, 1991); Center Game (Bantam Books, 1989).

Allen Appel   Novelist, photographer, freelance journalist.
Recent Books: Twice Upon a Time (Carroll & Graf, 1988); Time After Time (Carroll & Graf, 1985).

E. J. Applewhite   Author, essayist, historian.
Recent Books: Paradise Mislaid (1991); Washington Itself: An Informed Guide to the Capital of the United States (Knopf, 1981).

Ellen Argo   Novelist.
Recent Books: The Yankee Girl (Putnam, 1980); The Crystal Star (Putnam, 1979).

Scott Armstrong   Author, journalist. Executive director, National Security Archive. Visiting Scholar of International Journalism, American University. Former staff writer, *The Washington Post*. Winner of President's Award, Washington Independent Writers (1991).

Recent Book: The Brethren: Inside the Supreme Court (with Bob Woodward, Simon & Schuster, 1979).

Bob Arnebeck   Author, journalist.

Recent Book: Through A Fiery Trial: Building Washington 1790–1800 (Madison Books, 1991).

Rick Atkinson   Author, journalist. Staff writer, *The Washington Post*. Pulitzer Prize, National Reporting, 1982.

Recent Book: The Long Gray Line (Houghton Mifflin, 1989).

Donald C. Bacon   Author, journalist. Assistant managing editor, *U.S. News & World Report*. Former staff writer, *The Washington Star*, *The Wall Street Journal* and Newhouse News Service.

Recent Books: Rayburn: A Biography (with D.B. Hardeman, Madison Books, 1989); Congress & You (1985).

Russell Baker   Author, columnist ("All Things Considered," *The New York Times*). Winner of two Pulitzer Prizes—Commentary (1979) and Autobiography (1983). Also winner of the Frank Sullivan Award (1976) and the George Polk Award (1979).

Recent Books: The Good Times (William Morrow, 1989); The Norton Book of Light Verse (ed., Norton, 1986); Growing Up (Congdon & Weed, 1982); The Rescue of Miss Yaskell & Other Pipe Dreams (Congdon & Weed, 1984).

Letitia Baldrige   Author, etiquette consultant. Former White House Social Secretary.

Recent Books: Letitia Baldrige's Complete Guide to the New Manners for the '90s (Rawson Associates, 1990); Letitia Baldrige's Complete Guide to a Great Social Life (Rawson Associates, 1987).

Michael Barone   Author, journalist.

Recent Books: Our Country (Free Press, 1990); The Almanac of American Politics (National Journal, 1987).

John M. Barry   Author, journalist. Former Washington editor, *Dun's Business Month*.

Recent Book: The Ambition & The Power: Jim Wright and the Will of the House (Viking, 1989).

Richard Bausch Novelist, short story writer, teacher. Professor of creative writing and literature, George Mason University.
Recent Books: The Fireman's Wife & Other Stories (Simon & Schuster/Linden Press, 1990); Mr. Field's Daughter (Simon & Schuster, 1989); Spirits & Other Stories (Simon & Schuster/Linden Press, 1987).

Robert Bausch Novelist, teacher. Professor of creative writing and literature, Northern Virginia Community College.
Recent Books: Almighty Me (Houghton Mifflin, 1990); The Lives of Riley Chance (St. Martin's Press, 1984); On the Way Home (St. Martin's Press, 1982).

Beryl Lieff Benderly Author, journalist.
Recent Books: Dancing Without Music: Deafness in America (Gallaudet University Press, 1990); The Myth of Two Minds: What Gender Means and Doesn't Mean (Doubleday, 1987); Thinking About Abortion (Dial Press, 1984).

Elizabeth Benedict Novelist.
Recent Books: The Beginner's Book of Dreams (Knopf, 1988); Slow Dancing (Knopf, 1985).

Lisa Berger Author, journalist. Former president, Washington Independent Writers.
Recent Books: The Healthy Company (Jeremy Tarcher, 1991); We Heard the Angels of Madness (with Diane Berger, William Morrow, 1991); Cashing In (Warner Books, 1989).

Laura Bergheim Author, editor, reviewer.
Recent Books: Weird, Wonderful America (Macmillan, 1988); The Map Catalog (with Joel Makower, Random House, 1986).

Michael R. Beschloss Author, historian. Adjunct historian, The Smithsonian Institution. Senior associate member, St. Anthony's College, Oxford.
Recent Books: The Crisis Years: Kennedy and Khrushchev, 1960–1963 (HarperCollins, 1991); Eisenhower: Centennial Life (Harper & Row, 1990); Mayday: Eisen-

hower, Kruschev and the U–2 Affair (Harper & Row, 1986); Kennedy & Roosevelt: The Uneasy Alliance (Norton, 1980).

Tom Bethell   Author, journalist.
Recent Books: The Electric Windmill (Regnery Gateway, 1987); Television Evening News Covers Inflation (Media Institute, 1980).

Richard N. Billings   Author, journalist, editor. Former editor, *Life* and *The Congressional Quarterly*.
Recent Books: Schirra (with Walter M. Schirra, Quinlan Press, 1988); So Close to Greatness: A Biography of William C. Bullitt (with Will Brownell, Macmillan, 1987); Sara & Gerald: Villa America and After (with Honoria Donnelly, Henry Holt, 1984); The Plot to Kill the President (with G. Robert Blakey, Times Books, 1981).

Wolf Blitzer   Author, journalist, television commentator (CNN). Washington Bureau Chief, *The Jerusalem Post*.
Recent Books: Territory of Lies (Harper & Row, 1989); Between Washington & Jerusalem (Oxford University Press, 1985).

Sidney Blumenthal   Author, journalist, columnist. Staff writer, *The Washington Post*. Former writer, *The New Republic*.
Recent Books: Our Long National Daydream: A Political Pageant of the Reagan Era (Harper & Row, 1988); The Rise of the Counter-Establishment: From Conservative Ideology to Political Power (Times Books, 1986); The Permanent Campaign: Inside the World of Elite Political Operatives (Beacon Press, 1980).

Carl Bode   Author, poet, teacher, journalist.
Recent Books: H.L. Mencken: A Biography (Johns Hopkins University Press, 1986); Practical Magic: Poems (Swallow/Ohio University Press, 1981).

Larry Bond   Novelist, author.
Recent Books: Vortex (Warner Books, 1991); Red Phoenix (Warner Books, 1990).

Daniel Boorstin   Author, historian. Librarian of Congress (1975–87). Winner of numerous awards, including the Pulitzer Prize for History (1974).

Recent Books: Hidden History: Exploring Our Secret Past (Harper & Row, 1989); Image: A Guide to Pseudo-Events in America (Atheneum, 1988); The Discoverers: A History of Man's Search to Know His World & Himself (Random House, 1983).

Robert H. Bork   Judge, attorney, constitutional scholar, Supreme Court nominee.
Recent Books: The Tempting of America: The Political Seduction of the Law (Free Press, 1989); The Antitrust Paradox (Basic Books, 1980).

Tom Boswell   Author, journalist, columnist. Sports Section, *The Washington Post.* Winner of the American Society of Newspaper Editors Award (1981).
Recent Books: Game Day (Doubleday, 1990); The Heart of the Order (Doubleday, 1989); Strokes of Genius (Doubleday, 1987); Why Time Begins on Opening Day (Doubleday, 1984); How Life Imitates the World Series: An Inquiry Into the Game (Doubleday, 1982).

Walter Boyne   Author, retired Air Force colonel. Former director, National Air & Space Museum.
Recent Books: The Wild Blue (with Steven L. Thompson, Ivy Books, 1990); Trophy for Eagles (Ivy Books, 1989).

Howard Bray   Author, journalist. Former executive director, Fund for Investigative Journalism. Past president, Washington Independent Writers.
Recent Book: Pillars of the Post: The Making of a News Empire in Washington (Norton, 1980).

David Brinkley   Author, journalist, television news commentator ("This Week With David Brinkley," ABC-TV). Former co-anchor, *The Huntley-Brinkley Report*; former co-anchor (with John Chancellor), *NBC Nightly News.* Winner of ten Emmy Awards and three George Foster Peabody Awards.
Recent Book: Washington Goes to War (Knopf, 1988).

David Broder   Author, journalist. Staff writer, *The Washington Post.* Member of the Washington Post Writers Group. Winner of the Pulitzer Prize for Commentary (1973).
Recent Books: Behind the Front Page: A Candid Look at How the News Is Made (Simon & Schuster, 1987);

Changing of the Guard: Power & Leadership in America (Simon & Schuster, 1980); The Pursuit of the Presidency (Putnam, 1980).

Ethan Bronner Author, journalist. Reporter, *The Boston Globe*. Winner of the *Washingtonian* Book Award (1989).
Recent Book: Battle for Justice: How the Bork Nomination Shook America (Norton, 1989).

Bruce Brooks Novelist, author (children's books).
Recent Books: The Moves Makes the Man (Harper Junior Editions, 1989); Midnight Hour Encores (Harper Keypoint, 1987).

Art Buchwald Author, essayist, syndicated columnist. Winner of the Pulitzer Prize for Commentary (1982). Former Paris columnist, The New York Herald Tribune.
Recent Books: Whose Rose Garden Is It Anyway? (Putnam, 1989); I Think I Don't Remember (Putnam, 1987); You Can Fool All of the People All of the Time (Putnam, 1985); While Reagan Slept (Putnam, 1983); The Bollo Caper: A Furry Tail for Children of All Ages (Putnam, 1983); Laid Back in Washington (Putnam, 1981).

John Buckley Novelist, journalist. Former press secretary, Jack Kemp's presidential campaign.
Recent Books: Statute of Limitations (Simon & Schuster, 1990); Family Politics (Simon & Schuster, 1988).

David Burnham Author, journalist. Former reporter, *The New York Times*.
Recent Books: A Law unto Itself: The IRS & The Abuse of Power (Random House, 1990); The Rise of the Computer State (Random House, 1983).

Sophy Burnham Author, novelist.
Recent Books: A Book of Angels (Ballantine, 1990); The Dogwalker (Warner Books, 1979).

Jeremy Campbell Author, journalist. Washington correspondent, *The London Evening Standard*.
Recent Books: The Improbable Machine (Simon & Schuster, 1990); Winston Churchill's Afternoon Nap: A Wide-Awake Inquiry into the Nature of Time (Simon &

Schuster, 1987); Grammatical Man: Information, Entropy, Language & Life (Simon & Schuster, 1982).

Lou Cannon Author, journalist. Staff writer, *The Washington Post*. Member, Washington Post Writers Group.
Recent Books: President Reagan: Role of a Lifetime (Simon & Schuster, 1990); Reagan (Putnam, 1982).

Lincoln Caplan Author, journalist. Frequent contributor to *The New Yorker*.
Recent Books: Open Adoption (Farrar, Straus & Giroux, 1990); The Tenth Justice: The Solicitor General and the Rule of Law (Knopf, 1987); The Insanity Defense and the Trial of John W. Hinckley, Jr. (David Godine, 1984).

Jean Carper Author, journalist, columnist. Former television correspondent and producer, Cable News Network.
Recent Books: The Food Pharmacy: Dramatic New Evidence That Food Is Your Best Medicine (Bantam Books, 1988); Jean Carper's Total Nutrition Guide (Bantam Books, 1987); The All-In-One Calorie Counter (Bantam Books, 1987); Health Care USA (Prentice-Hall, 1987); The National Medical Directory (Prentice-Hall, 1986).

Hodding Carter Author, journalist, television commentator. Former spokesperson, U.S. State Department.
Recent Books: The New American South (Bantam Books, 1991); The Reagan Years (Braziller, 1988).

Linda Cashdan Novelist.
Recent Book: Special Interests (St. Martin's Press, 1990).

Elena Castedo Novelist.
Recent Book: Paradise (Grove-Weidenfeld, 1990).

Grace Cavalieri Poet, author, radio host. Hosts "The Poet & The Poem," WPFW-FM Radio.
Recent Books: Trenton (1990); Bliss (Hillmunn Roberts, 1986); Creature Comforts (Word Works, 1982); Swan Research (Word Works, 1979).

Diane Chamberlain Novelist.
Recent Books: Lovers & Strangers (Jove, 1990); Private Relations (Jove, 1989); Secret Lives (1987).

Elaine Raco Chase   Novelist.
Recent Books: Designing Women & Video Vixens (Leisure Books, 1991); Rules of the Game (Dorchester, 1990); Dark Corners (Bantam Books, 1988); Dangerous Places (Bantam Books, 1987).

Nien Cheng   Author.
Recent Book: Life & Death In Shanghai (Grove Press, 1986).

Lynne Cherry   Novelist, author/illustrator (children's books).
Recent Books: Archie, Follow Me (Dutton, 1990); The Great Kapok Tree (Harcourt Brace Jovanovich, 1990); Who's Sick Today? (Dutton, 1988).

Alan Cheuse   Novelist, author, radio commentator. Book critic, National Public Radio ("All Things Considered"). Professor of creative writing, George Mason University.
Recent Books: The Light Possessed (1991); The Tennessee Waltz & Other Stories (Gibbs Smith, 1990); Fall Out of Heaven: An Autobiographical Journey Across Russia (Gibbs Smith, 1987); The Grandmother's Club (Peregrine Smith, 1986).

Tom Clancy   Novelist, author.
Recent Books: The Sum of All Fears (Putnam, 1991); Clear & Present Danger (Putnam, 1989); The Cardinal of the Kremlin (Putnam, 1988); Patriot Games (Putnam, 1987); Red Storm Rising (Putnam, 1986); The Hunt For Red October (Naval Institute Press, 1984).

Shirley Cochrane   Poet, teacher, short-story writer. Teaches writing courses at Georgetown University and the Writer's Center. Winner of PEN Syndicated Fiction Award.
Recent Book: Family & Other Strangers (Word Works, 1989).

James E. Cohen   Novelist, author, editor. Fiction instructor, The Writer's Center.
Recent Books: Disappearance (Atheneum, 1989); Mindbender (with Peter Ruby, Lynx Books, 1989).

William S. Cohen   Novelist, author, poet, U.S. Senator (R-Maine).

Recent Books: One-Eyed Kings (Doubleday, 1991); Men of Zeal: A Candid Story of the Iran-Contra Hearings (with Sen. George J. Mitchell, William Morrow, 1988); Of Sons & Seasons (Hamilton Press, 1987); The Double Man (with Gary Hart, William Morrow, 1985).

Judy Colbert & Ed Colbert   Authors, journalists, travel writers. Co-Publishers, *QuickTrips Travel Letter.*
Recent Books: Places to Go with Children in Washington, DC (Chronicle Books, 1991); Factory Outlet Guide to the Middle Atlantic States (Globe Pequot, 1990); Maryland: Off the Beaten Path (Globe Pequot, 1990); Virginia: Off the Beaten Path (Globe Pequot, 1989); The Spa Guide (Globe Pequot, 1988).

Michael Collier   Poet, teacher. Professor of literature, University of Maryland.
Recent Books: The Folded Heart (University Press of New England, 1989); The Clasp & Other Poems (University Press of New England, 1986).

James Conaway   Novelist, author, journalist.
Recent Book: Napa (Houghton Mifflin, 1990).

Anne Conover   Author, editor. Former writer/editor with Johns Hopkins Press and the Library of Congress.
Recent Book: Caresse Crosby: From Black Sun to Roccasinibalda (Capra Press, 1989).

A. Craig Copetas   Author, journalist. National correspondent, *Regardie's.*
Recent Book: Metal Men: Marc Rich and the $10 Billion Scam (Putnam, 1985).

John Cribb   Author, journalist.
Recent Book: The I-95 Field Guide (Madison Books, 1989).

Tom Crouch   Author, historian.
Recent Books: The Bishop's Boys: A Life of Wilbur & Orville Wright (Norton, 1989); A Dream of Wings (Smithsonian Books, 1989).

Marcus Cunliffe   Author, historian.
Recent Books: American Presidents and the Presidency (Houghton Mifflin, 1986); The Literature of the United States (Penguin, 1986, 4th ed.).

Ann Darr   Poet, author.
Recent Books: Do You Take This Woman? (Washington Writers' Publishing House, 1986); Riding with the Fireworks (Alice Jones Books, 1981); Cleared for Landing (Dryad Press, 1978).

Leon Dash   Author, journalist. Staff writer, *The Washington Post.*
Recent Book: When Children Want Children: The Urban Crisis of Teenage Childbearing (William Morrow, 1989).

Jeffrey Davidson   Author, journalist.
Recent Books: Breathing Space: Living & Working at a Comfortable Pace in a Sped-Up Society (MasterMedia, Ltd., 1991); How to Have a Great Year Every Year (Berkley, 1991); Selling to the Giants: How to Become a Key Supplier to Large Corporations (Tab/McGraw-Hill, 1991); Blow Your Own Horn: How to Get Ahead and Get Noticed (Berkley, 1990); Power & Protocol for Getting to the Top (Shapolsky, 1990); Avoiding the Pitfalls of Starting Your Own Business (Walker, 1988).

Benjamin O. Davis, Jr.   Author, U.S. Air Force general (retired). Commander, Tuskegee Airmen (World War II).
Recent Book: Benjamin O. Davis, Jr.: An Autobiography (Smithsonian Institution Press, 1991).

Deborah Davis   Author, journalist.
Recent Books: Katherine the Great: Katherine Graham and The Washington Post (National Press, 1987); The Children of God: The Inside Story (Zondervan, 1984).

Ken DeCell   Author, journalist, editor. Editor, *Washingtonian.*
Recent Book: The 13 Keys to the Presidency (with Allan J. Lichtman, Madison Books, 1990).

Arnaud de Borchgrave   Novelist, journalist, editor. Editor-in-chief, *The Washington Times.*
Recent Books: Monimbo (with Robert Moss, Simon & Schuster, 1983); The Spike (with Robert Moss, Crown, 1980).

Beth DeFrancis   Author, journalist.
Recent Book: The Writer's Guide to Metropolitan Washington: Where to Sell What You Write (Woodbine House, 1991).

Mollie Dickenson   Author, journalist.
Recent Book: Thumbs Up!: The Life & Courageous Comeback of White House Press Secretary Jim Brady (with Jim Brady, William Morrow, 1987).

Paul Dickson   Author, journalist. Former president, Washington Independent Writers. Winner of Philip M. Stern Award, Washington Independent Writers (1986).
Recent Books: Timelines (Addison-Wesley, 1991); What Do You Call A Person From . . .? (Facts on File, 1990); The Dickson Baseball Dictionary (Facts on File, 1989); Family Words: The Dictionary for People Who Don't Know a Frone from a Brinkle (Addison-Wesley, 1988); The Library in America (Facts on File, 1986); On Our Own (Facts On File, 1985).

John Dinges   Author, journalist.
Recent Books: Our Man in Panama (Random House, 1990); Assassination on Embassy Row (with Saul Landau, Pantheon, 1980).

Dusko Doder   Author, journalist. Former Moscow Bureau Chief, *The Washington Post.*
Recent Books: Gorbachev: Heretic in the Kremlin (with Louise Branson, Viking/Penguin, 1990); Shadows & Whispers: Power Politics Inside the Kremlin from Brezhnev to Gorbachev (Random House, 1986); The Yugoslavs (Random House, 1978).

Robert J. Donovan   Author, journalist. Former Bureau Chief, *The Los Angeles Times* and *The New York Herald Tribune.*
Recent Books: Confidential Secretary (Dutton, 1988); The Second Victory: The Marshall Plan & the Postwar Revival of Europe (Madison Books, 1987); Nemesis: Truman & Johnson in the Coils of War in Asia (St. Martin's Press, 1984); Tumultuous Years: The Presidency of Harry S. Truman, 1949–53 (Norton, 1982).

Frederick Downs   Author, novelist, journalist, former government official.

Recent Books: The Killing Zone (Berkley, 1987); Aftermath (Berkley, 1985).

Elizabeth Drew   Author, journalist, television commentator ("Inside Washington"). Regular contributor to *The New Yorker* and former Washington editor, *The Atlantic Monthly*.
Recent Books: Election Journal: The Political Events of 1987–88 (William Morrow, 1988); Campaign Journal: The Political Events of 1983–84 (Macmillan, 1985); Politics & Money: The New Road to Corruption (Macmillan, 1983).

Bruce Duffy   Novelist.
Recent Book: The World As I Found It (Ticknor & Fields, 1987).

Pete Earley   Author, journalist. Former staff writer, *The Washington Post*.
Recent Books: Family of Spies: Inside the John Walker Spy Ring (Bantam Books, 1988); The Keys to the Kingdom (Bantam Books, 1988).

Gregg Easterbrook   Author, novelist, journalist. Contributing editor, *Newsweek*.
Recent Book: This Magic Moment (St. Martin's Press, 1986).

Terry Eastland   Author, journalist, editor. Resident scholar, National Legal Center for the Public Interest.
Recent Books: Ethics, Politics and the Independent Counsel (National Legal Center Publications, 1989); The Conservation Paradox: Counting by Race Equality from the Founding Fathers to Bakke and Weber (Basic Books, 1979).

Thomas B. Edsall   Author, journalist.
Recent Books: Power & Money (Norton, 1989); The New Politics of Inequality (Norton, 1985).

Laura Elliott   Author, journalist. Senior writer, *Washingtonian*.
Recent Book: Shattered Dreams (with Charlotte Fedders, Harper & Row, 1987).

Sally Emerson   Novelist.
Recent Book: Fire Child (Viking, 1990).

Steven Emerson Author, journalist, editor. Senior editor, *U.S. News & World Report*. Winner of the Investigative Reporters & Editors Award (1988).
Recent Books: The Fall of Pan Am 103 (with Brian Duffy, Putnam, 1990); Secret Warriors: Inside the Covert Operations of the Reagan Era (Putnam, 1988); The American House of Saud: The Secret Petrodollar Connection (Franklin Watts, 1985).

Margaret Engel Author, journalist. Executive director, Alicia Paterson Foundation. Reporter, *The Washington Post*. Neiman Fellow.
Recent Book: Food Finds: America's Best Local Foods and The People Who Make Them (with Allison Engel, Harper & Row, 1986).

Jack Erickson Author, publisher. Nationally recognized authority on beer and brewing techniques.
Recent Books: Star Spangled Beer: A Guide to America's New Microbreweries and Brewpubs (RedBrick Press, 1987); Great Cooking with Beer (RedBrick Press, 1989); A Mission to Serve (RedBrick Press, 1989).

Pete Exton Author, journalist, editor.
Recent Books: A Shunpiker's Guide to the Northeast: Washington to Boston Without Turnpikes or Interstates (EPM Publications, 1988); Milestones into Headstones: Mini-Biographies of 50 Fascinating Americans Buried in Washington, DC (with Dorsey Kleitz, EPM Publications, 1985).

James Fallows Author, journalist, editor. Washington editor, *The Atlantic*. Former editor, *The Washington Monthly*. Former associate editor, *Texas Monthly*. Winner of the American Book Award (1981).
Recent Books: Human Capital (Houghton Mifflin, 1989); More Like Us: Making America Great Again (Houghton Mifflin, 1989); National Defense (Random House, 1981).

John Feinstein Author, journalist. Sports writer, *Sports Illustrated*. Former staff writer, *The Washington Post*.
Recent Books: Forever's Team (Random House, 1989); A Season Inside: One Year in College Basketball (Villard Books, 1988); A Season on the Brink: A Year with Bob Knight & the Indiana Hoosiers (Macmillan, 1986).

Randall Fitzgerald   Author, journalist. Former founding editor, *Second Look* magazine. Former reporter, Jack Anderson & Capitol Hill News Service.
Recent Books: When Government Goes Private: Successful Alternatives to Public Services (Universe Books, 1988); Porkbarrel (with Gerald Lipson, Cato Institute Press, 1984); The Complete Book of Extraterrestrial Encounters (Collier Books, 1979).

Roland Flint   Poet, teacher, author. Instructor, Georgetown University.
Recent Books: Stubborn (University of Illinois Press, 1990); Sicily (Wesleyan Press, 1987); Resuming Green: Selected Poems 1965–1982 (Dial Press, 1983); Say It (Dryad Press, 1979).

Carolyn Forche   Poet, teacher. Instructor, George Mason University.
Recent Books: The Country Between Us (Harper & Row, 1982); Gathering the Tribes (Yale University Press, 1976).

Thomas G. Foxworth   Author, novelist, airline pilot.
Recent Books: Passengers (with Michael J. Lawrence, Doubleday, 1983); The Speed Seekers (Doubleday, 1976).

Linda Bird Francke   Author, journalist, editor. Former contributing editor, *New York Magazine*. Former editor, *Newsweek*.
Recent Books: A Woman of Egypt (with Jihan Sadat, Simon & Schuster, 1987); Ferraro: My Story (with Geraldine Ferraro, Bantam Books, 1985); First Lady from Plains (with Rosalynn Carter, Houghton Mifflin, 1984); Growing Up Divorced: Children of the 80's (Simon & Schuster, 1983).

Jeffrey A. Frank   Author, novelist, editor. Editor, Outlook, *The Washington Post*.
Recent Book: The Creep (1991).

Jon Franklin   Author, teacher, science writer. Professor of journalism, University of Maryland. Winner of two Pulitzer Prizes—Feature Writing (1979) and Explanatory Journalism (1985). Also winner of the James T. Grady Medal (1975) and the Helen Carringer Award (1984).

Recent Books: Molecules of the Mind: The Brave New Science of Molecular Psychology (Atheneum, 1987); Shocktrauma (with Alan Doelp, St. Martin's Press, 1980).

Candida Fraze   Novelist.
Recent Book: Renifleur's Daughter (Henry Holt, 1987).

Margot Fromer   Author, novelist, journalist. President, Chesapeake Chapter, Sisters in Crime.
Recent Books: Gift of Death (Berkley, 1992); Scalpel's Edge (1990).

John Rolfe Gardiner   Novelist, short-story writer.
Recent Books: The Incubator Ballroom (Knopf, 1991); In the Heart of the Whole World (Knopf, 1988).

Frank Getlein   Author, journalist, editor.
Recent Books: John Safer (J.J. Binns, 1982); Mary Cassatt (Abbeville, 1980); The Washington, DC Art Review: The Art Explorers Guide to Washington (Vanguard Press, 1980).

Robert Gettlin   Author, journalist.
Recent Book: Silent Coup (with Len Colodny, St. Martin's Press, 1991).

Georgie Anne Geyer   Author, journalist.
Recent Books: Guerrilla Prince (Little, Brown, 1991); Buying the Night Flight: The Autobiography of a Woman Foreign Correspondent (Delacorte Press, 1983).

Jack Gillis   Author, consumer advocate, teacher. Part-time faculty, George Washington University.
Recent Books: The Car Book 1991 (HarperCollins, 1990); The Car Repair Book (with Tom Kelly, HarperCollins, 1990); The Used Car Book 1989 (Harper & Row, 1988); How to Keep Your Car Almost Forever (Putnam, 1987); The Childwise Catalog (with Mary Fise, Pocket Books, 1986).

Vic Gold   Novelist, author, journalist. National correspondent, *Washingtonian*.
Recent Books: The Body Politic (with Lynne Cheney, St. Martin's Press, 1988); Looking Forward: The George Bush Story (Doubleday, 1987).

Marita Golden Novelist, author, television producer. Creative writing instructor, George Mason University. Founder and president, Afro-American Writers Guild. Former associate producer, WNET-TV, New York.

Recent Books: Long Distance Life (Doubleday, 1989); A Woman's Place (Doubleday, 1986); Migrations of the Heart (Anchor Press, 1983).

Ronald L. Goldfarb Author, attorney, literary agent.

Recent Books: The Writer's Lawyer: Essential Legal Advice for Writers and Editors In All Media (with Gail Ross, Times Books, 1989); Jails: The Ultimate Ghetto (Anchor Press, 1975).

James M. Goode Author, historian. Former curator, Smithsonian Institution Building.

Recent Books: Best Addresses: A Century of Washington's Distinguished Apartment Houses (Smithsonian Institution Press, 1988); Capital Losses: A Cultural History of Washington's Destroyed Buildings (Smithsonian Institution Press, 1979); The Outdoor Sculpture of Washington, DC: A Comprehensive Historical Guide (Smithsonian Institution Press, 1974).

Stephen Goodwin Novelist, teacher. Director of Literature Program, National Endowment for the Arts. Former professor of creative writing and English literature, George Mason University.

Recent Books: The Greatest Masters: The 1986 Masters & Golf's Elite (Harper & Row, 1988); Blood of Paradise (Dutton, 1979).

James S. Gordon Author, teacher. Professor, Georgetown University.

Recent Books: The Golden Guru: The Strange Journey of Bhagwan Shree Rajneesh (Greene, 1988); Stress Management (Chelsea House, 1989); Holistic Medicine (Chelsea House, 1988).

Joseph C. Goulden Author, journalist. Former reporter, *Dallas News*. Former Washington Bureau Chief, *Philadelphia Inquirer*. Winner of Philip M. Stern Award, Washington Independent Writers (1991).

Recent Books: Fit To Print: A.M. Rosenthal & His Times (Lyle Stuart, 1988); The Dictionary of Espionage (as Henry Sabecket, Stein & Day, 1986); The Death

Merchants (Simon & Schuster, 1984); Korea: The Untold Story of the War (Times Books, 1982).

James Grady Novelist, screenwriter. Former staff writer, Jack Anderson.
Recent Books: Steeltown (Bantam Books, 1989); Just A Shot Away (Bantam Books, 1987); Hard Bargains (Macmillan, 1985); Runner in the Street (Macmillan, 1984).

Eloise Greenfield Author, novelist (children's books). Winner of the Coretta Scott King Honor Book Award (1990).
Recent Books: Grandpa's Face (Putnam, 1988); Nathaniel Talking (Writers & Readers, 1989); Africa Dream (Harper & Row, 1989).

John Greenya Author, journalist, novelist.
Recent Books: Blood Relations: The Exclusive Inside Story of the Benson Family Murders (Harcourt Brace Jovanovich, 1987); Are You Tough Enough? (with Anne Burford, McGraw-Hill, 1986); The Real David Stockman (St. Martin's Press, 1986); Guns Don't Die, People Do (with Pete Shields, Arbor House, 1981).

William Greider Author, journalist, columnist. Contributing editor, *Rolling Stone*. Former assistant managing editor, *The Washington Post*.
Recent Books: The Trouble With Money (Whittle Direct Books, 1990); Secrets of the Temple: How the Federal Reserve Runs the Country (Simon & Schuster, 1987); The Education of David Stockman & Other Americans (Dutton, 1982).

Patricia Griffith Novelist, teacher.
Recent Books: The Great Saturday Night Swindle (1987); Tennessee Blue (Crown, 1981).

Martha Grimes Novelist, mystery writer, poet, teacher. Visiting professor, The Writing Seminars, Johns Hopkins University. Former professor of literature, Montgomery College. Winner of the Nero Wolfe Award (1983).
Recent Books: Send Bygraves (Little, Brown, 1990); The Old Silent (Little, Brown, 1989); The Five Bells & Bladebone (Little, Brown, 1987); I Am the Only Running Footman (Little, Brown, 1986); The Deer Leap

(Little, Brown, 1985); Help the Poor Struggler (Little, Brown, 1985); The Dirty Duck (Little, Brown, 1984); Jerusalem Inn (Little, Brown, 1984); The Anodyne Necklace (Little, Brown, 1983); The Old Fox Deceiv'd (Little, Brown, 1982); The Man With a Load of Mischief (Little, Brown, 1981).

Jonathan Groner   Author, attorney. Editor, *The Legal Times.*
Recent Book: Hilary's Trial: The Morgan Case: A Child's Ordeal in America's Legal System (1991).

Jerry Hagstrom   Author, journalist. Contributing editor, *National Journal.*
Recent Books: Beyond Reagan: The New Landscape of American Politics (Norton, 1988); The Book Of America (with Neal Pierce, Norton, 1983).

Lynn Haney   Author, editor, lecturer, screenwriter. Coordinator, *The Georgetown Courier Creative People Series* (Georgetown Public Library).
Recent Book: Naked at the Feast: The Biography of Josephine Baker (Dodd Mead, 1980).

Louis Harlan   Author, historian. Professor at University of Maryland. Winner of the Pulitzer Prize for Biography (1989).
Recent Book: Booker T. Washington, Vol. 2: The Wizard of Tuskegee (Oxford University Press, 1989).

Gilbert Harrison   Author, editor, biographer. Former owner and editor, *The New Republic.*
Recent Books: The Enthusiast: A Life of Thornton Wilder (Fromm International Publications, 1986); A Timeless Affair: The Life of Anita McCormick Blaine (University of Chicago Press, 1979).

Jeffrey W. Harrison   Poet, author, editor.
Recent Book: The Singing Underneath (Dutton, 1988).

Richard Harteis   Poet, teacher.
Recent Books: Marathon (Norton, 1989); Internal Geography (Carnegie-Mellon University Press, 1987); Morocco Journal: Love, Work, Play (Carnegie-Mellon University Press, 1981).

Robert Hazen   Author, scientist, teacher. Research scientist, Carnegie Institution's Geophysical Laboratory. Professor of earth science, George Mason University.
   Recent Books: Science Matters: Achieving Scientific Literacy (with James Trefil, Doubleday, 1990); The Breakthrough: The Race for the Superconductor (Ballantine, 1989).

Anthony Hecht   Poet, literary critic, teacher. Professor of creative writing and literature, Georgetown University. Consultant in Poetry, Library of Congress (1982–84). Winner of the Pulitzer Prize for Poetry (1968).
   Recent Books: The Transparent Man (Knopf, 1990); Collected Earlier Poems (Knopf, 1990); Obbligati: Essays in Criticism (Atheneum, 1986); A Love for Four Voices (Penman Press, 1983); The Venetian Vespers (Atheneum, 1979).

Marcy Heidish   Novelist, author, freelance editor. President, Approach/Avoidance Editing Service. Teacher of creative writing, Georgetown University. Winner of NEA Creative Writing Fellowship and Sam S. Schubert Playwriting Award.
   Recent Books: Deadline (St. Martin's Press, 1990); Miracles (New American Library, 1984); The Secret Annie Oakley (New American Library, 1983); Witnesses (Houghton Mifflin, 1980).

Robin Marantz Henig   Author, journalist, medical writer. Regular contributor, "Body & Mind," *The New York Times Magazine.*
   Recent Books: How A Woman Ages (Ballantine, 1985); Your Premature Baby (Rawson Associates, 1983); The Myth of Senility: The Truth About the Brain & Aging (Doubleday, 1981).

Carl F. H. Henry   Author, theologian.
   Recent Books: Carl Henry at His Best (Multnomah, 1990); Christian Countermoves in a Decadent Culture (Multnomah, 1986); Horizons of Science: Christian Scholars Speak Out (Harper & Row, 1978).

Herblock   Author, editorial cartoonist. Cartoonist, *The Washington Post,* since 1946. Former editorial cartoonist, *Chicago Daily News.* Winner of the Pulitzer Prize for Editorial Cartooning three times (1942, 1954, 1979).

Also winner of the Elijah Lovejoy Award (1986), Franklin Roosevelt Freedom Medal (1987) and other honors.

Recent Books: Herblock at Large (Pantheon, 1987); Herblock Through the Looking Glass (Norton, 1984); Herblock on All Fronts (New American Library, 1980).

Seymour M. Hersh   Author, journalist. Former reporter, *United Press International* and *The New York Times* (1972–79). Contributing editor, *The Atlantic*. Winner of the Pulitzer Prize for International Reporting (1970) and four George Polk Awards (1970, 1974, 1975, 1981).

Recent Books: "The Target is Destroyed": What Really Happened To Flight 007 & What America Knew About It (Random House, 1986); The Price of Power: Kissinger in the White House (Summit Books, 1983).

Mark Hertsgaard   Author, journalist.

Recent Books: On Bended Knee: The Press & The Reagan Presidency (Farrar, Straus & Giroux, 1988); Nuclear Inc.: The Men and the Money Behind Nuclear Energy (Pantheon, 1983).

Christopher Hitchens   Author, journalist, editor. Washington editor, *Harper's*. Columnist for *The Nation*.

Recent Books: Blood, Class and Nostalgia (Farrar, Straus & Giroux, 1990); Monarchy (Random House, 1990); Prepared for the Worst (Hill & Wang, 1988).

Max Holland   Author, editor, journalist.

Recent Book: When the Machine Stopped (Harvard Business School Press, 1989).

Herman Holtz   Author, editor, consultant.

Recent Books: The Complete Work-At-Home Companion (Prima Publishing, 1990); The Consultant's Guide to Proposal Writing (Wiley, 1990); Writing Winning Proposals With Your PC (Scott Foresman, 1989); Advice: A High-Profit Business (Prentice-Hall, 1986).

Ann Hood   Novelist.

Recent Books: Three-Legged Horse (Bantam, 1989); Waiting to Vanish (Bantam Books, 1988); Somewhere Off the Coast of Maine (Bantam Books, 1987).

David Hoof   Novelist.

Recent Book: Foley Effects (New American Library, 1989).

Roy Hoopes Author, journalist. Washington Bureau Chief, *Modern Maturity*. Former editor at *Washingtonian*, *National Geographic* and *High Fidelity*.
Recent Books: The Making of a Mormon Apostle: The Story of Rudger Clawson (with David S. Hoopes, Madison Books, 1989); Ralph Ingersoll: A Biography (Atheneum, 1985); Cain: A Biography of James M. Cain (Holt, 1982); Political Campaigning (Franklin Watts, 1979).

Sandy Horwitt Author, journalist, legislative consultant.
Recent Book: Let Them Call Me Rebel: Saul Alinsky, His Life & Legacy (Knopf, 1989).

Carolyn Hougan Novelist, author.
Recent Books: The Romeo Flag (Simon & Schuster, 1989); Shooting in the Dark (Simon & Schuster, 1984).

Jim Hougan Author, journalist. Washington correspondent, *Intelligence* (Paris).
Recent Book: Secret Agenda (Random House, 1984).

Russell Warren Howe Author, novelist, journalist. Former foreign correspondent, *The Washington Post*. President, Foreign Policy Correspondents Association.
Recent Books: The Hunt for Tokyo Rose (Madison Books, 1990); The Koreans: Passion and Grace (Harcourt Brace Jovanovich, 1988); Mata Hari—The True Story (Dodd Mead, 1986); Weapons: The International Game of Arms, Money & Diplomacy (Doubleday, 1980).

David Hubler Author, novelist, freelance travel writer.
Recent Books: The Politician's Health Diet & Sex Guide (Tribeca/Comus, 1989); You Gotta Believe (NAL/Signet, 1983).

Mark Hulbert Author, columnist, editor, publisher. Editor, *The Hulbert Financial Digest*. President, Minerva Books. Regular columnist, *Forbes* ("The Wall Street Irregular").
Recent Books: The Hulbert Guide to Financial Newsletters (New York Institute of Finance, 1991); Interlock: The Untold Story of American Banks, Oil Interests, The Shah's Money, Debts & The Astounding Connection Between Them (Richardson & Snyder, 1982).

David Ignatius   Novelist, journalist, editor. Editor, Outlook, *The Washington Post*. Former Middle East correspondent, *The Wall Street Journal*.
Recent Books: Siro (Farrar, Straus & Giroux, 1991); Agents of Innocence: A Spy Story (Norton, 1987).

Walter Isaacson   Author, journalist, editor. Senior editor, *Time*.
Recent Book: The Wise Men: Six Friends and the World They Made (with Evan Thomas, Simon & Schuster, 1986).

Brooks Jackson   Author, journalist. Staff writer, *The Wall Street Journal*.
Recent Book: Honest Graft: Big Money & The Political Process (Knopf, 1988).

Josephine Jacobsen   Poet, author.
Recent Books: On The Island: New & Selected Stories (Persea Books, 1989); The Sisters: New & Selected Poems (Bench Press, 1987); Adios, Mr. Moxley: Thirteen Stories (Book Service Associates, 1986); The Chinese Insomniacs: New Poems (University of Pennsylvania Press, 1981).

Philip K. Jason   Poet, author.
Recent Books: Nineteenth-Century American Poetry (Dryad Press, 1989); Near the Fire (Dryad Press, 1983); Thawing Out (Dryad Press, 1979).

Pamela Jekel   Novelist, author.
Recent Books: The Last of the California Girls (Zebra Books, 1989); Columbia (Berkley, 1987).

Rod Jellema   Poet, author.
Recent Book: Eighth Day: New and Selected Poems (Dryad Press, 1984).

Haynes Johnson   Author, journalist, television commentator. Winner of the Pulitzer Prize for National Reporting (1966).
Recent Books: Sleepwalking Through History: America in the Reagan Years (Norton, 1991); The Landing: A Novel of Washington & WW II (with Howard Simons, Villard, 1986); In the Absence of Power: Governing America (Viking, 1980).

Rochelle Jones   Author, journalist. Former press secretary/ health care adviser, Rep. Claude Pepper (D-Fla.).
Recent Books: The Super Meds: How Private For-Profit Medical Organizations Are Controlling Our Health Care & What to do About It (Scribner's, 1987); The Big Switch: New Careers, New Lives After 35 (McGraw-Hill, 1980).

Beth Joselow   Poet, author.
Recent Books: Broad Daylight (Story Line Press, 1989); The April Wars (SOS Books, 1983); Gypsies (Washington Writers Publishing House, 1979).

Larry Kahaner   Author, journalist, novelist. Licensed private investigator, Kane International Associates. Also writes under the name Larry Kane.
Recent Books: Naked Prey (Zebra Books, 1991); Cults That Kill: Probing the Underworld of Occult Crime (Warner Books, 1988); On the Line: The Men of MCI Who Took on AT & T, Risked Everything and Won! (Warner Books, 1986); The Phone Book: The Most Complete Guide to the Changing World of Telephones (with Alan Green, Penguin, 1983).

Robert G. Kaiser   Author, journalist. Staff writer, *The Washington Post.*
Recent Books: Russia (1984); Russia from the Inside (Dutton, 1980); Great American Dreams: A Portrait of the Way We Are (Harper & Row, 1979).

Gloria Kamen   Novelist, author (children's books).
Recent Books: Edward Lear: King of Nonsense (Macmillan, 1990); Paddle, Said the Swan (Macmillan, 1989); The Ringdoves: From the Fables of Bidpai (Macmillan, 1988).

Fred Kaplan   Author, historian.
Recent Books: The Wizards of Armageddon: Strategists of the Nuclear Age (Simon & Schuster, 1983); Dubious Specter: A Skeptical Look at the Soviet Nuclear Threat (Institute for Policy Studies, rev. ed., 1980).

Stanley Karnow   Author, journalist, syndicated columnist (*King Features*). Former reporter for *Time, Washington Post, New Republic* and *NBC News.*
Recent Books: In Our Image: America's Empire in the

Phillipines (Random House, 1989); Vietnam: A History (Viking, 1983).

Walter Karp   Author, historian.
   Recent Books: Liberty Under Seige: American Politics, 1976–88 (Henry Holt, 1988); The Politics of War (Harper & Row, 1979).

D. Mark Katz   Author, Civil War photo historian. Media relations manager, American Legion. Former editor & publisher, *Incidents of the War* magazine (1984–87).
   Recent Books: Witness to an Era: The Life and Photographs of Alexander Gardner (Viking Studio Books, 1991); Custer in Photographs (Random House/Bonanza, 1990).

Caroline H. Keith   Author, historian, editor. Former editor, *The Maryland Historian.*
   Recent Book: For Hell and a Brown Mule: The Biography of Senator Millard E. Tydings (Madison Books, 1991).

Kitty Kelley   Author, journalist, celebrity biographer. Former staffer, *The Washington Post.* Winner of Outstanding Author Award, American Society of Journalists & Authors (1987). Winner of the Philip M. Stern Award, Washington Independent Writers (1987).
   Recent Books: Nancy Reagan: The Unauthorized Biography (Simon & Schuster, 1991); His Way: The Unauthorized Biography of Frank Sinatra (Bantam Books, 1986); Elizabeth Taylor: The Last Star (Simon & Schuster, 1981).

Brian Kelly   Author, editor, journalist. Editor, *Regardie's.*
   Recent Books: The Four Little Dragons (with Mark London, Simon & Schuster, 1989); Amazon (with Mark London, Harcourt Brace Jovanovich, 1983).

Marguerite Kelly   Author, journalist, columnist ("The Family Almanac").
   Recent Book: The Mother's Almanac II: Your Child From 6–12 (Doubleday, 1989).

Orr Kelly   Novelist, author, journalist.
   Recent Book: King of the Killing Zone (Norton, 1989).

Tom Kelly Author, journalist, editor. Feature writer, *The Washington Times*. Former reporter and contributing editor, *Washingtonian* and *Washington Daily News* (1954–65).
Recent Book: The Imperial Post: The Meyers, The Grahams & The Paper That Rules Washington (William Morrow, 1983).

Roger Kennedy Author, editor, scholar. Director, National Museum of American History.
Recent Books: Rediscovering America (1990); Greek Revival America (Stewart, Tabori & Chang, 1989).

Ronald Kessler Author, journalist. Winner of sixteen major journalism awards, including two George Polk Awards. Former staff writer, *The Washington Post* and *The Wall Street Journal*.
Recent Books: Escape from the CIA (Simon & Schuster, 1991); The Spy in the Russian Club (Scribner's, 1990); Moscow Station: How the KGB Penetrated the American Embassy (Scribner's, 1989); Spy vs. Spy: Stalking Soviet Spies in America (Scribner's, 1988); Adnan Khashoggi: The Story of the World's Richest Man (Warner Books, 1986); The Life Insurance Game (Holt, 1985).

Michael Kilian Novelist, author, journalist. Washington columnist, *Chicago Tribune*.
Recent Books: Dance on a Sinking Ship (Bantam Books, 1989); By Order of the President: Who Is Running the United States of America? (St. Martin's Press, 1986); Blood of the Czars (St. Martin's Press, 1985); Northern Exposure (St. Martin's Press, 1983); The Valkyrie Project (St. Martin's Press, 1981).

James J. Kilpatrick Author, journalist, columnist, television commentator ("Inside Washington").
Recent Books: A Bestiary of Bridge (Andrews & McMeel, 1986); The Writer's Art (Andrews & McMeel, 1985); The Ear Is Human: A Handbook of Homophones & Other Confusions (Andrews & McMeel, 1985).

Florence King Author, novelist.
Recent Books: Lump It or Leave It (St. Martin's Press, 1990); Reflections in a Jaundiced Eye (St. Martin's Press, 1989); Confessions of a Failed Southern Lady (St. Mar-

tin's Press, 1985); When Sisterhood Was in Flower (Viking, 1982).

Larry King   Author, television and radio talk show host, syndicated columnist.
  Recent Books: Tell Me More (Putnam, 1990); Mr. King, You're Having a Heart Attack (with B.D. Cohen, Delacorte Press, 1989); Tell it to the King (with Peter Occhiogrosso, Putnam, 1988); Larry King (with Emily Yoffe, Simon & Schuster, 1982).

Larry L. King   Novelist, author, playwright, screenwriter, actor. Winner of many awards, including Tony Award, TV Emmy (1981), Helen Hayes Award, Stanley Walker Journalism Award and Mark Twain Citation (1969).
  Recent Books: Because of Lozo Brown (Viking, 1988); None But a Blockhead: On Being a Writer (Viking, 1986); Warning: Writer at Work (Texas Christian University Press, 1985); Of Outlaws, Con Men, Whores, Politicians and Other Artists (Viking, 1980). *Plays*: The Golden Shadows Old West Museum; The Night Hank Williams Died; The Kingfish; Christmas: 1933; The Best Little Whorehouse in Texas.

Michael Kinsley   Author, journalist, columnist. Editor, *The New Republic*.
  Recent Book: Curse of the Giant Muffins & Other Washington Maladies (Summit Books, 1987).

Peter Klappert   Poet, teacher. Professor of creative writing and literature, George Mason University.
  Recent Books: The Idiot Princess of the Last Dynasty (Knopf, 1984); Fifty-Two Pick-Up (Orchises Press, 1984).

Philip Klass   Author, journalist. Senior editor, *Aviation Week & Space Technology*.
  Recent Books: UFO Abductions: A Dangerous Game (Prometheus Books, 1988); UFOs: The Public Deceived (Prometheus, 1986).

John J. Kohut   Author, political consultant.
  Recent Books: Beyond News of the Weird (with Chuck Shepherd and Roland Sweet, Plume, 1991); More News of the Weird (with Chuck Shepherd and Roland

Sweet, Plume, 1990); News of the Weird (with Chuck Shepherd and Roland Sweet, Plume, 1989).

Joyce R. Kornblatt Novelist, short-story writer, teacher. Professor of literature and creative writing, University of Maryland.
Recent Books: Breaking Bread (Dutton, 1987); White Water (Dell, 1987); Nothing to Do With Love (Viking, 1981).

Mary Lynn Kotz Author, journalist. Contributing editor, *Artnews*. Former reporter, United Press International.
Recent Books: Rauschenberg Himself (Abrams, 1990); Marvella: A Personal Journey (with Marvella Bayh, Harcourt Brace Jovanovich, 1979).

Nick Kotz Author, journalist, teacher. Professor of journalism, American University School of Communications. Former staff writer, *The Washington Post*. Winner of the Pulitzer Prize for National Reporting (1968) and the National Magazine Award (1983).
Recent Book: Wild Blue Yonder: Money, Politics and the B–1 Bomber (Pantheon, 1987).

Charles Krauthammer Author, journalist, columnist, television commentator ("Inside Washington"). Columnist, *The New Republic*. Regular contributor, *Time*. Winner of the Pulitzer Prize for Commentary (1987).
Recent Books: Cutting Edges: Making Sense of the '80s (Paragon House, 1988); Intervention & The Reagan Doctrine (Carnegie-Mellon Press, 1985).

Irving Kristol Author, journalist, political analyst.
Recent Book: Reflections of a Neoconservative: Looking Back, Looking Ahead (Basic Books, 1983).

Donald Lambro Author, journalist, political analyst.
Recent Books: Land of Opportunity: The Entrepreneurial Spirit in America (Little, Brown, 1986); Washington, City of Scandals: Investigating Congress and Other Big Spenders (Little, Brown, 1984); Fat City: How Congress Wastes Your Taxes (Regnery Gateway, 1980).

Jane Leavy Novelist, author, journalist (sports).
Recent Book: Squeeze Play (Doubleday, 1990).

Merrill Leffler   Poet, publisher, teacher. Publisher, Dryad Press.
Recent Books: Partly Pandemonium, Partly Love (Dryad Press, 1982); Changing Orders: Poetry From Israel (1979).

Jim Lehrer   Novelist, author, journalist, television news anchor (MacNeil-Lehrer News Hour, PBS-TV).
Recent Books: Lost & Found (Putnam, 1991); The Sooner Spy (Putnam, 1990); Crown Oklahoma (Putnam, 1989); Kick the Can (Putnam, 1988). *Plays*: Chili Queen.

Kate Lehrer   Novelist.
Recent Book: Best Intentions (Little, Brown, 1987).

Robert Lehrman   Novelist. Director of speechwriting, Federal National Mortgage Association.
Recent Books: Defectors (Arbor House/William Morrow, 1988); Juggling (Berkley, 1988).

Matthew Lesko   Author, journalist, information specialist. President, Information USA.
Recent Books: The Investor's Information Sourcebook (Harper & Row, 1988); Getting Yours: The Complete Guide to Government Money (Penguin, 1987, 3rd ed.); Information USA (Viking, 1986); Lesko's New-Tech Sourcebook (Harper & Row, 1986); The Marketing Sourcebook (with Wendy Lesko, Warner Books, 1984).

Mary Lide   Novelist, historian, poet. Winner of the *Romantic Times'* New Historical Fiction Award (1984).
Recent Books: Tregaran (St. Martin's Press, 1989); Isobelle (Warner Books, 1988); A Royal Quest (Warner Books, 1987), Gifts of the Queen (Warner Books, 1985); Ann of Cambray (Warner Books, 1984).

Neil C. Livingstone   Author, journalist, commentator.
Recent Books: The Complete Security Guide for Executives (1990); The Cult of Counterterrorism (Warner Books, 1989); Fighting Back (Lexington Books, 1986); The War Against Terrorism (Lexington Books, 1982).

Chris Llewelyn   Poet. Winner of the Walt Whitman Award (1986), Academy of American Poets.
Recent Book: Fragments from the Fire: The Triangle

Shirtwaist Company Fire of March 25, 1911 (Viking, 1987).

Milton Lomask   Author, biographer, historian, teacher.
Recent Books: The Biographer's Craft (Harper & Row, 1986); The Spirit of 1787: Aaron Burr: Conspiracy & Years of Exile (Farrar, Straus & Giroux, 1982); The Making of Our Constitution (Farrar, Straus & Giroux, 1980); Aaron Burr: The Years from Princeton to Vice President (Farrar, Straus & Giroux, 1979).

James Blair Lovell   Author, biographer, journalist.
Recent Book: Anastasia: The Lost Princess (Regnery Gateway, 1991).

Arnost Lustig   Novelist, short-story writer, playwright, teacher. Professor of creative writing, literature and film history, American University.
Recent Books: Indecent Dreams (Northwestern University Press, 1988); Diamonds in the Night (Northwestern University Press, 1986); The Unloved: From The Diary of Perla S. (Arbor House, 1985); Night & Hope (Northwestern University Press, 1985).

Edward Luttwak   Author, military historian. Former Pentagon official.
Recent Books: Strategy: The Logic of War & Peace (Harvard University Press, 1987); On the Meaning of Victory: Essays on Strategy (Simon & Schuster, 1986); The Pentagon and the Art of War (Simon & Schuster, 1985); The Grand Strategy of the Soviet Union (St. Martin's Press, 1983).

Kenneth Lynn   Author, scholar, literary biographer.
Recent Books: Hemingway (Simon & Schuster, 1987); A Divided People (Greenwood Press, 1977).

Roderick MacLeish   Novelist, author, commentator (National Public Radio).
Recent Books: Crossing at Ivalo (Little, Brown, 1990); Prince Ombra (Congdon & Weed, 1982); The First Book of Eppe: An American Romance (Fawcett, 1981).

Robert MacNeil   Author, journalist, television anchor. Co-host of MacNeil-Lehrer News Hour.
Recent Book: Wordstruck (Penguin, 1990).

Jeff MacNelly   Author, editorial cartoonist. Created comic strip "Shoe." Winner of the Pulitzer Prize for Editorial Cartooning three times (1972, 1978, 1985).
   Recent Books: Shake the Hand, Bite the Taco: A New Shoe Book (St. Martin's Press, 1989); A Cigar Means Never Having to Say You're Sorry (St. Martin's Press, 1989); Shoe Goes to Wrigley Field (Bonus Books, 1988); Too Old for Summer Camp & Too Young to Retire (St. Martin's Press, 1988); The Greatest Shoe on Earth (Henry Holt, 1985); The Shoe Must Go On (Holt, 1984); A Shoe for All Seasons (Holt, 1983); On with the Shoe (Holt, 1982); The New Shoe (Avon, 1981); The Other Shoe (Avon, 1980).

Joel Makower   Author, journalist, book producer (Tilden Press). Winner of Philip M. Stern Award, Washington Independent Writers (1990).
   Recent Books: The Green Consumer (1990); The Air & Space Catalogue (Random House, 1990); Woodstock: The Oral History (Doubleday, 1989); The Map Catalog (Random/Vintage, 1987); Trend Watching: How the Media Create Trends and How to Be the First to Uncover Them (with John E. Meriam, Amacom, 1988); Boom!: Talkin' 'Bout Our Generation (Contemporary Books, 1986); Office Hazards: How Your Job Can Make You Sick (Tilden Press, 1981).

David C. Martin   Author, novelist, journalist.
   Recent Books: Best Laid Plans: The Inside Story of America's War Against Terrorism (with John Walcott, Harper & Row, 1988); A Wilderness of Mirrors (Harper & Row, 1980).

Judith Martin   Author, novelist, syndicated columnist ("Miss Manners").
   Recent Books: Miss Manners' Guide for the Turn-of-the-Millennium (Pharos Books, 1989); Common Courtesy (Atheneum, 1985); Style & Substance (Atheneum, 1986); Miss Manners' Guide to Rearing Perfect Children (Atheneum, 1984); Miss Manners' Guide to Excrutiatingly Correct Behavior (Atheneum, 1982); Gilbert: A Comedy of Manners (Atheneum, 1982).

Christopher Matthews   Author, journalist, columnist, television and radio commentator (CBS Morning News, Mutual Broadcasting). Washington Bureau Chief, *San*

Francisco Examiner. Columnist, King Features. Former senior aide, House Speaker Tip O'Neill.
Recent Book: Hardball: How Politics Is Played, Told by One Who Knows the Game (Summit Books, 1988).

Barbara Matusow Author, journalist, editor, television producer (NBC-TV, CBS-TV). Senior writer, *Washingtonian*. Former senior editor, *Washington Journalism Review*.
Recent Book: The Evening Stars: The Making of the Network News Anchor (Houghton Mifflin, 1983).

Kathleen Maxa Author, journalist.
Recent Books: The Prize Pulitzer: The Scandal That Rocked Palm Beach (with Roxanne Pulitzer, Villard Books, 1988); "This is Judy Woodruff at the White House" (with Judy Woodruff, Addison-Wesley, 1982).

Jane Mayer Author, journalist. Former White House correspondent, *The Wall Street Journal*.
Recent Book: Landslide: The Unmaking of the President, 1984–1988 (with Doyle McManus, Houghton Mifflin, 1988).

Charles McCarry Novelist, author, journalist. Editor, *National Geographic*. Former CIA intelligence officer.
Recent Books: Second Sight (Dutton, 1991); The Bride of the Wilderness (NAL Books, 1988); For the Record: From Wall Street to Washington (with Donald Regan, Harcourt Brace Jovanovich, 1988); Caveat (with Alexander Haig, Macmillan, 1984); The Last Supper (Dutton, 1983); The Better Angels (Dutton, 1979).

Abigail Q. McCarthy Novelist, author, columnist.
Recent Books: One Woman Lost (with Jane Muskie, Atheneum, 1986); Circles: A Washington Story (Doubleday, 1977).

Coleman McCarthy Author, journalist, columnist (*The Washington Post*).
Recent Book: Involvements: One Journalist's Place in the World (Acropolis Books, 1984).

Eugene McCarthy Author, poet, columnist, politician. Former U.S. Senator (D-Minn.) from 1959–71. Former presidential candidate in 1968.
Recent Books: America Revisited (Doubleday, 1991);

Required Reading: A Decade of Political Wit & Wisdom (Harcourt Brace Jovanovich, 1988); Up 'Til Now: A Memoir of the Decline of American Politics (Harcourt Brace Jovanovich, 1987); The Ultimate Tyranny: The Majority Over The Majority (Harcourt Brace Jovanovich, 1980); Ground Fog & Night: Poems (Harcourt Brace Jovanovich, 1979).

Diana McClellan Author, columnist, editor. Washington editor, *Washingtonian*. Former gossip columnist, "The Washington Ear."
Recent Book: Ear on Washington: A Chrestomathy of Scandal, Rumor and Gossip Among the Capital's Élite (Arbor House, 1982).

David McCullough Author, historian, journalist. Narrator of *The Civil War* (PBS Television). Host, Smithsonian World. Chairman, Advisory Board, *American Heritage*. Former staff writer, *Time* (1956–61). Winner of the National Book Award for History (1977) and the American Book Award for Biography (1982).
Recent Books: Brave Companions: Portraits in History (1991); The Johnstown Flood (Simon & Schuster, 1987); The Great Bridge (Simon & Schuster, 1983); Mornings on Horseback (Simon & Schuster, 1981); The Path Between the Seas: The Creation Of The Panama Canal, 1870–1914 (Simon & Schuster, 1979).

Victoria McKernon Novelist, author.
Recent Book: Osprey Reef (Carroll & Graf, 1990).

Doyle McManus Author, journalist. Washington correspondent, *The Los Angeles Times*.
Recent Book: Landslide: The Unmaking of the President, 1984–1988 (with Jane Mayer, Houghton Mifflin, 1988).

Larry McMurtry Novelist, author, screenwriter. Winner of the Pulitzer Prize for Fiction (1986). Co-owner of Booked Up, a bookstore in Georgetown.
Recent Books: Buffalo Girls (Simon & Schuster, 1990); Some Can Whistle (Simon & Schuster, 1989); All My Friends Are Going to Be Strangers (Simon & Schuster, 1989); Anything For Billy (Simon & Schuster, 1988); Texasville (Simon & Schuster, 1987); Film Flam: Essays on Hollywood (Simon & Schuster, 1987); Lonesome Dove (Simon & Schuster, 1985); The Desert Rose

(Simon & Schuster, 1983); Cadillac Jack (Simon & Schuster, 1982). *Films*: Hud, The Last Picture Show.

William McPherson Novelist, author, book reviewer, editor. Former editor, Book World, *The Washington Post* (1972–78). Former senior editor, William Morrow & Company (1966–69). Winner of the Pulitzer Prize for Criticism (1977).
  Recent Books: To the Sargasso Sea (Simon & Schuster, 1987); Testing the Current (Simon & Schuster, 1984).

William Meredith Poet. Winner of the Pulitzer Prize for Poetry (1988). Former Consultant in Poetry, Library of Congress (1978–80).
  Recent Books: Poems Are Hard to Read (University of Michigan Press, 1991); Partial Accounts: New and Selected Poems (Knopf, 1987); The Cheer (Knopf, 1980).

Lawrence Meyer Novelist, author, journalist. Editor, National Weekly Edition, *The Washington Post.*
  Recent Books: Israel Now: Portrait of a Troubled Land (Delacorte Press, 1982); False Front (Viking, 1979).

Barbara Michaels Novelist, mystery writer, children's author, book reviewer. Also writes under the name Elizabeth Peters. Judge, Edgar Awards (Mystery Writers of America).
  Recent Books: The Last Camel Died at Noon (1991); Into the Darkness (Simon & Schuster, 1990); Smoke and Mirrors (Berkley, 1990); Shattered Silk (Atheneum, 1986); Be Buried in the Rain (Atheneum, 1985); Someone in the House (Dodd, 1981); The Wizard's Daughter (Dodd, 1980).

E. Ethelbert Miller Poet, teacher. Director, Afro-American Studies Resource Center, Howard University.
  Recent Books: Where Are the Love Poems for Dictators? (Open Hand, 1987); Season of Hunger/Cry of Rain (Lotus, 1982).

Luree Miller Author, journalist, historian.
  Recent Books: Literary Villages of London (Starrhill Press, 1989); Late Bloom: New Lives for Women (Grossett & Dunlap, 1979).

May Miller   Poet, author.
Recent Books: The Ransomed Wait (Lotus, 1983); Halfway to the Sun (Washington Writers Pub, 1981).

Nathan Miller   Author, journalist, historian, biographer.
Recent Books: Spying for America: The Hidden History of U.S. Intelligence (Paragon House, 1989); F.D.R.: An Intimate History (Madison Books, 1991); The Roosevelt Chronicles (Madison Books, 1991).

Morton Mintz   Author, journalist.
Recent Books: President Ron's Appointment Book (with Margaret Mintz, St. Martin's Press, 1988); Quotations from President Ron (with Margaret Mintz, St. Martin's Press, 1987); At Any Cost: Corporate Greed, Women and the Dalkon Shield (Pantheon, 1985).

Dan E. Moldea   Author, journalist. Former president, Washington Independent Writers. Winner of Philip M. Stern Award, Washington Independent Writers (1989).
Recent Books: Interference: How Organized Crime Influences Professional Football (William Morrow, 1989); Dark Victory: Ronald Reagan, MCA and The Mob (Viking, 1986); The Hunting of Cain: A True Story of Money, Greed & Fratricide (Atheneum, 1983).

John S. Monagan   Author, biographer. Member of Congress (D-Conn.) from 1959 to 1973.
Recent Books: The Grand Panjandrum: Mellow Years of Justice Holmes (University Press of America, 1988); Horace: Priest of the Poor (Georgetown University Press, 1985).

William Moore   Novelist, attorney, mystery writer.
Recent Book: The Last Surprise (St. Martin's Press, 1990).

Edmund Morris   Author, biographer. Winner of the Pulitzer Prize for Biography (1980).
Recent Books: Theodore Rex (Random House); The Rise of Theodore Roosevelt (Putnam, 1979).

Sylvia J. Morris   Author, biographer.
Recent Book: Edith Kermit Roosevelt (Random House, 1990).

Faye Moskowitz Poet, short-story writer, essayist, teacher. Director, Creative Writing Program, George Washington University.
Recent Books: And the Bridge is Love (1991); Whoever Finds This, I Love You (David Godine, 1988); A Leak in the Heart (David Godine, 1985).

Kermit Moyer Novelist, author, teacher. Professor of English, American University.
Recent Book: Tumbling (University of Illinois Press, 1988).

Daniel P. Moynihan Author, journalist, U.S. Senator (D-N.Y.).
Recent Books: On the Law of Nations (Harvard University Press, 1990); Loyalties (Harcourt Brace Jovanovich, 1989); Came the Revolution: Argument in the Reagan Era (Harcourt Brace Jovanovich, 1988); Family and Nation (Harcourt Brace Jovanovich, 1986); Counting Our Blessings: Reflections on the Future of America (Little, Brown, 1980).

Bruce Allen Murphy Author, journalist.
Recent Books: Fortas: The Rise and Ruin of a Supreme Court Justice (William Morrow, 1987); The Brandeis/Frankfurter Connection: The Secret Political Activities of Two Supreme Court Justices (Oxford University Press, 1982).

Ralph Nader Author, lawyer, consumer advocate.
Recent Books: The Lemon Book: Auto Rights (with Clarence Dittow, Moyer Bell, 1990); More Action for a Change: Students Serving the Public Interest (Dembner Books, 1987); The Big Boys: Power and Position in American Business (with William Taylor, Pantheon, 1986); Who's Poisoning America? (Sierra Club Books, 1981).

John Naisbitt Author, columnist, trend analyst.
Recent Books: Megatrends 2000 (Warner Books, 1990); Reinventing the Corporation: Transforming Your Job and Your Company for the New Information Society (with Patricia Aburdene, Warner Books, 1985); Megatrends: Ten New Directions Transforming Our Lives (Warner Books, 1982).

Jim Naughton Novelist, journalist. Reporter, *The Washington Post*.

Recent Book: My Brother, Stealing Second (Harper & Row, 1990).

Phyllis Reynolds Naylor Novelist, author, children's and juvenile fiction writer.

Recent Books: Bernie and The Besseldorf Ghost (1990); Beetles, Lightly Toasted (Macmillan, 1987); The Baby, the Bed and the Rose (Clarion, 1987); The Year of the Gopher (Atheneum, 1987); Unexpected Pleasures (Putnam's, 1986); The Agony of Alice (Atheneum, 1985); The Dark of the Tunnel (Atheneum, 1985); Eddie, Incorporated (Atheneum, 1980); Revelations (St. Martin's Press, 1979).

Robert Nelson Author, scholar, economist. Policy analyst, U.S. Department of Interior. Former visiting scholar, Brookings Institution.

Recent Books: Reaching for Heaven on Earth: The Theological Meaning of Economics (Rowman & Littlefield, 1991); The Making of Federal Coal Policy (Duke University Press, 1983).

Robert A. Nisbet Author, historian.

Recent Books: The Quest for Community: A Study in the Ethics of Order and Freedom (1990); The Present Age: Progress and Anarchy in Modern America (Harper & Row, 1988); Roosevelt and Stalin: The Failed Courtship (Regnery Gateway, 1988); Conservation: Dream and Reality (University of Minnesota Press, 1986); The History of the Idea of Progress (Basic Books, 1980).

Michael Novak Author, columnist, novelist. George Frederick Jewitt Scholar in Religion and Public Policy, American Enterprise Institute.

Recent Books: This Hemisphere of Liberty: A Philosophy for the Americas (American Enterprise Institute, 1990); Free Persons and the Common Good (Madison Books, 1988); The Joy of Sports: End Zones, Bases, Baskets, Balls and the Consecration of the American Spirit (Hamilton Press, 1988); Human Rights and the New Realism: Strategic Thinking in a New Age (Freedom House, 1986); Toward a Theology of the Corporation (American Enterprise Press, 1981).

P. J. O'Rourke Author, journalist, travel writer. Former editor-in-chief, *The National Lampoon*.

Recent Books: Parliament of Whores: A Lone Humorist's Attempt to Explain the Entire Federal Government (Atlantic Monthly Press, 1991); Modern Manners: An Etiquette Book for Rude People (Atlantic Monthly Press, 1989); Holidays in Hell: In Which Our Intrepid Reporter Travels to the World's Worst Places and Asks "What's Funny About This?" (Atlantic Monthly Press, 1988); Republican Party Reptile (Atlantic Monthly Press, 1987); The Bachelor Home Companion: A Practical Guide to Keeping House Like a Pig (Pocket Books/ Simon & Schuster, 1987).

Peter J. Ognibene   Novelist, author, columnist.
Recent Book: The Big Byte (Ballantine, 1984).

Patrick Oliphant   Author, editorial cartoonist. Winner of the Pulitzer Prize for Editorial Cartooning (1967).
Recent Books: Nothing Basically Wrong (Andrews & McNeel, 1988); Up to There in Alligators (Andrews & McNeel, 1987); Between a Rock and a Hard Place (Andrews & McNeel, 1986); But Seriously Folks (Andrews & McNeel, 1983); Ban This Book! (Andrews & McNeel, 1982); Oliphant! A Cartoon Collection (Andrews & McNeel, 1980).

Mark Olshaker   Novelist, author.
Recent Books: Unnatural Causes (William Morrow, 1986); Einstein's Brain (Evans, 1981).

Jerry Oppenheimer   Author, journalist.
Recent Book: Barbara Walters: An Unauthorized Biography (St. Martin's Press, 1990).

Judy Oppenheimer   Author, journalist.
Recent Book: Private Demons: The Life of Shirley Jackson (Putnam, 1988).

Michele Orwin   Novelist.
Recent Book: Waiting For Next Week (Henry Holt, 1988).

Robert Pack   Author, journalist, poet, literary critic. Senior writer, *Washingtonian*.
Recent Books: Before It Vanishes (David Godine, 1989); The Octopus Who Wanted to Juggle (Galileo Press, 1990); Speaking Out (with Larry Speakes, Scribner's, 1988); Edward Bennett Williams for the Defense (Harper & Row, 1983).

Linda Pastan   Poet, teacher. Poet Laureate of Maryland. Professor of creative writing and literature, American University. Regular instructor at Bread Loaf Writers Conference.

Recent Books: Heroes in Disguise (Norton, 1991); The Imperfect Paradise (Norton, 1989); A Fraction of Darkness (Norton, 1985); PM/AM: New and Selected Poems (Norton, 1982); Waiting for My Life (Norton, 1981).

Richard Peabody   Poet, editor, publisher. Former editor and publisher of *Gargoyle Magazine* and Paycock Press.

Recent Books: Sad Fashions (Gut Punch Press, 1990); Echt & Ersatz (Paycock Press, 1985); Mavericks: Nine Independent Publishers (Paycock Press, 1983); I'm in Love with the Morton Salt Girl (Paycock Press, 1979).

William D. Pease   Novelist, attorney. Former federal prosecutor, Department of Justice.

Recent Book: Playing The Dozens (Viking, 1990).

John Pekkanen   Author, journalist. Senior writer, *Washingtonian.*

Recent Books: M.D.: Doctors Talk About Themselves (Delacorte Press, 1988); My Father, My Son (with Elmo Zumwalt Sr. & Jr., Macmillan, 1986); Donor: How One Girl's Death Gave Life to Others (Little, Brown, 1986).

Mark Perry   Author, journalist, editor. Editor, *The Veteran*, Vietnam Veterans Association of America. Former editor, *City Paper*. Former president, Washington Independent Writers.

Recent Book: Four Stars: The Joint Chiefs of Staff and the American Military (Houghton Mifflin, 1989).

Joseph Persico   Author, novelist, historian. Former chief speechwriter for Nelson A. Rockefeller. Former Foreign Service Officer.

Recent Books: Casey: From the OSS to the CIA (Viking, 1990); Edward R. Murrow: An American Original (McGraw-Hill, 1988); The Imperial Rockefeller (Simon & Schuster, 1982); Piercing the Reich (Viking, 1979).

Charles Peters   Author, journalist, editor. Editor, *The Washington Monthly*.

Recent Books: Tilting at Windmills: An Autobiography (Addison-Wesley, 1988); How Washington Really Works (1985).

Neal Pierce Author, journalist, columnist. Contributor and co-founder, *National Journal.*
Recent Book: The Book of America (with Jerry Hagstrom, Norton, 1983).

Anthony S. Pitch Author, editor, publisher. President, Mino Publications. Former senior writer, books division, *U.S. News & World Report.* Former correspondent, Associated Press.
Recent Books: Chained Eagle (with Everett Alvarez, Dell, 1991); Washington, D.C. Sightseers' Guide (Mino Publications, 1991); Congressional Chronicles (Mino Publications, 1990); Exclusively Presidential Trivia (Mino Publications, 1985); Exclusively First Ladies Trivia (Mino Publications, 1985); Exclusively Washington Trivia (Mino Publications, 1984).

Stanley Plumly Poet, essayist, teacher. Professor of English, University of Maryland.
Recent Books: The Boy on the Step (Ecco Press, 1989); Summer Celestial (Ecco Press, 1983).

Norman Polmar Author, biographer, naval expert.
Recent Books: World War II: America at War (1991); CNN Reports: War in the Gulf (with Thomas B. Allen and F. Clifton Barry, Turner Publishing, 1990); Merchants of Treason: America's Secrets for Sale (with Thomas B. Allen, Delacorte Press, 1988); Ship of Gold (with Thomas B. Allen, Macmillan, 1987); Guide to the Soviet Navy (Naval Institute Press, 1983); Rickover: Controversy and Genius (with Thomas B. Allen, Simon & Schuster, 1982).

Jan Pottker Author, biographer, business writer.
Recent Book: Dear Ann, Dear Abby: An Unauthorized Biography of Ann Landers and Abigail Van Buren (Dodd, Mead & Company, 1987).

John Prados Author, journalist, intelligence expert.
Recent Books: Keepers of the Keys: A History of the National Security Council from Truman to Bush (William Morrow, 1991); Pentagon Games (Harper & Row, 1987); Presidents' Secret Wars: The CIA and Pentagon Covert Operations Since World War II (William Mor-

row, 1986); The Soviet Estimate: U.S. Intelligence and Soviet Strategic Forces (Princeton University Press, 1986).

Peter Prichard   Author, journalist. Editor, *USA Today*.
Recent Book: The Making of McPaper: The Inside Story of USA Today (Andrews & McMeel, 1987).

William Prochnau   Novelist, author, journalist. Staff writer, *The Washington Post*. Alicia Patterson Fellow, 1988.
Recent Book: Trinity's Child (Putnam, 1983).

Sally Quinn   Novelist, journalist. Staff writer, Style Section, *The Washington Post*. Former co-anchor, CBS Morning News.
Recent Books: Happy Endings (Simon & Schuster, 1991); Regrets Only (Simon & Schuster, 1986).

Richard Rashke   Author, journalist, screenwriter.
Recent Books: Runaway Father (Harcourt Brace Jovanovich, 1988); Capitol Hill in Black and White (with Robert Parker, Jr., Dodd Mead, 1986); Stormy Genius: The Life of Aviation's Maverick Bill Lear (Houghton Mifflin, 1985); Escape from Sobibor (Houghton Mifflin, 1982); The Killing of Karen Silkwood (Houghton Mifflin, 1981).

Barbara Raskin   Novelist, short-story writer, teacher. Former adjunct professor of creative writing, American University. Past president, Washington Independent Writers. Winner of Philip M. Stern Award, Washington Independent Writers (1988).
Recent Books: Current Affairs (Random House, 1990); Loose Ends (St. Martin's Press, 1989); Hot Flashes (St. Martin's Press, 1987); Out of Order (Simon & Schuster, 1979).

Carolyn Reeder   Author, teacher. Winner of the Scott O'Dell Award (Historical Fiction, 1989) and the Jefferson Cup Award (1990).
Recent Books: Shades of Gray (Avon, 1989); Shenandoah Vestiges: What the Mountain People Left Behind (with Jack Reeder, Potomac Appalachian, 1980).

Rick Reichman   Author, teacher, screenwriter. Teaches screenwriting classes at Georgetown University and other locations.

Recent Book: Formatting Your Screenplay (Paragon House, 1991).

Robert Reiss Novelist, author, journalist. Former reporter, *The Chicago Tribune.* Staff associate, Bread Loaf Writers' Conference, 1983.
Recent Books: Saltmaker (Viking, 1988); Divine Assassin (Berkley, 1987); The Casco Deception (Little, Brown, 1983); Summer Fires (Simon & Schuster, 1980).

Richard M. Restak Author, psychiatrist, radio commentator (National Public Radio).
Recent Books: The Brain Has a Mind of its Own (1991); The Mind (Bantam Books, 1988); The Infant Mind (Doubleday, 1986); The Brain (Bantam Books, 1985); The Self Seekers (Doubleday, 1982).

Donald Ritchie Author, historian, Associate historian, Historical Office, United States Senate. Winner of the Forrest C. Pogue Award (Oral History).
Recent Books: Press Gallery: Congress and the Washington Correspondents (Harvard University Press, 1991); The Senate (Chelsea House, 1988); James M. Landis: Dean of the Regulators (Harvard University Press, 1980).

Selwa Roosevelt Author, editor. White House Chief of Protocol, (1981–89).
Recent Book: Keeper of the Gate (Simon & Schuster, 1990).

Alvin Rosenbaum Author, book producer, graphic designer. President, Alvin Rosenbaum Associates.
Recent Books: America's Meeting Places (Facts on File, 1984); The Young People's Yellow Pages (Putnam, 1983).

Betty Ross Author, journalist, travel writer.
Recent Books: Washington, D.C. Museums: A Ross Guide (Americana Press, 1992); New York City Museums: A Ross Guide (Americana Press, 1991).

Gail Ross Author, attorney, literary agent.
Recent Book: The Writer's Lawyer: Essential Legal Advice for Writers and Editors In All Media (with Ronald Goldfarb, Times Books, 1989).

Carl T. Rowan Author, columnist, television news commentator ("Inside Washington"). Former U.S. ambassador to Finland. Former director, U.S. Information Agency.
Recent Books: Breaking Barriers: A Memoir (Little, Brown, 1990); You Can't Get There From Here (Little, Brown, 1986).

Richard Rubenstein Author, teacher, political historian. Professor, George Washington University.
Recent Book: Alchemists of Revolution: Terrorism in the Modern World (Basic Books, 1987).

William Safire Author, novelist, columnist ("On Language"). Writes commentary and essays for *The New York Times.* Winner of the Pulitzer Prize for Commentary (1978).
Recent Books: Coming to Terms (Doubleday, 1991); Fumblerules (Doubleday, 1990); Language Maven Strikes Again (Doubleday, 1989); Words of Wisdom (Simon & Schuster, 1989); Freedom (Doubleday, 1987); Take My Word for It (Times Books, 1986); I Stand Corrected: More on Language (Times Books, 1984).

Arnold Sawislak Author, journalist. News Editor, *United Press International.*
Recent Books: Dwarf Rapes Nun, Flees in UFO (St. Martin's Press, 1985); Who Runs Washington? (with Michael Kilian, St. Martin's Press, 1982).

Jerrold Schechter Author, journalist. Former correspondent, *Time.* Former official, National Security Council.
Recent Book: The Palace File (with Nguyen Tien Hung, Harper & Row, 1986).

David Scheim Author, journalist.
Recent Book: Contract On America: The Mafia Murder of President John F. Kennedy (Shapolsky Publishers, 1988).

Andrew Bard Schmookler Author, political analyst. Policy adviser, Search for a Common Ground.
Recent Books: Sowings & Reapings: The Cycling of Good & Evil in the Human System (Knowledge Systems, 1989); Out of Weakness: Healing The Wounds That Drive Us to War (Bantam Books, 1988); The

Parable Of The Tribes: The Problem of Power in Social Evolution (Houghton Mifflin, 1986).

Martin Schram Author, journalist, television commentator (Cable News Network). National editor, *Washingtonian*. Former Washington Bureau Chief, *Newsday*. Former White House correspondent, *The Washington Post*.
   Recent Book: The Great American Video Game: Presidential Politics in the Television Age (William Morrow, 1987).

Benjamin Schutz Novelist, author, psychotherapist. Winner of the Shamus Award.
   Recent Books: A Fistful of Empty (Viking, 1991); Things We Do For Love (Scribner's, 1990); A Tax In Blood (Bantam Books, 1989).

Richard Schwartz Novelist, author, educator. Dean, Graduate School, Georgetown University.
   Recent Book: Frozen Stare (St. Martin's Press, 1990).

Elaine Sciolino Author, journalist.
   Recent Book: The Outlaw State: Saddam Hussein's Quest for Power and the Gulf Crisis (1991).

Meryle Secrest Author, journalist. Former reporter, *The Washington Post*.
   Recent Books: Salvador Dali (Dutton, 1986); Kenneth Clark: A Biography (Fromm International Publications, 1986); Being Bernard Berenson: A Biography (Holt, 1979).

Tom Shales Author, critic, columnist. Television critic, *The Washington Post*. Movie reviewer, National Public Radio. Winner of the Pulitzer Prize for Criticism (1988).
   Recent Books: Legends: Remembering America's Greatest Stars (Random House, 1990); On the Air! (Summit Books, 1982).

Elaine Shannon Author, journalist. Washington bureau reporter, *Time*.
   Recent Book: Desperados: Latin Drug Lords, U.S. Lawmen & the War America Can't Win (Viking, 1988).

Leonard Shapiro Author, editor, journalist. Sports Editor, *The Washington Post*.

Recent Books: Big Man On Campus: John Thompson and the Georgetown Hoyas (1990); Tough Stuff: Hall of Famer Sam Huff (St. Martin's Press, 1988).

Deborah Shapley   Author, journalist. Former reporter, *Science* and *Nature* magazines.

Recent Books: Promise & Power: The Life of Robert S. McNamara (Little, Brown, 1992); The Seventh Continent: Antarctica in a Resource Age (Resources for the Future, 1985).

Marilyn Sharp   Novelist. Former editorial assistant, *The New Yorker*.

Recent Books: Firebird (Dutton, 1987); Falseface (St. Martin's Press, 1984); Masterstroke (Marek, 1981); Sunflower (Marek, 1979).

Neil Sheehan   Author, journalist. Former Vietnam Bureau Chief, United Press International (1962–64). Former reporter for *The New York Times*. Winner of many major awards, including the Pulitzer Prize for Nonfiction (1988), the National Book Award for Nonfiction (1988), the Investigative Reporters & Editors Award (1988), the Page One Award and the Drew Pearson Award.

Recent Book: A Bright Shining Lie: John Paul Vann and America in Vietnam (Random House, 1988).

Susan Sheehan   Author, journalist. Staff writer, *The New Yorker*. Winner of the Pulitzer Prize for Nonfiction (1983).

Recent Books: A Missing Plane (Putnam, 1986); Kate Quinton's Days (Houghton Mifflin, 1984); Is There No Place on Earth for Me? (Houghton Mifflin, 1982).

Chuck Shepherd   Author, syndicated columnist ("News of the Weird," Universal Press Syndicate). Assistant professor of Strategic Management and Public Policy, George Washington University.

Recent Books: Beyond News of the Weird (with John J. Kohut and Roland Sweet, Plume, 1991); More News of the Weird (with John J. Kohut and Roland Sweet, Plume, 1990); News of the Weird (with John J. Kohut and Roland Sweet, Plume, 1989).

Susan Richards Shreve   Novelist, children's author, short-story writer, teacher. Professor of creative writing, George Mason University. Visiting professor, Columbia University.

Recent Books: Daughters of the New World (Doubleday, 1991); A Country of Strangers (Simon & Schuster, 1989); Queen of Hearts (Simon & Schuster, 1987); Lucy Forever & Miss Rosetree (Henry Holt, 1987); Dreaming of Heroes (William Morrow, 1984); The Flunking of Joshua T. Bates (Knopf, 1984); The Bad Dreams of a Good Girl (Knopf, 1982); Children of Power (Macmillan, 1979).

Christopher Simpson Author, journalist. Assistant director, documentary film *Hotel Terminus* (1989 Academy Award winner). Winner of the Investigative Reporters & Editors Award (1988). Winner of the Present Tense Award for History (1988), *Present Tense* magazine.
Recent Book: Blowback: America's Recruitment of Nazis & Its Effect on the Cold War (Weidenfeld & Nicholson, 1987).

Patsy Sims Author, journalist.
Recent Books: Can Somebody Shout Amen! (St. Martin's Press, 1988); Cleveland Benjamin's Dead (Dutton, 1981); The Klan (Stein & Day, 1978).

Michelle Slung Author, columnist. Editor, American Women Writers Series (NAL/Plume). Former columnist, Book World, *The Washington Post*.
Recent Books: The Only Child Book (Ballantine, 1989); Momilies & More Momilies (Ballantine, 1988); Crime on Her Mind (Pantheon, 1987); Momilies: As My Mother Used to Say (Ballantine, 1985).

Hedrick Smith Author, journalist, television commentator (PBS series "The Power Game" & "The Russians"). Chief Washington correspondent, *The New York Times*. Winner of the Pulitzer Prize for International Reporting (1974).
Recent Books: The New Russians (Random House, 1990); The Power Game: How Washington Really Works (Random House, 1987); The Russians (Times Books, 1983); Reagan the Man, the President (Macmillan, 1980).

Russell Jack Smith Author, analyst. Former Deputy Director for Intelligence, Central Intelligence Agency.
Recent Books: The Unknown CIA: My Three Decades with the Agency (Berkley, 1992); The Singapore

Chance (Bartleby Press, 1991); The Secret War (Dan River Press, 1986).

Susan Sonde Poet, author. Winner of the Capricorn Poetry Prize (1986).
Recent Books: In the Longboats With Others (New Rivers Press, 1988); Inland Is Parenthetical (Dryad Press, 1983).

Duncan Spencer Author, journalist, editor. Former staff writer, *The Washington Star*. Former editor, *Fathers* Magazine.
Recent Books: Facing the Wall: Americans at the Vietnam Veteran's Memorial (Macmillan, 1986); Conversations with the Enemy (with Winston Groom, Putnam, 1983).

Steve Spruill Novelist, author, journalist.
Recent Books: Painkiller: A Novel of Medical Terror (St. Martin's Press, 1990); Paradox Planet (Doubleday, 1988); The Imperial Plot (Tor Books, 1985).

James Srodes Author, journalist. Former president, Washington Independent Writers.
Recent Books: Takeovers (with Ivan Fallon, Pantheon, 1987); Dream Maker: The Rise and Fall of John Z. Delorean (with Ivan Fallon, Putnam, 1983).

Susan Stamberg Author, journalist, radio host (National Public Radio's "Weekend Edition"). Former NPR evening host, "All Things Considered."
Recent Book: Every Night at Five (Pantheon, 1982).

Suzanne Fisher Staples Novelist, journalist, children's author. Winner of Joan G. Sugarman Children's Book Award, Washington Independent Writers (1989).
Recent Book: Shabanu (Knopf, 1989).

Daniel Stashower Novelist, author.
Recent Books: Elephants in the Distance (William Morrow, 1989); The Adventure of the Ecto-Plasmic Man (William Morrow, -1985).

Philip M. Stern Author, journalist. Former deputy assistant Secretary of State. Founder, Center for Public Financing of Elections. Founding member, Washington Independent Writers.

Recent Books: The Best Congress Money Can Buy (Pantheon, 1988); Lawyers on Trial (Times Books, 1980).

Bradley Strahan   Poet, editor, publisher.
Recent Books: New Love Songs for an Age of Anxiety (Black Buzzard Press, 1989); Poems (Barbara Allen, 1982); Love Songs for an Age of Anxiety (Black Buzzard Press, 1986).

Michael Straight   Author, novelist, art historian. Former arts administrator, National Endowment for the Arts.
Recent Books: Nancy Hanks: An Intimate Portrait (Duke, 1988); After Long Silence (Norton, 1983); Caravaggio (Devon Press, 1979).

Paul N. Strassels   Author, columnist, editor, tax expert. Former editor-in-chief, Washington Tax & Business Report. Former official, Internal Revenue Service.
Recent Books: How to Make Your Money Matter: Answers to 1,001 Questions (Dow Jones-Irwin, 1990); Money Matters: The Hassle-Free, Month-by-Month Guide to Money Management (with William B. Mead, Addison-Wesley, 1986); Paul Strassels' Quick & Easy Guide to Tax Management (Dow Jones-Irwin, 1986); The 1986 Tax Reform Act (Dow Jones-Irwin, 1986); Strassel's Tax Savers (Times Books, 1985).

Dorothy Sucher   Novelist, author, mystery writer.
Recent Books: Dead Men Don't Give Seminars (St. Martin's Press, 1990); Dead Men Don't Marry (St. Martin's Press, 1989).

Harry G. Summers   Author, journalist, editor. Editor, *Vietnam Magazine.* Former military correspondent, *U.S. News & World Report.*
Recent Books: The Vietnam War Almanac (Facts On File, 1985); On Strategy: A Critical Analysis of the Vietnam War (Presidio Press, 1982).

Roland Sweet   Author, journalist. Editor, *Log Home Living.*
Recent Books: Beyond News of the Weird (with Chuck Shepherd and John J. Kohut, Plume, 1991); More News of the Weird (with Chuck Shepherd and John J.

Kohut, Plume, 1990); News of the Weird (with Chuck Shepherd and John J. Kohut, Plume, 1989).

Joel Swerdlow   Author, novelist, journalist.
Recent Books: To Heal a Nation (with Jan Scruggs, Harper & Row, 1985); Code Z (Putnam, 1979).

Tad Szulc   Author, journalist, novelist. Former foreign correspondent, *The New York Times* (1953–72).
Recent Books: Then & Now: How the World Has Changed Since World War II (William Morrow, 1990); Fidel: A Critical Portrait (William Morrow, 1986); Diplomatic Immunity (Simon & Schuster, 1981).

Strobe Talbott   Author, journalist, television commentator. Washington Bureau Chief, *Time*.
Recent Books: The Master of the Game: Paul Nitze and the Nuclear Peace (Knopf, 1988); Reagan & Gorbachev (with Michael Mandelbaum, Random House, 1987); Deadly Gambits: The Reagan Administration & the Stalemate in Nuclear Arms Control (Knopf, 1984); The Russians & Reagan (with Cyrus Vance, Random House, 1984).

Deborah Tannen   Author, teacher, researcher, sociolinguist. Professor of linguistics, Georgetown University.
Recent Books: You Just Don't Understand: Women & Men in Conversation (William Morrow, 1990); That's Not What I Meant!: How Conversational Style Makes or Breaks Your Relations with Others (William Morrow, 1986); Talking Voices: Repetition Dialogue & Imagery in Conversational Discourse (Cambridge University Press, 1989).

Henry Taylor   Poet, author, teacher. Professor of creative writing and literature, American University. Winner of Pulitzer Prize for Poetry (1986).
Recent Books: The Flying Change (Louisiana State University Press, 1985); Desperado (1979).

Paul Taylor   Author, journalist.
Recent Book: See How They Run (Random House, 1990).

Wallace Terry   Author, journalist, editor, radio and television commentator.

Recent Book: Bloods: An Oral History of the Vietnam War (Random House, 1984).

Phyllis Theroux   Author, columnist (*Parents*). Regular contributor, *The New York Times* and *The Washington Post.*
Recent Books: Night Lights: Bedtime Stories for Parents in the Dark (Viking, 1987); Peripheral Visions (William Morrow, 1982); California & Other States of Grace (William Morrow, 1980).

Bill Thomas   Author, editor, journalist. Editor, *Roll Call.* Former editor, *Dossier.*
Recent Book: Lawyers and Thieves (with Norman Roy Grutman, Simon & Schuster, 1990).

Evan Thomas   Author, journalist, editor. Washington bureau chief, *Newsweek.*
Recent Books: The Man to See: Edward Bennett Williams (1991); The Wise Men: Six Friends and the World They Made (with Walter Isaacson, Simon & Schuster, 1986).

Peggy Thomson   Novelist (children's books).
Recent Books: The King Has Horse's Ears (Simon & Schuster, 1989); Keepers & Creatures at the National Zoo (Harper, 1988); Auks, Rocks & The Odd Dinosaur (Harper & Row, 1986).

Susan Tichy   Poet, author, teacher. Professor, George Mason University.
Recent Books: A Smell of Burning Starts the Day (Wesleyan University Press, 1988); The Hands in Exile (Random House, 1983).

Susan Tolchin & Martin Tolchin   Susan Tolchin is professor of public administration at George Washington University. Martin Tolchin is a reporter for *The New York Times.*
Recent Books: Buying into America: How Foreign Money Is Changing The Face of Our Nation (Times Books, 1988); Dismantling America: The Rush to Deregulate (Houghton Mifflin, 1983).

James Traub   Author, journalist, editor.
Recent Books: Too Good to Be True: The Outlandish Story of Wedtech (Doubleday, 1990); The Billion Dollar

Connection: The International Drug Trade (Messner, 1983).

William Triplett   Author, journalist, playwright. Board member, Washington Independent Writers.
Recent Book: Flowering of the Bamboo: A Bizarre International Mystery (Woodbine House, 1985).

Sheldon Tromberg   Author, teacher, screenwriter.
Recent Book: Making Money, Making Movies (Vision Books, 1980).

Cathy Trost   Author, journalist. Reporter, *The Wall Street Journal.* Alicia Patterson Fellow, 1981.
Recent Book: Elements of Risk: The Chemical Industry & Its Threat to America (Times Books, 1986).

Anne Truitt   Author, novelist.
Recent Book: Daybook: The Journal of an Artist (Viking Penguin, 1984).

Patrick Tyler   Author, journalist. Staff writer, *The Washington Post.*
Recent Book: Running Critical: The Silent War, Rickover and General Dynamics (Harper & Row, 1986).

Morris K. Udall   Author, politician, U.S. Representative (D-Ariz.). Former presidential candidate, 1976.
Recent Books: Too Funny to Be President: Notes from the Life of a Politician (Henry Holt, 1988); The Job of the Congressman (with Donald Tacheron, Bobbs-Merrill, 1966).

Sanford J. Ungar   Author, journalist, teacher. Dean of the School of Journalism, American University.
Recent Books: Estrangement: America and the World (Oxford University Press, 1985); Africa: The People and Politics of an Emerging Continent (Simon & Schuster, 1985).

Paul Valentine   Novelist, author, journalist. Reporter (Police Beat), *The Washington Post.*
Recent Book: Crime Scene at "O" Street (St. Martin's Press, 1991).

Judith Viorst   Novelist, poet, author, essayist, children's author. Regular contributor to *Redbook* and other national magazines.

Recent Books: Forever 50 . . . and Other Negotiations (Simon & Schuster, 1989); Necessary Losses (Simon & Schuster, 1986); When Did I Stop Being 20 & Other Injustices: Selected Poems from Single to Mid-Life (Simon & Schuster, 1987); Love & Guilt & The Meaning Of Life (Simon & Schuster, 1979); Alexander & the Terrible, Horrible, No Good, Very Bad Day (Atheneum, 1972); The Tenth Good Thing About Barney (Atheneum, 1971).

Milton Viorst Author, journalist. Contributor to *The New Yorker*. Former staff writer, *The Washington Post*. Former chairman, Fund for Investigative Journalism.
Recent Books: Reaching for the Olive Branch (Indiana University Press, 1989); Sands of Sorrow: Israel's Journey from Independence to Client State (Harper & Row, 1987); Making a Difference: The Peace Corps at Twenty-Five (Weidenfeld & Nicholson, 1986); Fire in the Streets: America in the Nineteen Sixties (Simon & Schuster, 1981).

Marta Vogel Author, journalist. Former president, Washington Independent Writers.
Recent Books: The Babymakers (with Diana Frank, Carroll & Graf, 1988); Hassle-free Homework (Doubleday, 1989).

Janet Wallach Author, editor, journalist. Former reporter, *The Washington Post*.
Recent Books: Arafat: In the Eyes of the Beholder (with John Wallach, Lyle Stuart, 1990); Still, Small Voices (with John Wallach, Harcourt Brace Jovanovich, 1989); Looks That Work (Penguin, 1988).

John Wallach Author, editor, journalist. Winner of three Overseas Press Club Awards and the Edwin Hood Award (National Press Club).
Recent Books: Arafat: In the Eyes of the Beholder (with Janet Wallach, Lyle Stuart, 1990); Still, Small Voices (with Janet Wallach, Harcourt Brace Jovanovich, 1989).

Ben J. Wattenberg Author, novelist, editor, columnist. Senior Fellow, American Enterprise Institute. Co-editor, *Public Opinion* Magazine. Radio commentator, CBS-Radio ("Spectrum").
Recent Books: The Terrain of the Nineties (Free Press,

1990); The Birth Dearth (Pharos Books, 1987); The Good News is the Bad News Is Wrong (Simon & Schuster, 1984).

James Webb, Jr.   Novelist, author, government official. Secretary of the Navy (1987–88).
Recent Books: Something to Die For (William Morrow, 1991); A Country Such as This (Doubleday, 1983); A Sense of Honor (Prentice-Hall, 1981); Fields of Fire (Prentice-Hall, 1978).

Tim Wells   Author, editor, journalist. Former president, Washington Independent Writers.
Recent Books: Uneasy Verdicts: A Narrative History of the 1968 Democratic National Convention (Viking, 1989); 444 Days: The Hostages Remember (Harcourt Brace Jovanovich, 1985).

Patrick Welsh   Author, essayist, teacher.
Recent Book: Tales Out of School (Penguin, 1987).

Daniel R. White   Author, attorney, columnist.
Recent Books: The Official Lawyers Handbook (Simon & Schuster, 1990); Trials and Tribulations: Appealing Legal Humor (Catbird Press, 1989).

Reed Whittemore   Poet, author, teacher. Editor, *Delos.* Professor emeritus, English Department, University of Maryland. Former literary editor, *The New Republic.* Former Consultant in Poetry, Library of Congress (1964–65). Award of Merit, American Academy of Arts & Letters.
Recent Books: The Past, the Future, the Present: Poems, Selected & New (University of Arkansas Press, 1990); Whole Lives: Shapers of Modern Biography (Johns Hopkins Press, 1989); Pure Lives: The Early Biographers (Johns Hopkins Press, 1988); The Feel of the Rock: Poems of Three Decades (Dryad Press, 1982).

Les Whitten   Novelist, author, journalist. Former staff writer, *The Washington Post.* Former associate reporter, Jack Anderson.
Recent Books: The Lost Disciple: The Book of Demas (Atheneum, 1989); A Day Without Sunshine (Atheneum, 1985); A Killing Pace (Atheneum, 1983); The Alchemist (1983); Sometimes a Hero (Doubleday, 1979).

Wanda Wigfall-Williams Author, writer, health educator.
Recent Book: Hysterectomy: Learning the Facts, Coping With the Feelings (Kesend Publications, 1986).

George F. Will Author, journalist, columnist, television news commentator ("Inside Washington"). Contributing editor, *Newsweek*. Winner of the Pulitzer Prize for Commentary (1977).
Recent Books: Men at Work: The Craft of Baseball (Macmillan, 1990); Political Essays (Macmillan, 1990); The Morning After: American Successes & Excesses, 1981–86 (Free Press, 1986); Statecraft as Soulcraft: What Government Does (Simon & Schuster, 1983).

Juan Williams Author, journalist, columnist. Staff writer, *The Washington Post*.
Recent Book: Eyes on the Prize: America's Civil Rights Years, 1954–1965 (Viking, 1987).

George C. Wilson Author, journalist. Staff writer, *The Washington Post*.
Recent Books: Mud Soldiers: Life Inside the New American Army (Scribner's, 1989); Supercarrier: An Inside Account of Life Aboard the World's Most Powerful Ship, the USS John F. Kennedy (Macmillan, 1986).

Terence Winch Poet.
Recent Books: Contenders (Story Line Press, 1989); Irish Musicians—American Friends (Coffee House, 1985); Total Strangers (Coffee House, 1982).

David Wise Author, novelist, journalist, intelligence & espionage expert. Former Washington Bureau Chief, *The New York Herald Tribune*. Winner of the George Polk Award (1974) and the Page One Award (1969).
Recent Books: The Spy Who Got Away: The Inside Story of Edward Lee Howard, the CIA Agent Who Betrayed His Country's Secrets & Escaped to Moscow (Random House, 1988); The Samarkind Dimension (Doubleday, 1987); The Children's Game (St. Martin's Press, 1983); Spectrum (St. Martin's Press, 1981).

Jules Witcover Author, journalist, columnist (with Jack Germond, *Baltimore Evening Sun*). Former reporter for Newhouse Newspapers, *The Los Angeles Times* and *The Washington Post*.

Recent Books: The Sabotage of Black Tom: Imperial Germany's Secret War in America (Algonquin Books, 1989); Whose Broad Stripes & Bright Stars?: The Trivial Pursuit of the Presidency, 1988 (with Jack Germond, Warner Books, 1989).

Elder Witt   Author, journalist. Reporter, Congressional Quarterly. Winner of the American Book Award.
Recent Book: A Different Justice: Reagan & The Supreme Court (Congressional Quarterly, 1985).

Bob Woodward   Author, journalist. Assistant managing editor, investigative staff, *The Washington Post.* Winner of the George Polk Award (1972).
Recent Books: The Commanders (Simon & Schuster, 1991); Veil: The Secret Wars of the CIA, 1981–1987 (Simon & Schuster, 1987); Wired: The Short Life & Fast Times of John Belushi (Simon & Schuster, 1984); The Brethren (with Scott Armstrong, Simon & Schuster, 1979).

Herman Wouk   Novelist, playwright, author. Winner of the Pulitzer Prize for Fiction (1952).
Recent Books: Inside, Outside (Little, Brown, 1985); War and Remembrance (Little, Brown, 1978); The Winds of War (Little, Brown, 1971); Don't Stop the Carnival (Doubleday, 1965); Youngblood Hawke (Doubleday, 1962); This Is My God (Doubleday, 1959); Marjorie Morningstar (Doubleday, 1955); The Caine Mutiny: A Novel of World War II (Doubleday, 1952); The City Boy: The Adventures of Herbie Bookbinder (Doubleday, 1950).

Robin Wright   Author, journalist. Reporter, Washington Bureau, *The Los Angeles Times.* Foreign correspondent for many media organizations, including *The Times of London*, CBS, *The Washington Post* and *The Christian Science Monitor*. Alicia Patterson Fellow, 1975.
Recent Books: In the Name of God: The Khomeini Decade (Simon & Schuster, 1989); Sacred Rage: The Wrath of Militant Islam (Simon & Schuster, 1986).

Jonathan Yardley   Author, literary critic. Book critic, Book World, *The Washington Post.* Winner of the Pulitzer Prize for Criticism (1981).
Recent Books: Out of Step (1991); Our Kind of People: The Story of an American Family (Weidenfeld & Nicholson, 1989).

Book & Audio Publishers

> Publishing is a very mysterious business.
> **—THOMAS WOLFE**

The mystery of publishing, as Thomas Wolfe suggests, is that its practitioners must gaze far into the future to decide what books they will add to their lists today. A good book takes months to write, months to edit and more months to design and set into type. It then takes even longer to be printed, bound and shipped. On the day a book is finally released, its publisher is usually seeing the outcome of playing a hunch six months to three years ago on what his or her audience might pay money to read.

Because so much time can elapse between when a book manuscript is completed and when the book is actually released, publishers also worry that the book's author may not recall any details of what he or she has written. This form of temporary literary amnesia, known as "amnesius literarius gravis," can, according to one publisher, "drain the author's mind of all useful information about the book approximately five to eight seconds before having to conduct any important media interviews on the subject." While authors usually recover from this condition and go on to lead normal lives, the possibility of its occurrence can be an added source of stress for many publishers. Hence another part of the mystery that Wolfe describes.

While coping well with stress is certainly a key attribute of most successful publishers, their solvency also depends upon other important attributes like ingenuity, talent, ambition, market information, an appreciation for coordinated design and production, a knack for releasing well-timed publicity, good distribution and plenty of luck. The latter attribute is especially useful in publishing, and can probably account for more best-sellers than all of the other attributes combined.

This chapter contains information on 98 book and audio publishers with offices in the Washington metropolitan area. These publishers are grouped in two categories: general interest [nonfiction and/or fiction (34)] and specialty interest [(academic & public policy (23), audio publishers (2), educational & text materials (7), hobbies & diversions (4), literary (fiction & poetry, 6) and professional & business (19)].

Despite some overlap between the categories, the essential difference is that "general interest" publishers typically acquire most of their titles to sell to the general public through bookstores while "specialty publishers" develop most of their titles to distribute in various ways to such specialized audiences as librarians, scholars, poetry lovers, educators, hobbyists, business professionals and others.

In publishing, "general interest" publishers are also called "trade" publishers, because they develop books which can be sold through "the trade" (i.e., bookstores). Unfortunately, because the word "trade" is often used to describe specialized aspects of many business professions, its accepted usage in publishing can leave the impression that it is being used to describe a "specialty interest" publisher instead. This confusing use of terms is yet another confirmation of Wolfe's bewilderment regarding the mysteries of publishing.

Finally we come to the greatest mystery of all. Despite the wealth of outstanding writing talent available to publishers here in the nation's capital, there has been no dramatic increase in the number of local "general interest" or "trade" publishers listed in this chapter since it was originally published in 1989.

At that time, my prediction was that we would see the number of such publishers "at least double within the next five years." Under the circumstances, it might be better to modify that original prediction to read something like this: "In an area of the country where one would expect to see a large amount of trade publishing, we find a small but active group of trade publishers and a large number of published and unpublished local authors. Hopefully, the odds will improve for both sides during the next five years."

In any case, authors always do a better job of finding publishers than the other way around. This chapter may help. And if, for some unfortunate reason, your manuscript does get returned, just remember what Edna St. Vincent Millay said about all publishers:

A person who publishes a book willfully appears before the populace with his pants down. . . . If it is a good book, nothing can hurt him. If it is a bad book, nothing can help him.

GENERAL INTEREST

Nonfiction/Fiction

Acropolis Books   Nonfiction (current issues, environment, gardening, leisure and family, self-help, fashion and beauty, contemporary education, biography). Hardcover and paperback originals; adult subjects only.

John R. Hackl, President, 13950 Park Center Road, Herndon, VA 22071; (703) 709-0008/ FAX (703) 709-0942.

Bartleby Press   Nonfiction (history, international affairs, travel) and some fiction (adventure/espionage). Hardcover and paperback originals; adult and young adult subjects. Bartleby's new imprint, *Breakaway Books*, plans to publish a travel guide to Monaco and other travel titles. Averages 5 books p/year.

Jeremy Kay, Publisher, 11141 Georgia Avenue, Suite A6, Silver Spring, MD 20902; (301) 949-2443/ FAX (301) 949-2205.

Brassey's (U.S.)   Nonfiction (general interest and reference books on foreign policy, defense, international affairs, military history) and some fiction (adventure, espionage). Hardcover and paperback originals; adult subjects only. A Macmillan Publishing Company; sister company is Brassey's (U.K.) in London. Distributed by Macmillan, Inc. Averages 25–30 books p/year.

Dr. Franklin D. Margiotta, President/Director of Publishing, 8000 Westpark Drive, McLean, VA 22102; (703) 442-4535. Don McKeon, Associate Director of Publishing. Kim Borchard, Director of Marketing.

Columbia Books   Nonfiction (local reference guides, political subjects, current affairs). Paperback originals; adult subjects only. Averages 6 books p/year.

Arthur Close, President, 1212 New York Avenue NW, Suite 330, Washington, DC 20005; (202) 898-0662. John Russell, Vice President.

Corkscrew Press   Nonfiction (cookbooks, how-to books, humor) and some fiction. Paperback originals; adult subjects only. Averages 1–2 books p/year.

Richard Lippmann, President, 2915 Fenimore Road, Silver Spring, MD 20902; (301) 933-0407.

Elliott & Clark Publishing Nonfiction (illustrated history, natural history, photography, calendars). Hardcover and paperback originals; adult titles only. Averages 4 books p/year.

Doug Elliott, President, 1638 R Street NW, Suite 21, Washington, DC 20009; (202) 387-9805. Carolyn Clark, Vice President. Michael J. Crall, Marketing Director.

EPM Publications Nonfiction (Americana, history, cookbooks, crafts, quilt books, self-help, recreation, regional guides) and some fiction. Hardcover and paperback originals; adult and children's subjects. EPM also provides distribution and warehousing services for Editorial Experts, Concept Associates Videos, Hero Books and several other small to medium-sized publishers. Averages 8–12 books p/year.

Evelyn Metzger, President & Editor, 1003 Turkey Run Road, McLean, VA 22101; (703) 442-7810/ FAX (703) 442-0599.

Farragut Publishing Nonfiction (local reference, politics, cooking, sports). Paperback originals; adult subjects only. Averages 2–3 books p/year.

Dan Rapoport, President & Publisher, 2033 M Street NW, Washington, DC 20036; (202) 872-4009/ FAX (202) 872-4703.

Garrett Park Press Nonfiction (career guidance, reference, minority information and opportunities, international issues). Paperback originals; adult subjects only. Averages 5–7 books p/year.

Robert Calvert, Jr., Publisher, P.O. Box 190, Garrett Park, MD 20896; (301) 946-2553.

Great Ocean Publishers Nonfiction (literature, biography, health, philosophy, crafts, music, how-to, illustrated books, reference, self-help). Hardcover and paperback originals; adult and children's subjects. Averages 2–4 books p/year.

Mark Esterman, President & Editor-in-Chief, 1823 North Lincoln Street, Arlington, VA 22207; (703) 525-0909. Margaret Park, Executive Editor.

Hatier Publishing Nonfiction (French language publisher and distributor). Hardcover and paperback originals; adult and children's subjects. Subsidiary of Librarie Hatier. Distributor for Didier, Foucher, Hatier and Hatier-Didier USA. Averages 4 books p/year.

Jean-Louys Rabeharisoa, Vice President, 3160 O Street NW, Washington, DC 20007; (202) 333-4435.

Heritage Books Nonfiction (history, genealogy, how-to, reference). Hardcover and paperback originals; adult subjects only. Averages 100 books p/year.

Laird Towle, Editorial Director, 1540–E Pointer Ridge Place, Bowie, MD 20716; (301) 390-7708.

Hero Books Nonfiction (military history and strategy, national security, political science, history and military science, Soviet studies). Hardcover and paperback originals; adult subjects only. Distributed by EPM Publications. Averages 4–6 books p/year.

Guy P. Clifton, Publisher, 6832 Old Dominion Drive, McLean, VA 22101; (703) 591-6109.

Howells House Nonfiction (current affairs, contemporary history, biography, art, architecture, graphics). Hardcover and paperback originals; adult subjects only. Imprints include The Compass Press and Whalesback Books. Distributed to the trade by Paul & Company Publishers' Consortium (U.S. and Canada) and by Drake Marketing Services/Oxford (International). Averages 3–4 books p/year.

W.D. Howells, President & Publisher, P.O. Box 9546, Washington, DC 20016; (202) 333-2182.

Island Press Nonfiction (environment and conservation, natural resource management, public policy, careers, reference). Hardcover and paperback originals; adult subjects only. Island plans to launch a new imprint, as yet unnamed, to publish nonfiction *and* fiction titles on environmental ethics and philosophy, nature writing, the life sciences and cultural anthropology. IP is a division of the Center for Resource Economics. Averages 30 books p/year.

Charles Savitt, Publisher, 1718 Connecticut Avenue NW, Suite 300, Washington, DC 20009; (202) 232-7933/ FAX (202) 234-1328. Joe Ingram, Editor-in-Chief.

Kar-Ben Copies Nonfiction (Jewish life-cycle, holidays and customs, Judaica) and some fiction (Jewish adventure, fantasy, historical, religious). Hardcover and paperback originals; children's and juvenile subjects only. Averages 8–10 books p/year.

Judyth Groner, President, 6800 Tildenwood Lane, Rockville, MD 20852; (301) 984-8733/ FAX (301) 881-9195. Madeline Wikler, Vice President.

Madison Books Nonfiction (history, biography, popular culture, contemporary affairs, social sciences, local and national reference). Hardcover and paperback originals; adult subjects only. A subsidiary of University Press of America (UPA), Madison's two imprints are Scarborough House (formerly Stein and Day) and Hamilton Press. Distributed by National Book Network, another subsidiary of UPA. Averages 30–40 books p/year.

James E. Lyons, Publisher, 4720 Boston Way, Lanham, MD 20706; (301) 459-5308/ FAX 459-2118. Jennifer Smith, Managing Editor.

Mage Publishers Nonfiction (Persian art, history, literature) and some fiction (illustrated and bilingual collections of short stories, poetry, short fiction). Hardcover and paperback originals; adult and children's subjects. Averages 3–5 books p/year.

Mohammad Batmanglij, Publisher & Editor, 1032 29th Street NW, Washington, DC 20007; (202) 342-1642/ FAX (202) 342-9269. A. Sepehri, Assistant to the Publisher.

Mino Publications Nonfiction (guidebooks, souvenir books, maps on the nation's capital). Paperback originals; adult and children's subjects. Averages 1–2 books p/year.

Anthony Pitch, Publisher, 9009 Paddock Lane, Potomac, MD 20854; (301) 294-9514.

National Geographic Society Books Nonfiction (geography, natural history, travel/adventure, cultures, ecosystems, full-color illustrated and photography books). Hardcover and paperback originals; adult and children's subjects. Averages 1–3 books p/year.

William Gray, Director of Publishing, 1145 17th Street NW, Washington, DC 20036; (202) 857-7355/ FAX (202) 775-6141.

National Press Nonfiction (biography, law and legislation, cookbooks, sports, recreation) and some fiction

(adventure, historical mainstream, regional, suspense/
mystery, translations). Hardcover and paperback originals; adult and children's subjects. Imprints include
Garlic Press, Beach Books, Pandamonium Books, Full
Court Press Books, Plain English Press and Zenith
Editions. Distributed by National Book Network. Averages 20–25 books p/year.

Joel Joseph, President, 7200 Wisconsin Avenue, Suite
212, Bethesda, MD 20814; (301) 657-1616/ FAX (301)
657-8475. Edward Smith, Submissions Editor.

Potomac-Pacific Press   Nonfiction (politics, child care,
writing, reference). Paperback originals; adult subjects
only. Averages 5–7 books p/year.

George Mair, President, 1003 North Fairfax Street,
Suite 304, Alexandria, VA 22314; (703) 836-8259/ FAX
(703) 836-4084.

Preservation Press   Nonfiction (architecture, design,
history and American culture, building restoration, cultural preservation). Hardcover and paperback originals;
adult and children's subjects. Imprints include Building
Watchers Series, Great American Series Places, Landmark Reprint Series and others. Averages 6–9 books p/
year.

Buckley C. Jeppson, Director, National Trust For
Historic Preservation, 1785 Massachusetts Avenue NW,
Washington, DC 20036; (202) 673-4058/ FAX (202) 673-
4172. Pamela Dwight, Editorial Assistant.

Regnery Gateway   Nonfiction (politics, biography, current affairs, philosophy, economics, religion, business,
literary criticism). Hardcover and paperback originals;
adult subjects only. RG's sole imprint is Gateway Editions; its subsidiaries include Cahill & Company Reader's Catalogue and American Citizen Reader's Catalogue. Distributed by National Book Network. Averages
25 books p/year.

Alfred S. Regnery, Publisher, 1130 17th Street NW,
Suite 620, Washington, DC 20036; (202) 457-0978/ (800)
448-8311.

Scarborough House   Nonfiction (biography, history,
military history, self-help). Hardcover and paperback
originals; adult subjects only. An imprint of Madison
Books, Scarborough House (formerly Stein and Day) is

distributed to the trade by National Book Network. Averages 20 books p/yr.

James E. Lyons, Publisher, 4720 Boston Way, Lanham, MD 20706; (301) 459-5308/ FAX 459-2118. Jennifer Smith, Managing Editor.

Seven Locks Press Nonfiction (biography, reference, politics, civil rights, history, business and economics, international relations, journalism, sociology, regional guides). Hardcover and paperback originals; adult subjects only. SLP's sole imprint is Isidore Stephanus Sons Publishing. Distributed by Independent Publishers Group. Averages 8–10 books p/year.

James McGrath Morris, President & Publisher, P.O. Box 27, Cabin John, MD 20818; (301) 320-2130.

Starfish Press Nonfiction (local history, regional travel guides, illustrated books). Paperback originals; adult subjects only. Averages 1–2 books p/year.

David Shears, Publisher, 6525 32nd Street NW, P.O. Box 42467, Washington, DC 20015; (202) 244-2178. Nicholas Shears, Editor.

Starrhill Press Nonfiction (art and architecture, gardens and weather, classic literary day books, travel guides, performing arts, decoration, reference). Paperback originals; adult subjects only. Averages 4 books p/year.

Elizabeth Hill & Marty Starr, Co-Presidents, P.O. Box 32342, Washington, DC 20007; (202) 686-6703/ FAX (202) 686-0707.

Starwood Publishing Nonfiction (natural history, gardening, history, Americana, fine art photography, calendars). Hardcover originals; adult subjects only. Averages 5 books p/year.

Ruina W. Judd, President & CEO, 5230 MacArthur Boulevard NW, Washington, DC 20016; (202) 362-7404. Lynne Shaner, Editorial & Production Director. Sandra Trupp, Director of Sales and Marketing.

Stone Wall Press Nonfiction (nature, ecology, recreation, adventure travel, health and fitness, conservation, natural history). Hardcover and paperback originals; adult subjects only. Averages 2–4 books p/year.

Henry C. Wheelwright, President & Publisher, 1241

30th Street NW, Washington, DC 20007; (202) 333-1860. Theresa Sullivan, Assistant Publisher.

Three Continents Press Nonfiction (African, Caribbean, Asian and Middle Eastern literature and criticism, translations, Third World histories) and fiction (poetry, novels, short-story collections, plays and translations by non-Western authors only). Hardcover and paperback originals; adult subjects only. TCP's imprints include Critical Perspectives and Sun-Lit Books. TCP also distributes several foreign publishers, including Graham Brash Singapore, Forest Books (London), Heinemann (Modern Arab Writers) and others. Averages 30 books p/year.

Donald E. Herdeck, Publisher & Editor-in-Chief, 1901 Pennsylvania Avenue NW, Suite 407, Washington, DC 20006; (202) 223-2554. Usha Nagarajan, General Manager.

Time-Life Books Nonfiction (art, cooking, crafts, gardening, health, history, home repair, nature, parenting, photography, science, reference, other subjects of general interest). Hardcover originals; adult and children's subjects. Subsidiary of Time Warner, Inc. Divisions include Time-Life Video, Time-Life Music and Time Life for Children. Averages 50–60 books p/year.

John Fahey, President & CEO, 777 Duke Street, Alexandria, VA 22314; (703) 838-7000/ (800) 621-7026. Joe Ward, Publisher. Tom Ward, Managing Editor.

Twenty-First Century Books Nonfiction (biography, history, hobbies, nature and the environment, geography, travel, social issues for children and teens) and some fiction (illustrated children's books). Hardcover and paperback originals; adult and children's subjects. Subsidiary of Henry Holt and Company. Averages 8–10 books p/year.

Jeffrey Shulman, President, 38 South Market Street, Frederick, MD 21701; (301) 698-0210.

Vandamere Press Nonfiction (history, regional guides, careers, travel, parenting). Hardcover and paperback originals; adult and children's subjects. Averages 6–8 books p/year.

Art Brown, Publisher, P.O. Box 5243, Arlington, VA 22205; (703) 525-5488.

Woodbine House Nonfiction (consumer reference, science, travel, history, education, regional interest, parents' guides for children with special needs). Paperback originals; adult and children's subjects. Averages 8–10 books p/year.

Irvin Shapell, Publisher, 5615 Fishers Lane, Rockville, MD 20852; (301) 468-8800/ FAX (301) 468-5784. Susan Stokes, Editor.

SPECIALTY INTEREST

Academic & Public Policy

Alban Institute Press Nonfiction (religious, ecumenical and congregational subjects). Paperback originals; adult subjects only. Averages 7 books p/year.

Celia A. Hahn, Director of Publications, 4125 Nebraska Avenue NW, Washington, DC 20016; (202) 244-7320.

American Enterprise Institute Press Nonfiction (economics, foreign affairs, defense issues, government, politics, law, education, energy, health policy, philosophy, religion, tax policy). Hardcover and paperback originals; adult subjects only. Distributed by University Press of America and National Book Network. Averages 40 books p/year.

Christopher C. DeMuth, President, 1150 17th Street NW, Washington, DC 20036; (202) 862-5800. Edward Styles, Publications Director.

American University Press Nonfiction (public policy, communications, international relations, art history, political history). Hardcover and paperback originals; adult subjects only. Distributed by University Press of America. Averages 6–7 books p/year.

Dr. Frederick Jacobs, 4400 Massachusetts Avenue NW, McDowell Hall #117, Washington, DC 20016; (202) 885-3409/ FAX (202) 885-3453. Dr. Rita J. Simon, Editor, Public Policy Series. Sanford Ungar, Editor, Journalism History Series.

Brookings Institution Press Nonfiction (economics, government affairs, foreign policy). Hardcover and paperback originals; adult subjects only. Averages 30–35 books p/year.

Robert L. Faherty, Director of Publishing, 1775 Massachusetts Avenue NW, Washington, DC 20036; (202) 797-6250/ FAX (202) 797-6004. Caroline Lalire, Managing Editor.

Catholic University of America Press Nonfiction (history, biography, languages and literature, philosophy, religion, church-state relations, political theory, series of translations of ancient Fathers of the Catholic Church). Hardcover and paperback originals; adult subjects only. Averages 15–20 books p/year.

Dr. David J. McGonagle, Director, 620 Michigan Avenue NE, Washington, DC 20064; (202) 319-5052.

Center for Strategic & International Studies Nonfiction (national policy, foreign affairs, defense, strategic issues). Hardcover and paperback originals; adult subjects only. Averages 13–15 books p/year.

Nancy B. Eddy, Director of Publishing, 1800 K Street NW, Suite 400, Washington, DC 20006; (202) 775-3119.

Ethics & Public Policy Center Nonfiction (foreign policy, education, business, religion and society). Hardcover and paperback originals; adult subjects only. Averages 5 books p/year. Distributed by University Press of America.

Carol Griffith, Publications Manager, 1015 15th Street NW, Suite 300, Washington, DC 20005; (202) 682-1200.

Gallaudet University Press Nonfiction (scholarly, educational and general interest books on deafness and hearing impairments). Hardcover and paperback originals; adult, juvenile and children's subjects. Imprints include Clerc Books and Kendall Green Publications. Averages 15–20 books p/year.

Dr. Elaine Costello, Director & Editor-in-Chief, Gallaudet University, 800 Florida Avenue NE, Washington, DC 20002; (202) 651-5488/ (800) 451-1073. Ivey Pittle Wallace, Managing Editor.

George Mason University Press Nonfiction (scholarly books on various subjects in the humanities, sciences and social sciences). Hardcover and paperback originals; adult subjects only. Averages 10 books p/year.

James Fisher, Director, George Mason University,

4400 University Drive, Fairfax, VA 22030; (703) 323-3785.

Georgetown University Press   Nonfiction (scholarly and educational books on linguistics, languages, contemporary ethics, theology and other subjects). Hardcover and paperback originals; adult subjects only. Averages 15 books p/year.

John Staczek, Director, Georgetown University, Intercultural Center, Suite 111, Washington, DC 20057; (202) 687-6251/ 687-6063/ FAX (202) 687-5712. Patrice La Liberte, Senior Editor.

Howard University Press   Nonfiction (contributions and interests of African-Americans, scholarly books on the arts, history, communications, politics, religion, education, literature and other subjects). Hardcover and paperback originals; adult subjects only. Averages 7–9 books p/year.

Renee Mayfield, Managing Editor, Howard University, 2900 Van Ness Street, NW, Washington, DC 20008; (202) 806-8450. Fay Acker and Ruby Esslen, Senior Editors.

Institute for International Economics   Nonfiction (international economic policy, finance, trade, energy, investment, foreign debt and development). Hardcover and paperback originals; adult subjects only. Averages 9–12 books p/year.

Linda Griffin Kean, Director of Publishing, 11 Dupont Circle NW, Washington, DC 20036; (202) 328-9000.

Institute for Policy Studies   Nonfiction (politics, culture, economics). Paperback originals; adult subjects only. IPS also provides co-publishing and distribution services to several smaller presses. Averages 5–7 books p/year.

Miriam Smallhout, Director of Publications Program, 1601 Connecticut Avenue NW, Washington, DC 20009; (202) 234-9382.

Library of Congress   Nonfiction (scholarly books about the Library and its collections, catalogues, bibliographies, guides, checklists). Hardcover and paperback originals; adult subjects only. Distributed by the U.S. Government Printing Office. No outside submissions accepted. Averages 25–30 books p/year.

Dana J. Pratt, Director of Publishing, Library of Congress, Madison Building, Independence Avenue & 1st Streets SE, Room 604, Washington, DC 20540; (202) 707-5093.

Maryland Historical Press Nonfiction (biography, Americana, history). Hardcover and paperback originals; children's and juvenile subjects. Averages 4 books p/year.

Vera Rollo, Publisher, 9205 Tuckerman Street, Lanham, MD 20706; (301) 577-5308.

National Academy Press Nonfiction (health, science, technology). Hardcover and paperback originals; adult subjects only. A division of the National Academy of Sciences. No outside submissions accepted. Averages 175 books p/year.

Scott F. Lubeck, Director, 2101 Constitution Avenue NW, Washington, DC 20418; (202) 334-3324. Stephen Mautner, Executive Editor.

Naval Institute Press Nonfiction (naval and maritime subjects: professional, engineering, science, history, texts, technical and trade, Institute proceedings) and some fiction (naval adventure, history, war themes). Hardcover originals; adult subjects only. Averages 60 books p/year.

Thomas Epley, Press & Editorial Director, U.S. Naval Institute, Treble Hall, Annapolis, MD 21402; (301) 268-6110/ FAX (301) 269-7940. Paul Wilderson, Manager of Acquisitions.

Rowman & Littlefield Publishers Nonfiction (business, economics, environmental studies, geography, government, law, social and biological sciences, health services, history, literature, philosophy, policy studies, women's studies, technical, reference). Hardcover and paperback originals; adult subjects only. Imprints include Barnes & Noble Books and Littlefield Adams Quality Paperbacks. A division of University Press of America. Averages 90 books p/year.

James E. Lyons, Publisher, 4720 Boston Way, Lanham, MD 20706; (301) 306-0400/ FAX (301) 459-2118. Jonathan Sisk, Editor-in-Chief.

Smithsonian Institution Press Nonfiction (American history, natural science, anthropology, history of science and technology, aeronautics and astronautics, art and art history, regional interest, musicology, other subjects). Hardcover and paperback originals; direct mail books, reprints, videos and sound recordings. Adult subjects only. SI Press has one imprint, Smithsonian Books, and four divisions: University Press Division (80 books p/year), Direct Mail Division (2 books p/year), Federal Series Division (35 books p/year) and Smithsonian/Folkways Recordings. Averages 120 books p/year.

Felix C. Lowe, Director, 470 L'Enfant Plaza, Room 7100, Washington, DC 20560; (202) 287-3738/ (800) 678-2675. Daniel Goodwin, Editorial Director. Amy Pastan, Peter Cannell and Mark Hirsch, Acquisitions Editors, University Press Division.

University Press of America Nonfiction (scholarly monographs; college and graduate level textbooks on history, economics, business, psychology, political science, African studies, philosophy, religion, sociology, music, art, literature, drama, education; conference proceedings). Hardcover and paperback originals; adult subjects only. UPA's imprints include Abt Books and RF Publishing. UPA's subsidiaries include Madison Books, Hamilton Press, Rowman & Littlefield, Barnes & Noble Books, Littlefield Adams Quality Paperbacks, Scarborough House and National Book Network (NBN). UPA's divisions include British American Publishing Company, UPA Co-Publishing and UPA Publishers' Reprints. Through NBN, UPA distributes for 50 prominent American publishers. Averages 450-500 books p/year.

James E. Lyons, Publisher, 4720 Boston Way, Lanham, MD 20706; (301) 459-3366/ FAX (301) 459-2118. Jonathan Sisk, Editor-in-Chief.

University Publications of America Nonfiction (microforms, research collections, looseleafs). Hardcover originals, reprints; adult subjects only. Averages 50 books p/year. An imprint of Congressional Information Service.

Paul Kesaris, Vice President-UPA Editorial, 4520 East-West Highway, Bethesda, MD 20814. (301) 657-3200/ FAX (301) 657-3203. Betsey Covell, Managing Editor.

Urban Institute Press Nonfiction (economics, government, public policy, social sciences). Hardcover and paperback originals; adult subjects only. Distributed by University Press of America. Averages 25 books p/year.

Felicity Skidmore, Director of Publishing, 2100 M Street NW, Washington, DC 20037; (202) 857-8724.

Wilson Center Press   Nonfiction (international relations, political science, social science, the humanities). Hardcover and paperback originals; adult subjects only. Distributed by Johns Hopkins University Press. Averages 9–12 books p/year.

Richard C. Rowson, Publishing Director, Woodrow Wilson International Center for Scholars, 370 L'Enfant Promenade SW, Suite 704, Washington, DC 20024; (202) 287-3000/ FAX (202) 287-3772.

Audio Publishers

Audio Book Contractors   This publisher offers hundreds of literary classics, narrated onto unabridged, full-length audio tapes and packaged in durable albums. The "Classic Books on Cassettes Collection" for adults features full-length novels and short stories on tape by many distinguished classic authors, including Trollope, Henry James, Austen, Wharton, Arthur Conan Doyle, Hawthorne, Dickens, Flaubert, Stevenson, Twain, Conrad, Dreiser, Hardy, Wells and Woolf. The "Classic Books on Cassettes Collection for Children" features more than 60 well-known children's classics on tape. There is also an excellent "Ride With Me" series of audio tapes available for interstate journeys by car through 15 U.S. states. A free catalogue is available upon request.

Flo Gibson, President, Classic Books on Cassettes, P.O. Box 40115, Washington, DC 20016; (202) 363-3429/ FAX (202) 363-3429.

Recorded Books   This publisher offers a large selection of unabridged audio books in many categories, either for sale or rent (30–day maximum). Bestsellers, mysteries, history and classics are available. Each book is studio recorded by expert narrators. A free catalogue is available upon request.

Recorded Books, P.O. Box 409, Charlotte Hall, MD 20622; (800) 638-1304.

Tapes For Readers   Engaging conversations by this notable audio publisher with well-known authors about their writing, lives, opinions and ideas. Authors interviewed include Woody Allen, Maya Angelou, Isaac Asimov, Russell Baker, Saul Bellow, Art Buchwald, John Cheever, William Kennedy, Margaret Meade, James Michener, S.J. Perelman, Isaac Bashevis Singer, Tom Stoppard, John Updike, Tennessee Williams and Tom Wolfe (more than 100 in all). Free catalogue available.

Stephen Banker, Publisher, 5078 Fulton Street NW, Washington, DC 20016; (202) 362-4585.

Educational & Text Materials

Chadwyck-Healey Nonfiction (scholarly books, reference works, academic microform publications, CD-ROM publications). Hardcover and paperback originals; adult subjects only. Averages 15 books p/year.

Charles Chadwyck-Healey, Owner, 1101 King Street, Suite 180, Alexandria, VA 22314; (703) 683-4890. Alan Fox, Director of Customer Service.

Close Up Foundation Books Nonfiction (social studies, government, international relations, public policy, economics, American history, peace and security issues, supplemental high school materials). Hardcover and paperback originals; adult and juvenile subjects. Averages 7–10 books p/year.

Lynn Whittaker, Director of Publishing, 1235 Jefferson Davis Highway, Alexandria, VA 22202; (703) 706-3300/ FAX (703) 892–1118.

Gifted Education Press Nonfiction (adult literacy, education of the gifted, psychology, philosophy, parenting). Paperback originals; adult and children's subjects. Also publishes quarterly newsletter. Averages 5 books p/year.

Maurice Fisher, Publisher, 10201 Yuma Court, P.O. Box 1586, Manassas, VA 22110; (703) 369-5017.

Gryphon House Nonfiction (educational activity books, teaching materials, how-to projects). Paperback originals; children's subjects only (ages 1–5). Gryphon House provides distribution services for a number of smaller presses, including Building Blocks Press, Teaching Strategies and others. Averages 4–5 books p/year.

Kathleen Charner, President & Editor, 3706 Otis Street, Mt. Rainier, MD 20712; (301) 779-6200/ (800) 638-0928.

Learning Matters   Nonfiction (education and learning-related materials for parents and children, literacy projects, teacher training texts). Hardcover and paperback originals, as well as video, audio and electronic media materials; adult and children's subjects. Averages 5–6 titles p/year.

Mark Esterman, President, 1823 N. Lincoln Street, Arlington, VA 22207; (703) 525-0909.

Octameron Press   Nonfiction (career guides, college admission information, post-secondary education financing, other subjects). Paperback originals; adult and juvenile subjects. OP's subsidiary is Educational Access. Distributed nationally by Longman Trade. Averages 12 books p/year.

Anna Leider, Publisher, Octameron Associates, 1900 Mount Vernon Avenue, Alexandria, VA 22301; (703) 836-5480.

TJ Publishers   Nonfiction and fiction (books on sign language and deafness). Hardcover and paperback originals; adult and children's subjects. Also provides specialized distribution services for other publishers, including Bantam Books, Gallaudet University Press, Houghton Mifflin Company, Random House, St. Martin's Press and others. Averages 3 books p/year.

Angela K. Thomas, President, 817 Silver Spring Avenue, Silver Spring, MD 20910; (301) 585-4440.

Hobbies & Diversions

Denlinger's Publishers, Ltd.   Nonfiction (books about dogs and dog breeding). Hardcover and paperback originals; adult subjects only. Averages 12–15 books p/year.

William Denlinger, Publisher, P.O. Box 76, Fairfax, VA 22030; (703) 830-4646/ FAX (703) 830-5303.

Greenberg Publishing Company   Nonfiction (collecting and repairing toy trains, railroad histories, guides to other collectibles). Paperback originals; adult and children's subjects. Averages 15–20 titles p/year.

Bruce Greenburg, Publisher, 7566 Main Street, Sykesville, MD 21784; (301) 795-7447.

Half-Halt Press   Nonfiction (books about horses and equestrian subjects, including care, management, riding, biographies and translations). Hardcover and paperback originals; adult and children's titles. U.S. distributor for Kenilworth Press (U.K.). Averages 5 books p/year.

Elizabeth Carnes, Publisher, 6416 Burkittsville Road, Middletown, MD 21769; (301) 371-9110. James P. Farber, Jr., Administrative Editor.

Peeking Duck Books Nonfiction (personalized children's name books). Hardcover originals; children's titles only. Available by direct mail and in select children's specialty stores.

Orin R. Heend, President, P.O. Box 207, Arlington, VA 22210; (703) 525-2378.

RedBrick Press Nonfiction (beer and the microbrewing industry, food, travel). Hardcover and paperback originals; adult subjects only. Averages 2–3 books p/year.

Jack Erickson, Publisher, P.O. Box 2184, Reston, VA 22090; (703) 476-6420.

Literary (Fiction & Poetry)

Ariadne Press Fiction (novels) and some nonfiction (how-to books on writing fiction). Paperback originals; adult subjects only. Averages 1–2 books p/year.

Carol Hoover, President, 4817 Tallahassee Avenue, Rockville, MD 20853; (301) 949-2514.

Dryad Press Fiction (poetry, short stories, translations) and selected literary nonfiction. Paperback originals, reprints; adult subjects only. Averages 1–2 books p/year.

Merrill Leffler, President, 15 Sherman Avenue, Takoma Park, MD 20912; (301) 891-3729/ FAX (301) 454-0367.

Orchises Press Fiction (poetry) and nonfiction (literary textbooks, computer books). Paperback originals; adult subjects only. Averages 4–5 books p/year.

Roger Lathbury, Publisher, P.O. Box 20602, Alexandria, VA 22320; (703) 683-1243.

Washington Writers' Publishing House Fiction (poetry collections by local authors). Paperback originals; adult subjects only. Averages 1–2 books p/year.

Jean Nordhaus, President, P.O. Box 15271, Washington, DC 20003; (202) 543-1905. Jeannie Krohn, Director.

The Wineberry Press Fiction (collections of poetry). Paperback originals; adult subjects only. Averages 1 book p/year.

Elisavietta Ritchie, President, 3207 Macomb Street NW, Washington, DC 20008; (202) 363-8036.

The Word Works Fiction (contemporary poetry in single author editions). Paperback originals, occasional anthologies; adult subjects only. Averages 1–2 books p/year.

Karren Alenier & J.H. Beall & Robert Sargent & Barbara Goldberg, Poetry Editors, P.O. Box 42164, Washington, DC 20015.

Professional & Business

American Institute of Architects Press Nonfiction (illustrated and reference books on historical and contemporary architecture, construction technology, research, statistics, interior design). Hardcover and paperback originals; adult subjects only. Averages 7–9 books p/year.

John Ray Hoke, Jr., Publisher, AIA, 1735 New York Avenue NW, Washington, DC, 20006; (202) 626-7300/FAX (202) 626-7518. Cynthia G. Ware, Managing Editor.

American Psychiatric Press Nonfiction (psychiatry, behavioral and social sciences, medicine, reference, college texts). Hardcover and some paperback originals; adult subjects only. Averages 50 books p/year.

Ron McMillen, Director of Publishing, APA, 1400 K Street NW, Suite 1101, Washington, DC 20005; (202) 682-6268. Claire Reinburg, Editorial Director.

American Psychological Association Nonfiction (psychology, mental health, works for professionals in the field). Hardcover and paperback originals; adult subjects only. Averages 15–20 books p/year.

W. Ralph Eubanks, Director of Publishing, APA, 1200 17th Street NW, Washington, DC 20036; (202) 955-7600.

Aspen Publishers Nonfiction (health care, nursing, medicine, special education, allied health, physical and occupational therapy, gerontology, speech and hearing, psychology, family therapy, business and professional, law texts, reference materials). Hardcover and paperback originals, journals, newsletters and loose-leaf subscription services; adult subjects only. Member of the Worldwide Wolters-Kluwer Group. Averages 70 books p/year.

Michael B. Brown, VP & Publisher, 200 Orchard Ridge Drive, Gaithersburg, MD 20878; (301) 417-7500/FAX (301) 417-7550.

BNA Books Nonfiction (law and legal practice, taxation, management, arbitration, labor and employee relations, environment and safety). Hardcover and paperback originals; adult subjects only. Division of the Bureau of National Affairs. Averages 25–30 books p/year.

Richard Cornfield, Publisher, Bureau of National Affairs, 1250 23rd Street NW, Washington, DC 20037; (202) 452-4400. Randy Auerbach, Managing Editor.

CQ Press Nonfiction (politics and political science, reference guides, elections, American government, college textbooks). Hardcover and paperback originals; adult subjects only. CQ Press is an imprint of Congressional Quarterly. Averages 20 books p/year.

David Tarr, Director/Book Department, 1414 22nd Street NW, Washington, DC 20037; (202) 887-8642. Brenda Carter, Acquisitions Editor.

Editorial Experts Nonfiction (books on writing and editing, reference materials, directories, publishing information). Paperback originals; adult subjects only. Averages 6–8 books p/year.

Andrea Johnson, Director of Publishing, 66 Canal Center Plaza, Suite 200, Alexandria, VA 22314; (703) 683-0683.

Government Institutes Nonfiction (environmental law, health, safety, personnel, energy, reference, technical). Hardcover and paperback originals; adult subjects only. Averages 45 books p/year.

Ronald W. Schumann, Manager of Acquisitions, 4 Research Place, Rockville, MD 20850; (301) 251-9250.

Home Builder Press Nonfiction (residential and light commercial construction information, home design and construction, land development, multihousing construction and management, new home sales and marketing, remodeling). Hardcover and paperback originals; adult subjects only. Averages 10–12 books p/year.

Rosanne O'Connor, Director of Publishing, National Association of Home Builders, 15 & M Streets NW, Washington, DC 20005; (202) 822-0476.

Information Resources Press   Nonfiction (health, computer science, information, library science, reference, technical). Hardcover originals; adult subjects only. A division of Herner & Company. Averages 4–6 books p/year.

Gene Allen, VP & Publisher, 1110 N. Glebe Road, Suite 550, Arlington, VA 22201; (703) 558-8270/ FAX (703) 558-4979.

International Library–Law Book Publishers   Nonfiction (law books in the fields of advertising, insurance, business, finance, energy, government, political science, public utilities, tax, labor, the environment). Hardcover and paperback originals; adult subjects only. Divisions include International Law Library and Law Book Publishers. Averages 12–15 books p/year.

Donald J. Hoyes, President, 101 Lakeforest Boulevard, Suite 270, Gaithersburg, MD 20877; (301) 990-7755.

Kendall/Hunt Publishing Company   Nonfiction (medical education, professional development, certification programs, industry studies, training). Hardcover and paperback originals; adult subjects only. Averages 160 books p/year.

Emmett Dingley, Director of Publishing, 7223 Lee Highway, Suite 302, Falls Church, VA 22046; (703) 237-1907.

Kiplinger Books   Nonfiction (business, trend forecasting, personal finance, investments). Hardcover and paperback originals; adult subjects only. Distributed by National Book Network. Averages 3–5 books p/year.

David Harrison, Publisher, 1729 H Street NW, Washington, DC 20006; (202) 887-6680.

Lomond Publications   Nonfiction (science policy and business management for professionals). Hardcover originals; adult subjects only. Averages 3 books p/year.

Thomas Hattery, President & Publisher, P.O. Box

88, Mount Airy, MD 21771; (301) 829-1496/ (800) 443-6299.

Miles River Press Nonfiction (scholarly and general interest books on business management and communications). Paperback originals; adult subjects only. Averages 1–2 books p/year.

Peg Paul, President, 1009 Duke Street, Alexandria, VA 22314; (703) 683-1500.

Minerva Books Nonfiction (financial newsletter performance ratings, investment trends, other related subjects). Hardcover and paperback originals; adult subjects only. Averages 1–2 books p/year.

Mark Hulbert, President & Publisher, 316 Commerce Street, Alexandria, VA 22314; (703) 683-5905.

National Center for Nonprofit Boards Nonfiction (nonprofit board governance, legal and economic issues related to nonprofit associations). Hardcover and paperback originals; adult subjects only. Averages 5–6 books p/year.

Judith Greifer, Director of Publishing, 2000 L Street NW, Suite 411, Washington, DC 20036; (202) 452-6262.

Pasha Publications Nonfiction (energy, defense, foreign markets, the gas industry, space, reference). Paperback originals; adult subjects only. Averages 7–9 books p/year.

Doug Rekenthaler, Book Project Manager, 1401 Wilson Boulevard, Suite 900, Arlington, VA 22209; (703) 528-1244/ FAX (703) 528-1253.

Staff Directories, Ltd. Nonfiction (directories covering legislative, executive and judicial branches of the federal government, local and national reference books). Hardcover and paperback originals; adult subjects only. Averages 6–8 books p/year.

Ann L. Brownson, President, P.O. Box 62, Mount Vernon, VA 22121; (703) 739-0900/ FAX (703) 739-0234.

Literary Agents & Book Producers

Then there's the one about Jack, the writer, and his agent Morty. They both fall off a boat in the middle of the ocean and find themselves treading water.

Jack suddenly points and screams: "MORTY, IT'S A SHARK! WE'RE DONE FOR !!!"

The shark heads straight for them. Then, at the last second, it sees Morty, turns away and heads back into open water.

"What do you make of that?" says Jack.

"Professional courtesy," says Morty, flashing a smile.

—WRITER'S JOKE

In the seas of publishing, popular lore holds that literary agents are bloodthirsty sharks out to swallow writers whole. This is a convenient myth, perhaps originated by an angry publisher whose own plans for total author consumption became thwarted at the last minute by an agent's skillful contract changes. Whatever its origin, the myth is a bit galling for anyone who has worked as an agent, and begs to be revised.

Let's examine the facts. We are talking about an intelligent, sophisticated species here, one which has evolved a natural appetite for sharp, clear writing (or at least a good story). Each day, members of the species prowl magazines, newspapers, other "major media," gossip columns, lunching establishments and oceans of unpublished manuscripts, looking for blood in the water. The good morsels are few and far between. And even when an occasional feeding frenzy occurs, drawing more than one member of the species to a single hapless author, the chances of that author being gobbled up whole are very unlikely.

Instead, the author is usually permitted to keep as much as 85 *or even* 90 percent of all parts intact! This small sacrifice by the author is typically made following a successful negotiation between the author's agent and a mutually agreeable publisher. Now, let's face it. Even in the seas of life, few percentages get any better than that.

Why are good agents permitted to do this? Because

they help authors focus their book ideas, submit book proposals or completed manuscripts to editors they know or have worked with, negotiate publishing and subsidiary rights contracts, secure promotional and advertising considerations (before, during and after release), review royalty and residual statements for accuracy and much more. Nine-tenths of all agents are exclusively looking for manuscripts with "trade potential," meaning they hope to interest a "trade" (general interest) publisher in acquiring rights to the manuscript. And most agents are also interested in dealing with authors who have solid credentials as professional writers, with published work in magazines, newspapers or other media.

For all they do, agents typically request commissions of between 10 and 15 percent on all advances, royalties and other revenues their authors receive. While most agents provide services on commission in this manner, some agents may charge by the hour for their time or ask authors to pay reading and/or other up-front fees before going to work. Those local agents who do charge up-front fees or who contract their services by the hour are noted in this chapter's listings.

Many readers of this book may know more about literary agents than they do about book producers. Book producers act much like agents, but they also typically initiate their own projects, collaborate with one or more authors to sell, write and/or edit a manuscript and then provide design, production and even printing services to a publisher after the manuscript has been accepted for publication. In the publishing business, book producers perform many of the same functions that independent film producers perform in the feature film business. Because of higher overhead costs, book producers usually request higher commissions than literary agents.

This chapter contains listings for 13 local agents and 11 local book producers. Throughout the chapter, when the word "trade" is used, it refers to books of general interest and wide popular appeal which will be sold in bookstores. To contact anyone listed in this chapter, writers are *strongly* advised to start by mailing a query letter, book proposal and/or short manuscript sample along with a self-addressed, stamped envelope (SASE) to the address listed.

Don't send entire manuscripts (unless specifically asked to do so). Don't show up unannounced on an agent's doorstep. And before placing an ill-advised phone call, consider that your verbal explanation of a manuscript, no matter how compelling, will not convince an agent or book producer to represent it for you. What you describe over the phone will eventually need to be read and evaluated. It is, after all, what you've *written* that counts.

So, if your writing is read by an agent or a book producer and the phone rings, it means the fish are biting.

LITERARY AGENTS

Adler & Robin Books Handles "a wide range of trade nonfiction books; no fiction." Adult subjects only. Accepts no unsolicited manuscripts; send query letter or proposal with SASE. Works on commission.

Bill Adler, Jr., President, 2755 Ordway Street NW, Suite 415, Washington, DC 20008; (202) 363-7410. Peggy Robin, Vice President. Laraine Balk, Agent.

Robert B. Barnett Handles "all types of books, including autobiography, general fiction and nonfiction." Adult subjects only. Will read query letters, book outlines or proposals; please send SASE. If a project is accepted, charges an hourly fee for services.

Robert B. Barnett, Esq., Williams & Connolly, Hill Building, 839 17th Street NW, Washington, DC 20006; (202) 331-5034.

David Cutler & Associates Handles mostly trade nonfiction and some trade fiction books. Adult subjects only; no children's or juvenile titles. Accepts no unsolicited manuscripts; send 1–2-page query letter with SASE. Works on commission. Also provides publishing consultation services.

David Cutler, President, 2960 Chain Bridge Road (#110), Oakton, VA 22124; (703) 255-2886. Anita Gross, Consulting Editor. Dorian Patchin, Associate.

Ronald Goldfarb Handles "trade nonfiction and fiction books." Adult subjects only. Will review query letters, book outlines, proposals and manuscripts. Works on commission *and/or* charges hourly fees.

Ronald Goldfarb, Esq., Ronald Goldfarb & Associates, 918 16th Street NW, Washington, DC 20006; (202) 466-3030. Nina Graybill, Esq.

Larry Kaltman Literary Agency Handles "all types of trade books, both nonfiction and fiction." Adult subjects only. Will accept completed manuscripts. Works on commission *and* charges reading fees.

Larry Kaltman, 1301 South Scott Street, Arlington, VA 22204; (703) 920-3771.

Irene W. Kraas Handles "mostly trade fiction books and some nonfiction." Adult and children's subjects. Will accept completed manuscripts; please send SASE. Works on commission.

Irene W. Kraas, 1200 North Nash Street, Arlington, VA 22209; (703) 525-3323.

Literary Agency of Washington Handles "trade books of all kinds." Adult and children's subjects. Will also read and evaluate magazine articles and short stories. Prefers query letters, but will accept proposals and completed manuscripts. Works on commission *and* charges reading fees.

David Richards, Editorial Director, P.O. Box 577, Burtonsville, MD 20866; (301) 639-8214.

Literary & Creative Artists Agency Handles "seasoned fiction, nonfiction and TV/film screenplays covering such subjects as politics, health, adventure, true accounts of human experience/ drama, business and how-to, as well as cookbooks and children's stories." Accepts no unsolicited manuscripts; requires exclusive review. Query first with SASE. Works on commission.

Muriel Nellis & Jane Roberts, 3539 Albemarle Street NW, Washington, DC 20008; (202) 362-4688.

Gail Ross Handles "trade nonfiction books and selected fiction titles." Adult subjects only. Will read book proposals or outlines, along with published writing samples (if available). Please send SASE. Works on commission.

Gail Ross, Esq., Lichtman, Trister, Singer & Ross, 1666 Connecticut Avenue NW, Suite 501, Washington, DC 20009; (202) 328-1666/ FAX (202) 328-9162. Elaine English, Associate. Elizabeth Outka, Assistant.

The Sagalyn Literary Agency Handles "trade nonfiction books and some fiction." Adult subjects only. Will review query letters, proposals, outlines and manuscripts. Please send SASE. Works on commission.

Raphael Sagalyn, 1520 New Hampshire Avenue NW, Suite 300, Washington, DC 20036; (202) 797-9090. Lisa DiMona, Agent. Joanne Ira, Assistant Agent.

Leona P. Schechter Literary Agency Handles "many different kinds of books, especially fiction and serious political, business and economic nonfiction." Adult subjects only. Accepts no unsolicited manuscripts; will review query letters, book outlines and proposals. Works on commission.

Leona P. Schechter, 3748 Huntington Street NW, Washington, DC 20015; (202) 362-9040/ FAX (202) 362-4425.

Ann Tobias Handles "trade fiction and nonfiction books, with an exclusive emphasis on children's and juvenile titles." No adult subjects. Will read unsolicited manuscripts; please include SASE. Works on commission.

Ann Tobias, 307 South Carolina Avenue SE, Washington, DC 20003; (202) 543-1043.

Audrey Adler Wolf Handles "trade nonfiction, fiction and TV/film screenplays on a wide variety of subjects." Adult subjects only. Will review query letters, book outlines and proposals; please include SASE. Works on commission.

Audrey Adler Wolf, 1001 Connecticut Avenue NW, Washington, DC 20036; (202) 659-0088.

BOOK PRODUCERS

Archetype Press Produces "illustrated books on architecture, the arts and American culture for publication by trade and educational publishers, museums and associations." Provides services from concept through printing and post-production. Archetype also assists publishers in producing supplementary materials, such as catalogues, promotional items, posters, greeting cards and postcards.

Diane Maddex, President, 2828 10th Street NE, Washington, DC 20017; (202) 832-2828/ FAX (202) 832-6304. Marc Alain Meadows & Robert L. Wiser, Vice Presidents & Principals, Meadows & Wiser Graphics.

Big River Publishing Services Works with "trade publishers, academic publishers and government agencies in providing publishing services, from concept through finished product." Services include writing, editorial, indexing, design, production and printing coordination.

Brenda Brienza & Adele Gorelick, Co-Owners, 9342 Big River Run, Columbia, MD 21045; (301) 730-8744/ (301) 897-8814.

Community Scribes Handles "all phases of book production, from concept through final printing." Community Scribes specializes in writing, editing, graphics and production.

Suzanne Scott and Lynne Constantine, Co-Owners, 4600 S. Four Mile Run Drive, #636, Arlington, VA 22204; (703) 379-5820.

Directory Publishing Resources Specializes in "creating and producing directories. Services include product development, research, compilation, database planning, editorial services and book production and delivery."

Dianne Johansson-Adams, President, P.O. Box 19107, George Mason Station, Alexandria, VA 22320; (703) 329-8206/ FAX 960-9618.

Educational Challenges Founded in 1969, Educational Challenges specializes in "educational print products for early childhood through high school readers, with particular interest in at-risk and minority populations." Advocates student-oriented approaches. Distributes through catalogues and by contact with publishers.

Peg Paul, President, 1009 Duke Street, Alexandria, VA 22314; (703) 683-1500/ FAX (703) 683-0827.

Fastback Press Develops "series ideas and provides full production services, from manuscript to printed books." Specializes in mass-market paperbacks.

Linda Williams Aber & Louise Colligan, 9905 Doubletree Court, Potomac, MD 20854; (301) 279-2027.

Redefinition Undertakes "series projects, from concept through final production and printing." Specializes in illustrated books on various subjects, including baseball and gardening, and other blends of text and pictures.

Edward Brash, President, 700 North Fairfax Street, Alexandria, VA 22314; (703) 739-2110.

Alvin Rosenbaum Associates   Specializes in illustrated art and gift books, "produced with great attention to detail and artfully designed." Also handles popular reference, design and other nonfiction projects (hardcover and paperbacks). Provides training and consulting advice in electronic design and production.

Alvin Rosenbaum, President, 3107 Rolling Road, Chevy Chase, MD 20815; (301) 654-1988.

Strawtown Associates   Specializes in "developing books and other published products for children (8–13 years old), including mass-market paperbacks, trade activity books, posters, humor items and premiums." Offers full development services, from concept to camera-ready mechanicals.

Linda Williams Aber, 9905 Doubletree Court, Potomac, MD 20854; (301) 279-2027/ FAX (301) 762-5348.

Summerville Press   A "full-service consulting firm covering all aspects of publishing," Summerville Press provides "contract publishing and management consulting services in the areas of editorial, circulation, advertising sales and strategic planning." Emphasis on resolving the problems of undercapitalized publications and publishing ventures.

Margaret Byrne Heimbold, President, 2300 N Street NW, Suite 600, Washington, DC 20037; (202) 663-9071/ FAX (202) 223-1512.

Tilden Press   Produces trade hardcover and paperback books "on reference, business and consumer topics." Handles projects from concept to camera-ready design; also offers publishing consulting and marketing services. Does not accept unsolicited book proposals.

Joel Makower, President, 1526 Connecticut Avenue NW, Washington, DC 20036; (202) 332-1700.

Literary, Media & Writers' Organizations

Americans of all ages, all stations in life and all types of disposition are forever forming associations.
—ALEXIS DE TOCQUEVILLE

E ver since barrels of English tea were dumped into Boston Harbor, we Americans have achieved a special notoriety for our organizational abilities. We just can't seem to help it. The urge to congregate, to freely assemble, to exercise the inalienable right to mingle with others in a chosen field and trade ideas on how to get ahead in life runs deep in the American psyche.

As working professionals, American authors, poets, novelists, screenwriters, journalists, editors, publishers and others who have enjoyed success in communicating will openly confess to participating in this form of national self-expression.

Here in the nation's capital, for instance, there are at least 51 prominent literary, media and writers' organizations which contribute in some way to the preservation and continuance of the literary life. Also listed in this chapter are 16 key media organizations which help to protect First Amendment rights, resolve copyright issues or even provide legal assistance to working authors, editors and journalists, two well-known organizations committed to improving literacy and some 22 organizations which help to promote the better creation, production and dissemination of articles, books, films, magazines, newspapers, recordings, software and other products of writing.

In a city crawling with PACs, cutthroat lobbyists and special interest groups, the organizations listed in this chapter provide support, information and services to hundreds of literary, editorial and communications professionals. We should applaud and encourage these organizations in their efforts. Without them, writers, editors and publishers might be left to their own devices, thereby posing a significant threat to society and to themselves.

Advertising Club of Metropolitan Washington The Club is an organization of more than 1,200 professionals involved in all aspects of advertising and communications in the Washington metropolitan area. ACMW sponsors monthly luncheons, educational seminars and the ADDY Awards, which are given each year to local firms and individuals who do highly creative work in print and broadcast advertising.

Barbara Westland, President, Advertising Club of Metropolitan Washington, 7200 Wisconsin Avenue, Suite 200, Bethesda, MD 20814; (301) 656-2582 [656–CLUB].

Afro-Hispanic Institute The Institute promotes the study of Afro-Hispanic literature and culture, and assists in the research of blacks in Spanish-speaking nations.

Dr. Stanley A. Cyrus, President, 3306 Ross Place NW, Washington, DC 20008; (202) 966-7783.

American Agricultural Editors Association The AAEA is comprised of editors and editorial staff members of farm publications. Affiliate members are agricultural public relations/advertising personnel and state and local officials. Members: 625.

Paul Weller, Executive Secretary, American Agricultural Association, 1629 K Street NW, Suite 1100, Washington, DC 20006; (202) 785-6710.

American Association of Sunday & Feature Editors The AASFE is a specialized media group whose members are Sunday and feature newspaper editors. Bestows annual awards. Members: 120.

Mary Nahan, Administrative Secretary, Newspaper Center, P.O. Box 17407, Dulles Airport, Washington, DC 20041; (703) 648-1286.

American Copyright Council The ACC serves to educate the public about the value of copyrights and the harm caused by copyright infringement. It is a coalition of film, law, magazine, computer, publishing, music, recording and television organizations. Members: 25.

Fritz Attaway, Vice President & Secretary, 1600 I Street NW, Washington, DC 20006; (202) 293-1966.

American Film Institute The AFI is a nonprofit corporation dedicated to preserving and developing the nation's artistic and cultural resources in film. The Institute's goals are to increase recognition and understanding of the moving image as an art form, to assure preservation of the art form and to identify, encourage and develop talent (including screenwriters). Members: 140,000.

Jean Firstenberg, Director, John F. Kennedy Center for the Performing Arts, Washington, DC 20566; (202) 828-4000.

American Intellectual Property Law Association The AIPLA is a voluntary bar association of lawyers practicing in the fields of patents, trademarks and copyrights which is dedicated to aiding in the operation and improvement of U.S. patents, trademark and copyright systems. The Association offers a placement service and maintains 25 committees. Members: 5,500.

Michael Blommer, Executive Director, 2001 Jefferson Davis Highway, Suite 203, Arlington, VA 22202; (703) 521-1680.

American International Book Development Council AIBDC helps to promote access to American books abroad while encouraging the dissemination of foreign literature in the United States. The Council is also known as Helen Dwight Reid Educational Foundation.

William M. Childs, Executive Director, 4000 Albemarle Street NW, Washington, DC 20016; (202) 362-8131. Former U.N. Ambassador Jeane J. Kirkpatrick, President.

American Medical Writers Association AMWA is dedicated to the advancement and improvement of medical communication. It sponsors annual medical book awards and more than 50 workshops each year. Members: 3,300.

Lillian Sablack, Executive Director, 9650 Rockville Pike, Bethesda, MD 20814; (301) 493-0003.

American News Womens' Club Members of the ANWC are women journalists who cover news in all print and broadcast media, as well as women writing and editing for government agencies, nonprofit organizations or as freelancers. The Club encourages friendly understanding between members and their sources. Members: 450.

M. Virginia Daly, Executive Director, 1607 22nd Street NW, Washington, DC 20008; (202) 332-6770.

American Newspaper Publishers Association The ANPA serves newspapers and newspaper executives across the United States by (1) working to advance the cause of a free press; (2) encouraging the efficiency and economy of the newspaper publishing business in all departments and aspects; (3) promoting and conducting important research of use to newspapers; (4) gathering and distributing among ANPA member newspapers the most accurate, reliable and useful information available about the industry; and (5) promoting the highest standard in journalism. Members: 1,400.

Jerry W. Freidheim, President, The Newspaper Center, 1160 Sunrise Valley Drive, Reston, VA 22091; (703) 648-1000.

American Philatelic Society Writers Unit Members of the APSWU are editors, writers and columnists who specialize in covering stamps and stamp collecting. Members: 400.

George Griffenhagen, Secretary & Treasurer, 2501 Drexel Street, Vienna, VA 22180; (703) 560-2413.

American Press Institute API is an educational center dedicated to the continuing education and management training of newspaper men and women in the United States and Canada.

William L. Winter, Executive Officer, 11690 Sunrise Valley Drive, Reston, VA 22091; (703) 620-3611.

American Society of Newspaper Editors The ASNE represents the interests of directing editors who determine editorial and news policy on daily newspapers. Members: 1,000.

Lee Stinnett, Executive Director, 11600 Sunrise Valley Drive, Reston, VA 22091; (703) 648-1144.

American Women in Radio & Television Members of AWRT are women in administrative, creative or executive positions in the broadcasting industry (radio, television, cable and networks). Members: 3,000.

Susan K. Finn, President, 1101 Connecticut Avenue NW, Suite 700, Washington, DC 20036; (202) 429-5102.

Association for the Study of Afro-American Life & History The Association is an organization of historians, scholars and students interested in the research and study of African-Americans as a contributing factor in civilization. It encourages the study of African-American history and training in the social sciences, history and other disciplines. Members: 2,200.

Gail A. Hansberry, Executive Director, 1407 14th Street NW, Washington, DC 20005; (202) 667-2822.

Association of American Publishers (D.C. Office) The AAP monitors and promotes the U.S. publishing industry. Its members are actively engaged in the creation, publication and production of books or types of prints and AV materials. Members: 300.

Judith Platt, Diana Rennert & Carol Risher, Directors, 1718 Connecticut Avenue NW, Suite 700, Washington, DC 20009–1148; (202) 232-3335. Nicholas A. Veliotes, President (Main Office/NY).

Association of Railway Communicators The members of ARC are editors of house organs for the railroad industry and rail labor. Each year, the Association presents achievement awards for excellence in communication. Members: 90.

J. Ronald Shumate, Secretary & Treasurer, c/o Association of American Railroads, 50 F Street NW, Washington, DC 20001; (202) 639-2171.

Barbara Bush Foundation for Family Literacy Since 1989, the Foundation has helped to support many projects in schools and preschools which teach reading skills to parents while helping children learn to read. Named after the First Lady, who has long supported family literacy, the Foundation also supports and promotes local family literacy programs across the country while seeking to encourage literacy training for teachers and volunteers.

Benita Somerfield, Executive Director, 1002 Wisconsin Avenue NW, Washington, DC 20007; (202) 338-2006.

Black Women Playwrights' Group Members of the Group are women of African-American descent who meet monthly to share information about writing opportunities and study the craft of dramatic writing. Scripts-in-progress are read at each meeting and discussed. Once a year, the BWPG produces a professional reading of works by its members. Annual dues are $12.

Karen Evans, President, 1426 Irving Street NE, Washington, DC 20017; (202) 832-7329.

Bookbuilders of Washington Bookbuilders is concerned with all phases of book production, including typesetting, design, printing, binding and specialized techniques. Some members work for publishers, others supply services and products to publishers (printers, typesetters, binders, designers, paper manufacturers and distributors) and the rest provide editorial services such as proofreading and indexing. BW publishes a monthly newsletter and sponsors at least one field trip a year. A recent trade show ("New Columbia Exposition: Washington Books & Their Making") was well attended and got rave reviews.

Richard E. Farkas, President, c/o American Psychiatric Press, 1400 K Street NW, Suite 1101, Washington, DC 20005; (202) 682-6273.

Capital Press Club The Club seeks to expand opportunities for minorities within the news industry, while acting as a platform for leaders to convey opinions on issues affecting minorities in the United States. Members are black communications professionals from newspapers and news services nationwide. Members: 200.

Claryce Handy, President, P.O. Box 19403, Washington, DC 20036; (202) 429-5497.

Capital Press Women CPW runs monthly meetings and an annual conference to help foster professional development among local women journalists. It also publishes a quarterly newsletter, honors "Women of Achievement" at an annual spring dinner and fosters opportunities to build networks of associates. Members: 400.

Ruthann Saenger, President, 1448 Duke Street, Alexandria, VA 22314; (703) 684-6988.

Center for the Book Established in 1977, the Center for the Book uses the influence and resources of the Library of Congress to stimulate public interest in books, readings and libraries while encouraging the study of books and print culture. Its excellent roster of symposia, projects, lectures, exhibitions and publications is supported by tax-deductible contributions from corporations and individuals. The Center sponsors "Read More About It" messages on CBS Television, reading promotion projects on CBS and all other networks, National Book Week with the National Book Foundation (last week in January), an ambitious publications program and many other worthwhile programs. It has chapters in many U.S. states and in countries overseas.

John Y. Cole, Director, The Library of Congress, Washington, DC 20540; (202) 707-5221. Simon Michael Bessie, Chairman.

Center for Media & Public Affairs The Center conducts and analyses random, in-depth and rapid response media surveys to determine media impact on public opinion.

Dr. S. Robert Lichter, Co-Director, 2101 L Street NW, Suite 405, Washington, DC 20037; (202) 223-2942.

Chesapeake Regional Area Book Sellers (CRABS) An alliance of bookstore owners in the Washington/Baltimore area, CRABS sponsors programs and publishes materials designed to increase public awareness of the many outstanding bookstores and book-related operations throughout the region. Members: 75.

Liz Steingraber, President, 11 Sparrow Valley Court, Gaithersburg, MD 20879; (301) 840-9074.

City & Regional Magazine Association The CRMA sponsors professional development seminars and an annual conference for employees at city & regional magazines around the nation. It also hosts the annual CRMA White Awards Competition at the William Allen White School of Journalism (Kansas University). Members: 43.

Brandi Sullivan, 335 Commerce Street, Alexandria, VA 22314; (703) 548-5016.

Construction Writers Association Members of the CWA are writers and editors for print and broadcast media covering the building construction field. Associate members include public relations and advertising personnel connected with building construction. Members: 122.

E.E. Halmos, Jr., Secretary & Treasurer, P.O. Box 259, Poolesville, MD 20837.

Department of State Correspondents Association Members of the DSCA include newspaper, magazine, wire service, radio and television news correspondents who cover the U.S. State Department. Members: 130.

Norman Kempster, President, 2201 C Street NW, Suite 2310, Washington, DC 20520; (202) 887-7257.

Dog Writers' Association of America The DWAA provides information about dogs (sport breeding and ownership) and assists writers in gaining access to exhibitions. Members: 350.

Harold Sundstrom, President, 9800 Flint Rock Road, Manassas, VA 22111; (703) 369-2384.

Education Writers Association EWA is dedicated to improving the quality of education reporting nationwide and in helping to attract topnotch writers and reporters to the education field. Member services include conferences, seminars, publications, employment services, freelance referral, workshops and national awards. Members: 450.

Lisa J. Walker, Executive Director, 1001 Connecticut Avenue NW, Suite 310, Washington, DC 20036; (202) 429-9680.

Federal Publishers' Committee The Committee promotes and encourages cost-effective publications management within the federal government, including planning, marketing, writing, design, printing, distribution and other areas of publishing. FPC conducts symposia, offers speakers' bureau, maintains placement service and compiles statistics. Its members are professionals within the executive and legislative branches of the U.S. federal government who are involved in publishing. Members: 511.

John E. Mounts, Chairman, c/o National Center for Health Statistics, 3700 East-West Highway, Rm I–57, Hyattsville, MD 20782; (301) 436-8586.

Freedom of Information Clearinghouse The FOIC assists citizens seeking information from the federal government. It also collects and disseminates information on state and federal Freedom of Information (FOI) statutes.

Patti Goldman, Executive Director, 2000 P Street NW, P.O. Box 19367, Washington, DC 20036; (202) 785-3704.

Fund for Investigative Journalism The Fund's mission is to increase knowledge about the concealed, obscure or complex aspects of matters significantly affecting the public. FIJ makes grants to writers to enable them to probe abuses of authority and other abuses of power. To date, more than 35 books have been written with Fund support.

John Hanrahan, Executive Director, 1755 Massachusetts Avenue NW, Suite 504, Washington, DC 20036; (202) 462-1844.

Fund for Objective News Reporting The FONR is a nonpartisan organization which works to correct biases in the major news media. It also provides grants to journalists doing media research.

Executive Director, Fund for Objective News Reporting, 713 D Street SE, Washington, DC 20003; (202) 547-9404.

Gridiron Club of Washington Founded in 1885, this prestigious and well-known club of journalists from daily newspapers devotes itself to crafting hilarious skits and songs which satirize life in America. The culmination of the Club's efforts is a well-publicized gala, during which the members' best material is performed for the President of the United States, the First Lady and many honored "roastees." The size of the Gridiron Club is always limited to 60 full members and is *by invitation only.* There are 85 "associated" members and a handful of "limited" members in the Club, all of whom are also asked to join. Despite its name, the Club has absolutely nothing to do with football.

Penny Dixon, Executive Secretary, Capital Hilton, 16th & K Streets NW, Washington, DC 20036; (202) 783-7787.

Guild of Book Workers A national nonprofit organization, the Guild was founded in 1906 to foster the hand book arts, such as binding, calligraphy, illumination and paper decorating. It currently sponsors exhibits, lectures and workshops. Members: 750.

Frank Mowery, President, Folger Shakespeare Library, 201 East Capitol Street SE, Washington, DC 20003; (202) 544-4600.

Information Industry Association The IIA is a full-service trade association which conducts an active government relations and public policy program seeking to safeguard the interests of a healthy and competitive information industry. The Association, which sponsors seminars, roundtables and conferences, also publishes a bimonthly newsletter as well as various other trade publications.

J. Angerman, Information Industry Association, 555

New Jersey Avenue NW, Suite 800, Washington, DC 20001; (202) 639-8262.

International Copyright Information Center The Center assists publishers in developing nations to contact U.S. publishers regarding the licensing of translation and English-language reprint rights to U.S. books. ICIC is one of several national information centers on copyright clearance in major publishing countries throughout the world.

Carol Risher, Director, Association of American Publishers (D.C. Office), 1718 Connecticut Avenue NW, Washington, DC 20009–1148; (202) 232-3335.

International Science Writers Association The ISWA is comprised of journalists and freelancers who write frequently on scientific subjects. Its primary objective is to provide contacts and to enable members to assist each other when working in a foreign country. The ISWA also works to improve science media facilities, gain recognition for members and maintain and improve standards of science writing.

Howard Lewis, Secretary & Treasurer, 7310 Broxburn Court, Bethesda, MD 20817; (301) 656-0022.

Jesuits in Communications in the United States Through the JCUS, members of the Society of Jesus (Jesuits) in the United States can learn more about various areas of communication, including writing, editing, radio and television.

James J. Conn, Executive Secretary, 1424 16th Street NW, Suite 300, Washington, DC 20036; (202) 462-0400.

Lewis Carroll Society of North America Members of the Society are collectors, authors, publishers and others interested in the life and works of Charles Lutwidge Dodgson (1832–1898), who wrote under the pen name of Lewis Carroll. The LCSNA's purpose is to encourage study of the author, to publish journals and books about his work and to become a recognized center for Carroll studies. Members: 350.

Edward Guiliano, President, 617 Rockford Road, Silver Spring, MD 20902; (301) 593-7077.

Literary Friends of the D.C. Public Library This active group of Washington writers and book lovers helps to promote appreciation of the written word by supporting the operations of the Martin Luther King, Jr. Public Library in Washington. LFDCPL, which sponsors many outstanding programs throughout the year, has also organized the Washington Writers Collection, which is on display in the library's Washingtoniana Room. Members: 650.

Betty Parry, President, Literary Friends of the DC Public Library, 901 G Street NW, Washington, DC 20001; (202) 727-1101.

Magazine Publishers of America   MPA is a national association representing the consumer magazine industry whose membership publishes a total of nearly 1,000 magazines. The organization provides many services to its members, including education and professional development. MPA also represents its members in Washington and throughout state legislatures on such important issues as taxes, advertising, copyright and the First Amendment. Members: 230.

George Gross, Executive Vice President for Government Affairs, MPA, 1211 Connecticut Avenue NW, Suite 406, Washington, DC 20036; (202) 296-7277.

Media Access Project   The Project is a public-interest law firm working to assure that the media will inform the public fully and fairly on important national issues. MAP participates in conferences and seminars, advises local and national organizations and represents those groups in their efforts to gain access to media.

Andrew Jay Schwartzman, Executive Director, 2000 M Street NW, Washington, DC 20036; (202) 232-4300.

The Media Institute   The Institute promotes understanding of the American media and communications, conducts research into various aspects of the media and communications industry and maintains a program of conferences focusing on media performance, the role of new technologies and communications policy issues. It also sponsors a regular luncheon discussion series on media topics.

Patrick D. Maines, Executive Director, 3017 M Street NW, Washington, DC 20007; (202) 298-7512.

Motion Picture Association of America (D.C. Office)   The MPAA is the trade association for major motion picture producers and distributors. It administers the motion picture industry's system of self-regulation, while seeking to further production and distribution of motion pictures for theatrical, home video and television use in the United States. Members: 60.

Jack Valenti, President, 1600 I Street NW, Washington, DC 20006; (202) 293-1966.

Beatrice M. Murphy Foundation The Foundation encourages the reading, appreciation and further production of African-American literature. It also awards scholarships to the disadvantaged, assists authors and provides other information on African-American literature.

Beatrice M. Murphy, Executive Director, 2737 Devonshire Place NW, Suite 222, Washington, DC 20008; (202) 387-6053.

Mystery Writers of America (D.C. Chapter) Local mystery writers share their experiences (but not their plots) with colleagues in this congenial chapter of the national organization, which is based in New York. Featured speakers and panels are the primary order of business at the chapter's meetings, held the second Wednesday of each month.

Jacklyn Boice, President, D.C. Chapter, c/o 2085 National Press Building, Washington, DC 20045; (703) 892-4790.

National Alliance of Third World Journalists The NATWJ works to increase the quality and quantity of U.S. media coverage of the Third World. The Alliance acts as an informational bridge between minorities in the United States and the Third World, and helps U.S. journalists travel to Third World countries. It also provides speakers for functions, and schedules forums and seminars. Members: 500.

Leila McDowell & Gwen McKinney, Co-coordinators, P.O. Box 43208, Columbia Heights, Washington, DC 20010; (202) 462-8197.

National Association of Black Journalists The Association is dedicated to strengthening the ties between blacks in the black media and blacks in the white media. It also works to sensitize white media organizations to institutionalized racism in its coverage, while expanding black coverage and promoting professionalism among black journalists. Members: 1,200.

Linda A. Edwards, Director, 11600 Sunrise Valley

Drive, Reston, VA 22091; (703) 648-1270. Thomas Morgan III, President.

National Association of Black-Owned Broadcasters The Association represents the interests of existing and potential black radio and television stations. Its members are black broadcast station owners, black-formatted stations not owned by blacks and others. Members: 150.

James L. Winston, Executive Director, 1730 M Street NW, Washington, DC 20036; (202) 463-8970.

National Association of Government Communicators The NAGC works to make communication an essential government resource, by disseminating information, encouraging professional development, public awareness and exchange of ideas and improving internal communications. It maintains an active placement service and sponsors awards. Members: 600.

Debbie Trocchi, Executive Director, 80 South Early Street, Alexandria, VA 22304; (703) 823-4821.

National Association of Hispanic Journalists The Association helps to organize and support Hispanics involved in the media, and seeks recognition for achievements of Hispanics in the field. NAHJ also promotes fair and accurate media treatment of Hispanics, conducts an annual census of Hispanics in media and offers such services as scholarships, seminars, training workshops and special awards. Members: 700.

Frank Newton, Executive Director, 634 National Press Building, 529 14th Street NW, Washington, DC 20045; (202) 783-6228.

National Black Media Coalition The NBMC is a media advocacy group working to increase media access for blacks and other minorities through employment, ownership and programming. A frequent participant in FCC rulemaking, NBMC members speak before university and professional audiences, conduct training classes and work to negotiate positive affirmative action plans with media corporations. The Coalition maintains a full resource center and a job referral service. Members: 1,500.

Carmen Marshall, Executive Director, 38 New York Avenue NE, Washington, DC 20002; (202) 387-8155.

National Conference of Editorial Writers The NCEW works to "stimulate the conscience and the quality of the editorial page." It sponsors professional seminars, regional critique meetings, an annual meeting and a yearly foreign tour for members. The NCEW also publishes *The Masthead*, a quarterly journal, and co-sponsors the "Wells Award" for exemplary leadership in offering minorities employment in journalism. Members: 575.

Cora Everett, Executive Secretary, 6223 Executive Boulevard, Rockville, MD 20852; (301) 984-3015.

National League of American Pen Women Members of NLAPW are women authors, composers and artists who sponsor exhibits and contests in letters, music and art. The League maintains an extensive biographical archives, library and research programs. It also offers scholarships and conducts seminars. Members: 6,000.

Frances Hartman Mulliken, President, Pen Arts Building, 1300 17th Street NW, Washington, DC 20036; (202) 785-1997.

National Newspaper Association The Association's members are community weekly and daily newspapers. NNA sponsors competitions, presents awards and compiles statistics. It also holds an annual convention and trade show. Members: 5,000.

David C. Simonson, Executive Vice President, 1627 K Street NW, Suite 400, Washington, DC 20006; (202) 466-7200.

National Newspaper Foundation The NNF is the educational arm of the National Newspaper Association. It conducts a Blue Ribbon Newspaper Evaluation Program, as well as regional management seminars and conferences. NNF also presents awards and scholarships to journalism school students.

David C. Simonson, Executive Vice President, 1627 K Street NW, Suite 400, Washington, DC 20006; (202) 466-7200.

National Newspaper Publishers Association The NNPA presents an award each year to a black leader for distinguished contributions to black advancement in the media. The Association also sponsors an annual workshop, and maintains a "Hall of Fame." Members: 200.

Steve G. Davis, Executive Director, 948 National Press Building, 529 14th Street NW, Washington, DC 20045; (202) 662-7324.

National Press Club   The Club is a well-known private professional organization for journalists. It sponsors sports, travel and cultural events, as well as workshops and seminars, rap sessions with news figures and authors, press forums and newsmaker breakfasts and luncheons. NPC also awards prizes for consumer journalism, diplomatic writing, Washington coverage and newsletters. Each year, NPC holds a popular annual book sale and ongoing art exhibits. The Club maintains a computerized reference library and its own archives (from 1908), as well as the archives of the Women's National Press Club/Washington Press Club (1919–1985). Members: 4,800.

Harry Bodaan, General Manager, National Press Building, 529 14th Street NW, Washington, DC 20045; (202) 662-7500. Barbara Vandergrift, Librarian.

National Press Foundation   The NPF provides grants, fellowships and seminars for journalists and educators to help foster excellence in journalism. It also provides workshops and mentoring relationships to attract minority high school students to choose careers in journalism, supports organizations dedicated to freedom of the press and conducts conferences and seminars for journalists, policymakers and the concerned public.

David Yount, President, 1282 National Press Building, 529 14th Street NW, Washington, DC 20045; (202) 662-7350.

Newsletter Association   Members of this organization are newsletter publishers representing small and large companies. The Association conducts research and prepares reports, represents members before Federal agencies, monitors legislation, compiles statistics, holds seminars and workshops and presents annual awards. Members: 883.

Frederick D. Goss, Executive Director, 1401 Wilson Boulevard, Suite 207, Arlington, VA 22209; (703) 527-2333.

The Newspaper Guild   The Guild sponsors an International Pension Fund, which provides retirement benefits to persons employed in the news industry. It also bestows its annual "Heywood Broun Award" for outstanding journalistic achievement. Members: 34,000.

Charles Dale Perlik, Jr., President, 8611 Second Avenue, Silver Spring, MD 20912; (301) 585-2990.

Overseas Writers Club Members of the Club are accredited American and foreign correspondents who regularly cover foreign affairs. The OWC has been meeting every two or three weeks for lunch since 1921. Its annual membership fees are $10. Members: 280.

John Wallach, President, c/o Hearst Newspapers, 1701 Pennsylvania Avenue NW, Washington, DC 20006; (202) 298-6920. Elaine Sciolino, Vice President.

PEN Syndicated Fiction Project An editorial panel from the Project selects approximately 50 short stories from those submitted during open reading period each January. Chosen stories are then syndicated to newspapers nationwide, published in the literary quarterly *American Short Fiction* and read on a weekly half-hour show on National Public Radio called "The Sound of Writing." Three of the year's ten best stories are also read by their authors during a special reading at the Library of Congress.

Caroline Marshall, Director, P.O. Box 15650, Washington, DC 20003; (202) 543-6322.

The Playwright's Forum The Forum is a three-tiered organization for playwrights and theater lovers. The Unit is where experienced playwrights hone their craft. The Forum is an apprentice program of five limited enrollment groups. Associates are people who have a strong interest in theater. The Forum publishes a newsletter, hosts in-house and public readings, offers free theater tickets and special classes and sponsors an Annual Playwrights' Conference.

Ernest Joselovitz, President & Administrator, P.O. Box 11488, Washington, DC 20008; (301) 816-0569.

Poetry Committee of Greater Washington, DC The Committee promotes the appreciation and writing of poetry in the Washington area. Each year, it confers its Poetry Committee Book Award on an area writer who has published a collection of poetry in the previous year. The Committee also sponsors an annual "Celebration of Washington Poetry," held the first week in May.

Gigi Bradford, c/o Folger Shakespeare Library, 201 East Capitol Street SE, Washington, DC 20003; (202) 544-7077.

Producers Council The Council is comprised of individuals and firms engaged in producing motion pictures, videotapes, slide shows and audio presentations for outside clients. The organization lobbies Congress, maintains a professional training institute and offers symposia. Members: 45.

Harry R. McGee, Executive Vice President, 3150 Spring Street, Fairfax, VA 22031; (703) 273-7200.

Reading Is Fundamental No single literacy program can claim greater success in teaching all kids to read than RIF, which presently sponsors some 4,000 programs in communities throughout the United States. RIF volunteers have taught thousands of children to love books while helping parents to encourage reading at home.

Ruth Graves, President, 600 Maryland Avenue SW, Washington, DC 20560; (202) 287-3220.

Recording Industry Association of America The RIAA establishes manufacturing and recording standards, and certifies sales figures for recording awards in various categories. Also operates an antipiracy intelligence bureau and presents annual awards to individuals or institutions which have encouraged cultural activities in the United States. Members: 41.

Angela Croio, Public Relations Director, 1020 19th Street NW, Suite 200, Washington, DC 20036; (202) 775-0101.

Reporters Committee for Freedom of the Press The Committee provides free legal advice to reporters whose First Amendment rights are threatened by subpoenas and other legal pressures. It offers legal defense and research services for journalists and media lawyers. Members: 2,500.

Jane E. Kirtley, Executive Director, 1735 I Street, NW, Suite 504, Washington, DC 20006; (202) 466-6313.

Society of American Travel Writers The SATW is a group of editors, writers, broadcasters, photographers and PR representatives working to provide travelers with accurate reports on destinations, facilities and services. The Society encourages the preservation of historic sites and conservation of nature, and presents annual awards to honor efforts to conserve, preserve and beautify America. SATW also provides a referral service and a job bank. Members: 850.

Ken Fischer, Administrative Coordinator, 1155 Connecticut Avenue NW, Suite 500, Washington, DC 20036; (202) 429-6639.

Society of Professional Journalists (Sigma Delta Chi) The oldest and largest organization for journalists in the country, Sigma Delta Chi conducts development seminars, sponsors several awards and internships, holds annual contests, conducts forums on free press and publishes a monthly newsletter (*The Quill*). Members: 17,000 (National).

Washington Professional Chapter, P.O. Box 19555, Washington, DC 20036; (202) 737-3139.

Society for Technical Communications STC members are individuals and organizations interested or involved in technical communications. The Society seeks to advance the theory and practice of technical communication in all media. It presents awards, and sponsors high school writing contests. Members: 12,000.

William C. Stolgitis, Executive Director, 815 15th Street NW, Washington, DC 20005; (202) 737-0035.

Software Publishers Association As the principal association of the microcomputer software industry, SPA examines and researches topics raised by growth in the industry. It also represents members' interest before the federal government, sponsors an awards program and operates a campaign to stop software theft and protect copyrights. Members: 250.

Ken Wasch, Executive Director, 1101 Connecticut Avenue NW, Suite 901, Washington, DC 20036; (202) 452-1600.

Washington Antiquarian Booksellers Association Membership in WABA includes open-shop and appointment-only booksellers of rare, antique and collectible books. The Association plans to publish a list of dealers in the Washington metropolitan area, and has organized a social and professional exchange which includes lectures and tours. WABA also plans to sponsor an annual charity booksale.

Carl Sickles, Chairman, c/o Book Alcove, 15976 Shady Grove Road, Gaithersburg, MD 20877; (301) 977-9166.

Washington Book Publishers WBP is an informal alliance of those who work in book design, editing, production, marketing and other publishing activities. The group meets regularly to discuss topics suggested by members, and provides an active job bank. Members: 275.

Mary Louise Hollowell, Membership Coordinator, % 2900 Q Street NW, Suite 102, Washington, DC 20007; (202) 338-7652.

Washington Directory Association WDA is a nonprofit organization comprised primarily of directory professionals: publishers, associations, government agencies, typesetters and consultants. Members share ideas, information, expertise and contacts regarding the successful production and printing of directories. Luncheon meetings are held the last Thursday of the month at the Arts Club of Washington, 2017 I Street NW. Regular attendance is the only WDA membership requirement.

Dianne Johansson-Adams, President, Washington Directory Association, P.O. Box 19107, Alexandria, VA 22320; (703) 329-8206. Tom Johnson, Treasurer.

Washington EdPress EdPress provides professional development for those active in publications and public relations. A majority of the organization's members work for associations or as freelancers. EdPress conducts monthly luncheons and informal brown-bag sessions, holds an annual workshop, publishes a monthly newsletter and maintains an active job bank. Members: 200.

Bita Lanys, c/o 1000 Connecticut Avenue NW, Suite 9, Washington, DC 20036; (202) 369-1522.

Washington Independent Writers WIW promotes the mutual interests of freelance writers and provides its members with a variety of services, including a newsletter (*The Independent Writer*), monthly workshops, a very active job bank, specialized publications about writing and publishing, regular social activities, a grievance committee, health insurance and legal and financial services plans. A number of WIW "Small Groups" meet around town during the week (usually in members' homes) to discuss aspects of the writing life. WIW's annual Spring Conference is a major literary event. Members: 2,000.

Isolde Chapin, Executive Director, 220 Woodward

Building, 733 15th Street NW, Washington, DC 20005; (202) 347-4973.

Washington Journalism Center WJC seeks new methods in journalism education and new approaches to public affairs reporting to increase the potential for journalistic excellence. The organization also sponsors conferences for journalists to discuss key issues.

Don Campbell, Director, 2600 Virginia Avenue NW, Suite 502, Washington, DC 20037; (202) 337-3603.

Washington Romance Writers This local chapter of the Romance Writers of America holds monthly meetings where members can meet editors and agents, talk shop and trade information on educational resources and on the market. Critique groups of WRW meet regularly, and members receive a monthly newsletter. Members: 200.

Susan Brack, President, P.O. Box 21311, Kalorama Station, Washington, DC 20009; (703) 476-0520.

White House Correspondents Association Members of WHCA are newspaper, magazine and television/radio correspondents engaged exclusively in news work at the White House. Members: 600.

Edgar A. Poe, Executive Director, 1067 National Press Building, 529 14th Street NW, Washington, DC 20045; (202) 737-2934.

Women in Communications WIC works toward providing equality for women and men in all communications professions and for First Amendment rights. The organization holds annual and regional conferences, publishes a monthly magazine, monitors legislation and participates in coalitions with other media and national women's organizations. The D.C. chapter publishes a monthly newsletter (*Byline*), maintains an active job bank and sponsors regular ongoing programs. Members: 300 (D.C. Chapter).

Susan Lowell Butler, Executive VP, 2101 Wilson Boulevard, Suite 417, Arlington, VA 22201; (703) 528-4200 (National Office).

Emile Davio, President, WIC D.C. Chapter, P.O. Box 19795, Washington, DC 20036; (703) 525-2226.

Women in Film and Video (D.C. Chapter) WFV is a national organization of women active in the film and video fields. The D.C. chapter produces a bimonthly newsletter, sponsors public forums and educational programs and produces a popular biennial film festival called "Women Make Movies." WFV also sponsors a monthly workshop for aspiring screenwriters. Members: 500.

Lucinda Ebersole, P.O. Box 19272, Washington, DC 20036; (202) 232-2256.

Women's Institute for Freedom of the Press   Members of WIFP are women journalists and others concerned with the expansion of all women's roles in the major national and local news media. The Institute conducts research and disseminates information.

Martha Leslie Allen, Director, 3306 Ross Place NW, Washington, DC 20008; (202) 966-7783.

Women's Media Project   The Project was started by the Legal Defense and Education Fund of the National Organization of Women (NOW) to eliminate sex role stereotyping in the media and to increase participation of women and minorities in broadcasting. WMP conducts public education and community action campaigns, monitors compliance with equal employment legislation, encourages development and distribution of radio and TV programming offering realistic images of women and conducts research in broadcast employment.

Alisa Shapiro, Director, 1333 H Street NW, 11th Floor, Washington, DC 20005; (202) 682-0940.

Women's National Book Association (D.C. Chapter)   WNBA serves to bring authors together with readers while championing the role of women in the world of books. WNBA supports and brings to public attention the contributions of women writers, booksellers, librarians, editors and publishers, while providing a stimulating forum for issues relating to the book world. The chapter's newsletter, *Signature*, is regarded by many as one of the best sources of writing jobs in the Washington area. Members: 220.

Diane Ullius, President, WNBA-Washington Chapter, c/o 5621 6th Street South, Arlington, VA 22204; (703) 931-8610.

World Press Freedom Committee   The Committee is comprised of journalistic organizations who have united to oppose state control of the media, especially in Third

World countries. The WPFC has sponsored more than 90 programs in Africa, Asia, Latin America and the Caribbean.

Dana R. Bullen, Executive Director, 11600 Sunrise Valley Drive, Reston, VA 20091; (703) 648-1000.

The Writers' Center The Center's main goal is to help the general public participate in the creation, distribution and enjoyment of literature and the graphic arts. It offers courses on every aspect of writing and graphic design, allows members access to typesetting and printing equipment and operates the Book Gallery, which sells magazines and books by local writers and small press publishers. The Writer's Center also sponsors frequent readings by local and visiting writers and poets, and publishes the monthly newsletter *Carousel*. Members: 1,500.

Jane Fox, Executive Director, 7815 Old Georgetown Road, Bethesda, MD 20814; (301) 654-8664.

Readings, Resources & Recognition

> Books have to be read (worse luck it takes so long a time). It is the only way of discovering what they contain. A few savage tribes eat them, but reading is the only method of assimilation revealed to the West.
>
> **—E.M. FORSTER**

> The profession of book writing makes horse racing seem like a solid, stable business.
>
> **—JOHN STEINBECK**

Reading and writing are usually intimate, private acts. But they can also be happily shared with others.

Literary readings, lectures and programs are plentiful in the Washington area, giving audiences a choice of some 25 regular series each year in which a favorite author is likely to be featured. The area's 12 literary magazines help to create a public forum for literary dialogue and exchange, while 31 writing contests, grants and awards based here allow local and national authors to be publicly recognized for their work.

The region has at least 17 writing courses, conferences and seminars where writers can build confidence while sharpening their skills. And there is also the fun of attending at least 12 local book fairs and sales each year, which brings out the bargaining skills in just about every biblioholic I know.

LITERARY READINGS, LECTURES & PROGRAMS

Knowledgeable book publicists consider the nation's capital a "must" during author promotion tours, partly because turnout at book signings and other literary events is usually good and also because there are many national and international media opportunities available. In the publicist's jargon, Washington is what's known

149

as a "double hit," a "major market" to be "exploited."
Many authors describe it in different terms. Either way,
it's a rewarding experience to be embraced by local
readers, as many local and out-of-town authors will
readily attest.

Usually free of charge, literary readings, lectures and
programs are to be found throughout the entire Washington metropolitan area. They are hosted by organizations, public and private libraries, universities, bookstores and literary groups. Some are held in people's
homes. One popular summer series even meets outside
a famous log cabin in Rock Creek Park. As in other
cities, it is considered common courtesy to purchase a
book by the author if copies are on sale.

To plan ahead, consult the *Washington Post Book
World*'s "Literary Calendar" the first Sunday of every
month. Many suburban and community newspapers
throughout the area feature listings of upcoming literary
events. Another excellent resource is the local *Poetry
Hotline* (202) 291-7638 [291–POET], which is updated
weekly and has a detailed listing of poetry events held
throughout the metropolitan area.

American University Visiting Writer's Reading Series
Well-known visiting writers read from their works for
faculty, students and the public in this popular series.
Past readings have featured Stanley Kunitz, Richard
Yates, John Irving, Linda Pastan, Allen Ginsburg, Wil-
liam Stafford and Grace Paley. All readings are free.

Henry Taylor & Richard McCann, Co-Directors,
MFA Program in Creative Writing, Gray Hall (Room
227), American University, 4400 Massachusetts Avenue
NW, Washington, DC 20016; (202) 885-2977/78.

Ascension Poetry Reading Series
This series focuses on
black and Third World writers living in the United
States, especially new writers. Each year, an average of
six readings are held at various locations throughout the
city. Recent readings have featured Alice Walker, June
Jordan, Ishmael Reed, Lucille Clifton, Jessica Hagedorn
and Kimiko Hahn. All readings are free and open to the
public.

E. Ethelbert Miller, Director, Ascension Poetry
Reading Series, P.O. Box 441, Howard University,
Washington, DC 20054; (202) 232-3066.

Chapters' Authors Series
Chapters, the popular down-
town literary bookstore, holds an average of one literary

reading or event each week. To keep up on days and times, ask to be put on Chapters' mailing list and you will receive free copies of the store's *Literary and Other To Do's* newsletter. Authors who are interested in reading at Chapters should ask their publishers or publicity representatives to contact either of store's owners. All readings are free and open to the public.

Robin Diener & Terri Merz, Co-Owners, Chapters: A Literary Bookstore, 1512 K Street NW, Washington, DC 20005; (202) 347-5495.

Creative People Series   This biweekly lecture series features prominent area writers, artists, poets and other creative figures. The series runs from October to May, and also includes workshops on journalism, fiction writing and screenwriting. Most events are held at the Georgetown Public Library. Lectures and refreshments are free, but a donation to the Friends of the Georgetown Public Library is appreciated.

Lynn Haney, Director, 3539 R Street NW, Washington, DC 20007; (202) 338-6595.

Folger Evening Poetry Series   Started in 1968, the oldest privately run poetry series in the city brings distinguished poets to Washington from around the world. Past readings have featured Derek Wolcott, Octavio Paz, Marilyn Hacker, Yehuda Amic'hai, Rita Dove, Seamus Heaney, Joseph Brodskey and Peter Sacks. All readings begin at 8 pm, often preceded by small group seminars with the poets and followed by a reception. Readings are open to the public, with tickets available in advance or at the door.

Gigi Bradford, Poetry Coordinator, Folger Shakespeare Library, 201 E. Capitol Street SE, Washington, DC 20003; (202) 544-7077.

George Mason University Readings   GMU's English Department and the student-run Writers' Club (whose members are undergraduate and graduate creative writing students) co-sponsor as many as ten major author readings during the school year. Richard Wilbur, Adrienne Rich and Norman Mailer are among the authors who have read from their work. Usually held at GMU's Student Union 2 Building. All readings are free and open to the public.

Roger Lathbury, Director, Writing Program, George

Mason University, 4400 University Drive, Fairfax, VA 22030; (703) 323-2936.

Jenny Moore Fund for Writers With the George Washington University Department of English, the Fund offers an average of three to four readings each semester by writers from the area and around the country. Recent readings have featured Jamaica Kincaid, Alan Cheuse and U.S. Poet Laureates Mark Strand and Howard Nemerov. All readings are free and open to the public.

Department of English, George Washington University, 2013 G Street NW, Washington, DC 20052; (202) 994-6180.

Jewish Community Center Readings Series Each year, the Center invites four to six local and national authors to discuss their work. All authors featured have written books of Jewish interest. The JCC also hosts occasional readings and literature study courses emphasizing Jewish heritage. All readings and lectures are free and open to the public.

Ms. Tommy Feldman, Director, Literary Arts Development, 6125 Montrose Road, Rockville, MD 20850; (301) 881-0100.

Joaquin Miller Cabin Poetry Series At the log cabin once owned by the famed "Poet of the Sierras," poetry lovers can enjoy outdoor readings under the stars from mid-June through the end of July. Focusing chiefly on local poets, the series features readings by two poets followed by a reception at a nearby home. Past presenters have included Lucille Clifton, Kweli Smith, Minnie Bruce Pratt, Roland Flint and Pulitzer Prize-winner Henry Taylor. Held every Tuesday at 7:30 pm at the Miller Cabin site in Rock Creek Park. All readings are free and open to the public.

Joaquin Miller Cabin, Beach & Military Drives, Picnic Area #6, Rock Creek Park, Washington, DC 20011. For more information, call Jacklyn Potter at (202) 726-0971.

Lammas Books & More Reading Series This downtown bookstore has regular readings by feminist authors, generally held every other Sunday at 2 pm. Poetry readings are most common, but you'll also hear fiction and essays. Wine and snacks are served. The store's free quarterly newsletter lists details of upcoming events. A donation of $2 is requested for readings by out-of-town authors; otherwise programs are free.

Lammas/Dupont Circle, 1426 21st Street NW, Washington, DC 20036; (202) 775-8218.

Library of Congress Literary Reading Series From October to May, nationally known poets and authors are invited to read from their work. Past readings have featured Garrison Keillor, Herman Wouk and Tom Stoppard and poets Gwendolyn Brooks, Howard Nemerov and E. Ethelbert Miller. The free evening readings, usually two a month, are frequently introduced by the U.S. Poet Laureate and followed by a reception. On occasion, tickets are required.

Nancy Galbraith, Director, Poetry & Literature Program, First & East Capitol Streets SW, Washington, DC 20540; (202) 707-5394.

Lunchtime Author Series The Literary Friends of the D.C. Public Library sponsor regular author lunchtime discussions every Tuesday at 12 noon in the library's main lobby. Local authors of fiction, nonfiction and poetry are invited to read from and talk about their work. All readings and lectures are free and open to the public.

Jewel Ogonji, Library Services, M.L. King Memorial Library, 901 G Street NW, Washington, DC 20001; (202) 727-1186. *Lunchtime Author Series Organizer*: Avideh Shashaani, (301) 654-9191.

Montpelier Cultural Arts Center From September through November, and sometimes in the spring, the Center sponsors an average of three poetry and fiction readings. Free and open to the public, the readings are usually held either Friday evenings or Sunday afternoons.

Montpelier Cultural Arts Center, 12826 Laurel-Bowie Road, Laurel, MD 20708; (301) 953-1993.

National Archives Author Lecture Series The Archives hosts at least two lectures each month by authors who have published recent books on American history or current events. Lectures are usually held around noon, and are free and open to the public. For details on upcoming lectures, call the "Events Line" at (202) 501-5000 or ask to be mailed a free monthly calendar of events.

National Archives, Pennsylvania Avenue between 7th and 9th Streets NW, Washington, DC 20408; (202) 501-5525.

PEN/Faulkner Reading Series   These readings, held from October through May, are presented by respected and popular authors to benefit the PEN/Faulkner Award and are co-sponsored by the Folger Shakespeare Library. Past participants include Arthur Miller, William Styron, E.L. Doctorow, Pat Conroy, T. Coraghessan Boyle, Terry McMillan and Grace Paley. The winner of the previous year's PEN/Faulkner Award is always invited to read from his or her work. Each reading is held on a Friday evening, followed by a short question-and-answer period and ending with a reception and book signing. Admission is $10.

Janice Delaney, Executive Director, PEN/Faulkner Award, The Folger Shakespeare Library, 201 E. Capitol Street SE, Washington, DC 20003; (202) 544-7077.

"The Poet & The Poem"   Airing every Sunday evening from 8 to 9 pm on WPFW 89.3 FM, this lively radio program features readings and discussions with well-known local and international poets. Hosted by local poet Grace Cavalieri, "The Poet & The Poem" is also distributed nationally.

Grace Cavalieri, c/o WPFW-FM, 702 H Street NW, Washington, DC 20001; (202) 783-3100.

Poetry/PM   Twice a month during the spring and fall, the International Monetary Fund Visitors' Center hosts lunchtime poetry readings with a focus on international poets. All readings begin at 1 pm, and are free and open to the public.

IMF Visitors Center, 700 19th Street NW, Washington, DC 20431; (202) 623-6869.

Politics & Prose Readings   This popular bookstore specializes in discussions with nonfiction writers and readings by fiction writers. Free semi-monthly newsletter announces all upcoming literary events. Politics & Prose also holds mini-courses and sponsors two book clubs that meet twice a month. All readings are free and open to the public.

Politics & Prose, 5015 Connecticut Avenue NW, Washington, DC 20008; (202) 364-1919.

Smithsonian Resident Associates Program There are always several exciting literary events and programs scheduled among the many offerings provided by the Smithsonian Institution's Resident Associate Program (RAP). Such prominent writers as Joyce Carol Oates, Harold Bloom, Neil Sheehan, Robert MacNeil, Gus Lee and Nikki Giovanni have all been invited to speak and read from their work at recent RAP events. For details on upcoming events, either join RAP or request a copy of its newsletter, *The Smithsonian Associate.*

Resident Associates Program, Smithsonian Institution, 1100 Jefferson Drive SW, Washington, DC 20560; (202) 357-3030.

Strathmore Hall Literary Luncheon Series Sponsored by the Friends of the Library, Montgomery County, MD, this lecture series has featured such prominent authors as Stanley Karnow, Jonathan Yardley, Phyllis Naylor, Dr. Elena Castedo, E. Ethelbert Miller and Dori Sanders. Lunch is served in the splendid Strathmore Hall Arts Center in Bethesda, and each of the four annual lectures is held the second Thursday of October, November, March and April from 11:30 am to 1:30 pm. Admission is charged.

Friends of the Library, 99 Maryland Avenue, Rockville, MD 20850–2389; (301) 217-3810.

TTU Press Poetry Reading Series This regular poetry reading series, sponsored by TrimTab University Press, can be enjoyed the first Sunday of each month at Takoma Traders, 7071 Carroll Avenue in Takoma Park, MD. Readers (past and scheduled) include poets Mary Ann Daly, Jacklyn Potter, Ann Darr, Hilary Tham and Grace Cavalieri. Work by readers has also been selected for publication in an anthology of the series.

D.J. Hoffman, P.O. Box 5915, Takoma Park, MD 20913; (301) 891-2886.

University of Maryland Readings Series The university's English Department sponsors "Writers Here and Now," twice-a-month readings by prominent poets and novelists. Authors who have read in the series include poets Louise Gluck, Gerald Stern and Rita Dove and novelists Russell Banks and Marilynne Robinson. All readings are free and open to the public.

Department of English, University of Maryland, College Park, MD 20740; (301) 405-3809.

Vintage Poets Sarah's Circle, an organization providing housing and special programs for low-income seniors, holds monthly poetry readings or workshops from September through June. Held the second Saturday of the month, each session features a published poet from the Washington area. All readings and workshops are free and open to the public.

Program Coordinator, Sarah's Circle, 2551 17th Street NW, Washington, DC 20009; (202) 332-1400.

Visions International Poetry Reading Series The publisher of the poetry magazine *Visions* presents monthly readings by local and out-of-town poets at two locations: The Art Barn [2401 Tilden Street NW, near Beach Drive in Rock Creek Park; (202) 426-6719] and the Reston Community Center [Colts Neck Road, Reston, VA; (703) 476-4500]. Readings at Reston Community Center are free; a small donation is requested for readings at the Art Barn.

Bradley Strahan, Director, Visions International, 1110 Seaton Lane, Falls Church, VA 22046; (703) 521-0142.

The Writer's Center Local and visiting poets read from their work on Sundays at 2 pm, followed by a reception. Coffeehouse readings for local poets are also held once a month. *Carousel*, the Center's free bimonthly newsletter, prints reviews and lists a calendar of events and information for all writers. All readings are free and open to the public.

Dr. Allan Lefcowitz, Artistic Director, The Writer's Center, 7815 Old Georgetown Road, Bethesda, MD 20814; (301) 654-8664.

LITERARY MAGAZINES

In any community, literary magazines help readers and writers find each other more readily. These magazines also give many promising young writers a chance to be published, while frequently airing provocative views of the world that challenge mainstream thought.

Aerial This poetry magazine is published once or twice each year (118 pp). Subscriptions are $17.50 for three issues; sample copies $7. Please enclose SASE with submissions. *Aerial* also presents a regular reading series at Bick's Books, 2309 18th Street NW, in Washington, DC.

Rod Smith, Editor, P.O. Box 25642, Washington, DC 20007.

Belles Lettres: A Review of Books by Women This quarterly magazine features interviews, essays, fiction, rediscoveries and retrospectives. Both scholarly and popular works are reviewed in the genres of fiction, nonfiction, poetry, biography and criticism. Subscriptions for individuals are $20/year or $35/two years; for institutions, $40/year; for students, $15/year. Sample issues are $5 each.

Janet Mullaney, Editor, 1115 Captain's Walk Court, Potomac, MD 20878; (301) 294-0278.

Black Buzzard Review Published by Visions International, *Black Buzzard Review* features poems written originally in English and mostly by American poets. The magazine is published once a year ($4.50/issue).

Bradley Strahan, Director, Visions International, 1110 Seaton Lane, Falls Church, VA 22046; (703) 521-0142.

Delos Published three times a year by the Center for World Literature, *Delos* reflects the purpose of the Center, a nonprofit organization established in 1987 "to maintain and invigorate the world's literatures by making their best works widely available in other than their original languages." Each issue of the magazine contains nearly 150 pages of poetry (with translations) and other writing from around the world. Subscriptions for individuals are $20/year or $36/two years; for institutions, $25/year or $45/two years; for students $15/year. Single issues are $5 each.

Reed Whittemore, Editor, P.O. Box 2880, College Park, MD 20741.

The Federal Poet This poetry magazine is published semi-annually by the Federal Poets, the D.C. chapter of the National Federation of State Poetry Societies and the Academy of American Poets. Subscriptions are $10/year. The Federal Poets meet at 2 pm on the third Saturday of each month. Poets and guests are welcome.

Frank Goodwin, Editor, P.O. Box 65400, Washington, DC 20035; (301) 292-1053.

Folio: A Literary Journal This journal of fiction, poetry, interviews, essays and artwork is published twice a year by the creative writing program at American University. Manuscript submissions are welcome from U.S. and foreign writers; reading period for submissions is between September 1 and March 15. Subscriptions are $10/year; back issues are available for $4.50 each.

Editor, *Folio*, Department of Literature, The American University, 4400 Massachusetts Avenue NW, Washington, DC 20016; (202) 885-2971.

GW Review Published by George Washington University, this literary magazine accepts submissions in short fiction, poetry, essays and graphic arts. Subscriptions are $4/year; single issues are $3.

Editor, *GW Review*, P.O. Box 20, Marvin Center, George Washington University, 800 21st Street NW, Washington, DC 20052.

Lip Service This poetry magazine "encourages submission of quality poetry from poets everywhere." It is published twice a year by Lip Service, a nonprofit organization established in 1987. Subscriptions are $4/year.

Editor, P.O. Box 23231, Washington, DC 20026.

Phoebe The literary magazine of George Mason University, *Phoebe* accepts work in poetry, fiction, nonfiction and photography. Subscriptions are $8/year; single issues are $3.25.

Editor, *Phoebe*, George Mason University, 4400 University Drive, Fairfax, VA 22030; (703) 323-3730.

The Plum Review This biannual literary magazine publishes previously unpublished poetry from around the world, as well as poetry reviews and interviews with prominent poets. Subscriptions are $10/year; single issues are $5.

Mike Hammer & Christina Daub, Editors, P.O. Box 3557, Washington, DC 20007; (202) 466-4578. *London Office*: c/o Sophie Ahmeen, 20 Waldemar Avenue, London SW6 5NA.

Poet Lore This magazine of poetry, translation and criticism celebrated its 100th anniversary in 1989. Now published by the Writer's Center, *Poet Lore* comes out four times a year. Subscriptions for individuals are $12/

year; for institutions, $20/year; for Writer's Center members, $8/year. Single issues are $4.50; sample issue costs $4. Submissions are welcome.

Editor, *Poet Lore*, The Writer's Center, 7815 Old Georgetown Road, Bethesda, MD 20814; (301) 654-8664.

Visions International This magazine of poetry, reviews and original artwork features many translations and poems from other countries. It is published three times a year. Subscriptions are $14/year; regular issues are $4.50; special issues are $6.

Bradley Strahan, Director, Visions International, 1110 Seaton Lane, Falls Church, VA 22046; (703) 521-0142.

WRITING COURSES, CONFERENCES & SEMINARS

Writing well is rather like cooking well—you can always use a little more flavor, a dash of subtlety, a pinch of irony, a teaspoon of wit or perhaps some other measure of style that will make your final creation irresistible. For those who hunger to improve their literary skills, there are a number of outstanding writing courses, conferences and seminars being offered each year in the Washington area.

The American University

Creative Writing An MFA degree in creative writing is offered through the Creative Writing Program within the Literature Department. Co-directors Henry Taylor and Richard McCann lead a staff of eight full- and part-time writing instructors. The program requires 48 semester hours, or about two-and-a-half years, to complete. There are three workshops offered each semester for which nonstudents can apply, but preference is given to enrolled writing students.

Henry Taylor & Richard McCann, Co-Directors, MFA Program in Creative Writing, Room 227, Gray Hall, The American University, 4400 Massachusetts Avenue NW, Washington, DC 20016; (202) 885-2977/78.

Journalism Bachelor's and master's degrees in communications are offered through the School of Communication, with focus on journalism and public affairs. Duration of the undergraduate program is four years. The M.A. program typically lasts ten months, and is for full-time students only.

Graduate Journalism Committee, School of Communication, The American University, 4400 Massachusetts Avenue, NW, Washington, DC 20016; (202) 885-2060/78.

Professional Development Workshops The Office of Continuing Studies offers on-site writing and editing programs for organizations, corporations or government agencies. Courses can be offered for academic credit or noncredit, and last anywhere from several hours to fourteen weeks. Tailored to the needs and interests of the host organization, workshops are taught for the most part by American University faculty.

Program Representative, Office of Continuing Studies, The American University, 4400 Massachusetts Avenue, NW, Washington, DC 20016; (202) 885-3990.

Editorial Experts

Workshops on Publication Skills Editorial Experts is a well-known local editorial and publishing firm that offers a full range of excellent workshops on improving publication skills. The courses, usually one to three days long, are taught by staff and many area publication professionals.

Claire Coyne, Manager, Training Division, Editorial Experts, 85 S. Bragg Street, Suite 400, Alexandria, VA 22312; (703) 683-0683.

Georgetown University

Certificate Program in Editing & Publications Georgetown's Professional Development Program offers evening courses in the principles of writing and editing, graphic design and printing, advanced editing, copyediting, proofreading and developing resource skills. The courses usually last eight to twelve weeks.

Renee Rodgers, Director, Professional Development Program, 306 Intercultural Center, Georgetown University, Washington, DC 20057; (202) 687-6218.

George Mason University

Creative Writing Program   Students can choose to pursue any of three writing-related degrees at GMU: B.A. in English, with concentration in writing (minimum 12 hours); M.A. in English, with concentration on writing fiction or poetry (minimum 30 hours); and MFA in writing, specializing in poetry or fiction (minimum 48 hours). Program faculty members include novelists Richard and Robert Bausch, Susan Richards Shreve, Marita Golden, Alan Cheuse and Vassily Aksyonov; poets Carolyn Forche, C.K. Williams, Peter Klappert and Susan Tichy; and playwright Paul D'Andrea. The program has also invited distinguished visiting writers to teach each year, among them Carlos Fuentes, Edmund White and John Gardener.

Roger Lathbury, Director, Creative Writing Program, English Department, George Mason University, 4400 University Drive, Fairfax, VA 22030; (703) 323-2936. Geri Dolan, Program Secretary.

Extended Studies   Adults who want to take any GMU writing course without enrolling in a degree program can do so by registering through Extended Studies. Credit given can also be applied toward a degree program in future.

George Mason University, School for Continued & Alternative Learning, 4400 University Drive, Fairfax, VA 22030; (703) 323-2436.

George Washington University

Creative Writing   This program offers a B.A. in English, with a minor in Creative Writing. There are five creative writing instructors in the program.

Faye Moskowitz, Department of English, George Washington University, Washington, DC 20052; (202) 994-6180.

Publication Specialist Program   The PSP is a year-long, graduate-level certificate program of mostly evening courses covering all aspects of brochure, newsletter, magazine and book publishing. There is also a certificate program in desktop publishing available.

Kate McIntyre, Program Director, Publication Specialist Program, George Washington University, 801

22nd Street, NW, Suite T409, Washington, DC 20052; (202) 994-7273.

Howard University

Book Publishing Institute The BPI is an intensive five-week certificate program which covers all the basics of book publishing. Key publishing executives conduct lectures and workshops on editing, design and production, marketing and financial management. Also covered are such specialty areas as children's, university, textbook and direct-mail publishing. Enrollment is limited and competitive.

Avis Taylor, Program Administrator, Book Publishing Institute, Howard University Press, 2900 Van Ness Street, NW, Washington, DC 20008; (202) 806-8465.

Smithsonian Institution

Resident Associates Program The RAP sponsors an extensive range of lectures and courses in the arts and humanities, taught by Smithsonian experts as well as other distinguished scholars and guest speakers. Each year, offerings always include something literary. Literary guests in the past have included Judith Viorst, T. Coraghessan Boyle, Joyce Carol Oates and Umberto Eco. Academic credit is given by the University of Maryland for selected courses.

Resident Associates Program, Smithsonian Institution, 1100 Jefferson Drive, SW, Washington, DC 20560; (202) 357-3030.

University of the District of Columbia

English Composition & Rhetoric This program, which offers an academic degree, is designed to be of use to scholars, teachers and practicing writers.

Renee Housman, Assistant Professor, Department of English Studies, UDC, 4200 Connecticut Avenue, NW, Washington, DC 20008; (202) 282-7522.

University of Maryland

Creative Writing The Department of English offers a two-year Masters of Fine Arts degree in Creative Writing, as well as an extensive selection of creative writing courses at the undergraduate level. Among the eight full-time professors who teach creative writing are novelist Joyce Kornblatt, poets Stanley Plumly, Phillis Levin and Michael Collier and novelist/translator Howard Norman.

Creative Writing Program, Department of English, University of Maryland, College Park, MD 20742; (301) 405-3819.

College of Journalism The College offers B.A. and M.A. degrees in several specializations, both print and broadcast. Students can also pursue a Ph.D. in public communications. A number of the college's 27 faculty members double as staff on the *Washington Journalism Review*, which is published by the college.

Greg Steward, Assistant Dean for Undergraduate Studies, College of Journalism, University of Maryland, College Park, MD 20742; (301) 454-1815.

Washington Independent Writers

Spring Writers Conference The Conference is a one-day event, usually held in May, which offers a thoroughly comprehensive series of panels and workshops on all aspects of writing and publishing. Local and national authors, agents, publishers, editors and others involved in the literary life share their insights and candidly assess the current literary scene. Lunch and a reception give participants a chance to talk with conference guests. For the past several years, the Conference has been held at Mount St. Albans School, next to the Washington National Cathedral.

Washington Independent Writers, 733 15th Street NW, Suite 220, Washington, DC 20005; (202) 347-4973.

Freelance Basics Course Designed for established writers who want to freelance, this series of four evening classes covers all practical aspects of the freelance life, from writing query letters to doing one's taxes to successful marketing. The course, usually held during February, often includes at least one session in which writers can have their work critiqued. Participation is open to non-WIW members.

Washington Independent Writers, 733 15th Street NW, Suite 220, Washington, DC 20005; (202) 347-4973.

The Writer's Center

Writing & Publications Workshops The Center offers a full range of writing workshops in fiction, nonfiction, poetry, playwriting and screenwriting. Participants in all writing workshops submit manuscripts for critical evaluation by their peers. The Center also holds publications workshops in such areas as editing, typesetting, desktop publishing and basic graphic design. All workshops typically last between four and eight weeks, and are offered four times a year.

Jane Fox, Director, The Writer's Center, 7815 Old Georgetown Road, Bethesda, MD 20814; (301) 654-8664.

WRITING CONTESTS, GRANTS & AWARDS

Local authors can gain recognition and support from many regional and national writing contests, grants and award programs based in the nation's capital. Virtually every genre of writing is represented here, with the exception of such fictional categories as mystery and science fiction. No clues have been uncovered which help to explain this fact, either in this galaxy or in any other.

Alicia Patterson Foundation Fellowship Program for Journalists   The Foundation awards one-year grants to working print journalists, reporters, editors or photojournalists to pursue independent projects of significant interest. Between five and seven fellows are selected each year; each one-year grant carries a stipend of $30,000. Applicants must have at least five years of professional experience. Deadline: October 1.

Margaret Engel, Director, Alicia Patterson Foundation, 1001 Pennsylvania Avenue, NW, Suite 1250, Washington, DC 20004; (202) 393-5995.

American Historical Association Book Awards   Outstanding books of history are given awards each year by the AHA, which makes its selections from books published prior to May 15. Each award is $1,000.

Book Awards Committee, AHA, 400 A Street SE, Washington, DC 20003; (202) 544-2422.

AMWA Medical Book Awards Competition   The American Medical Writers Association (AMWA) presents awards for outstanding medical books in the following categories: books for physicians, books for allied health professionals and trade books for the lay public. Deadline: April 1.

Book Awards Committee, AMWA, 9650 Rockville Pike, Bethesda, MD 20814; (301) 493-0003.

American Sociological Association Book Awards Outstanding books of sociology are given awards each year by the ASA, which makes its selections from books published in the prior year.

Book Awards Committee, ASA, 1722 N Street NW, Washington, DC 20036; (202) 833-3410.

Author's Recognition Day & Special Awards Ceremony All local writers and authors are honored in a reception and special ceremonies hosted during November by the Literary Friends of the D.C. Public Library (LFDCPL) in the library's main hall. Special recognition is given to three local authors who have had notable books published in the previous year. People who have made major contributions to the literary life in the nation's capital are also honored. Past honorees have included Eloise Greenfield, Reed Whittemore, Josephine Jacobsen, O.B. Hardison, Myra Sklarew and Juan Williams.

Molly Raphael, Executive Assistant to the Director, M. L. King Public Library, 901 G Street NW, Washington, DC 20001; (202) 727-1101. Betty Parry, President, LFDCPL.

Felix Morley Memorial Prizes Prizes are given each year by the Institute for Humane Studies at George Mason University to "discover and encourage college-aged writers who reflect an interest in the classical liberal traditions of private property and free exchange." Entries can be either nonfiction articles, editorials, columns, essays, criticism or investigative pieces or fictional short stories. College-aged writers from the United States and abroad may submit their work. Deadline: June 15.

Morley Prize Secretary, Institute for Humane Studies, George Mason University, 4400 University Drive, Fairfax, VA 22030; (703) 323-1055.

Folio Fiction/Poetry Award Given each year, these awards for short fiction and poetry are co-sponsored by the American University and the university's literary magazine *Folio*. Both awards also include publication in the spring issue of the magazine. Work submitted for consideration must be unpublished. Deadline: March 1.

Department of Literature, American University, 4400 Massachusetts Avenue NW, Washington, DC 20016; (202) 885-2990.

Jefferson Cup Award The award is given each year by the Virginia Library Association to the author of an outstanding book written for young people in the fields of history, biography or historical fiction (1490 to present). Deadline: Mid- to late December.

Debbie Trocchi, Virginia Library Association, 80 S. Early Street, Alexandria, VA 22304; (703) 370-6020.

Larry Neal Writing Contest Sponsored by the D.C. Commission on the Arts and Humanities, the contest helps to recognize and reward the talents of local writers. Candidates, who must have lived in the District of Columbia for at least one year, can submit entries in only one of five categories: poetry, fiction, criticism, essays or dramatic writing. Awards are $500 each in all categories.

D.C. Commission on the Arts & Humanities, 410 8th Street NW, Suite 500, Washington, DC 20004; (202) 724-5613.

Mary Roberts Rinehart Fund The Fund awards annual grants to unpublished creative writers of fiction, poetry, drama, biography, autobiography or history with strong narrative quality. Two awards of $950 are given each year (fiction and poetry in odd years; nonfiction and drama in even years). Writers must be nominated by a sponsoring writer or editor. Deadline: November 30.

Roger Lathbury, Director, Mary Roberts Rinehart Fund, GMU, 4400 University Drive, Fairfax, VA 22030; (703) 323-2221.

National Awards for Educational Reporting Each year, the best educational reporting in the nation is honored at special ceremonies sponsored by the Education Writers Association. There are a total of seventeen categories in print, radio and television. Deadline: Mid- to late January.

Lisa J. Walker, Executive Director, Education Writers Association, 1001 Connecticut Avenue NW, Suite 310, Washington, DC 20036; (202) 429-9680.

National Press Foundation Annual Awards   Three awards are given each year by the Foundation for excellence in print and broadcast journalism. The Foundation also funds a variety of journalism awards given by the National Press Club, the American Association for the Advancement of Science and other organizations.

David Yount, President, National Press Foundation, 1282 National Press Building, Washington, DC 20045; (202) 662-7350.

PEN/Faulkner Award for Fiction   This prestigious award is given each year to five American authors who have published works of distinction in the previous calendar year. Recent award winners include T. Coraghessan Boyle (*World's End*), Richard Wiley (*Soldiers in Hiding*) and Peter Taylor (*The Old Forest & Other Stories*). The awards ceremony is held in May and open to the public. Deadline: December 31.

Janice Delaney, Executive Director, PEN/Faulkner Award, Folger Shakespeare Library, 201 E. Capitol Street SE, Washington, DC 20003; (202) 544-7077.

PEN/Malamud Award   This annual short-story award is given for a lifetime of achievement in writing short stories or for a collection of exceptional distinction published in the previous calendar year. The winner is chosen by a committee of PEN/Faulkner board members and literary executors of the Bernard Malamud Fund. Recent winners include John Updike, Saul Bellow and George Garrett. The awards ceremony is open to the public.

Janice Delaney, Executive Director, PEN/Faulkner Award, Folger Shakespeare Library, 201 E. Capitol Street SE, Washington, DC 20003; (202) 544-7077.

Phi Beta Kappa Book Awards   These awards are given each year for notable books published in the United States. The *Ralph Waldo Emerson Award* is given for outstanding interpretive studies of the intellectual and cultural condition of man. The *Christian Gauss Award* is given for an outstanding work of literary criticism or scholarship. The *Science Award* is given for outstanding interpretations of the physical or biological sciences or mathematics. Deadline: April 30. Award: $2,500.

Mary Mladinov, Phi Beta Kappa Book Awards, 1811 Q Street NW, Washington, DC 20009; (202) 265-3808.

Poet Lore Awards   This quarterly poetry magazine, published by the Writer's Center, sponsors two annual awards: the *John Andrews Narrative Poetry Award* (Deadline: November 30/Award: $250) for outstanding narrative poetry and the *Rose Lefcowitz Awards* ($150.00 each) for the best poem and criticism to appear in any volume.

Poet Lore, The Writer's Center, 7815 Old Georgetown Road, Bethesda, MD 20814; (202) 654-8664.

Poetry Committee Book Award   This cash award is given each year to a local poet for either a first or a second published collection of poems by any publisher or a book of poetry published by a small press. Deadline: April 1.

Poetry Committee, The Folger Shakespeare Library, 201 E. Capitol Street SE, Washington, DC 20003; (202) 544-7077.

Regardie's Annual Money/Power/Greed Fiction Writing Contest   These three annual prizes are given for "stories about money, power and greed, in the tradition of Fitzgerald's *The Great Gatsby*, Dreiser's *The Titan* and Dos Passos' *The Big Money*." Manuscripts should be from 2,000 to 10,000 words. The contest is co-sponsored and co-judged with the Sagalyn Literary Agency. Prizes: $3,000 (first place); $2,000 (second place) and $1,000 (third place). The three winning stories are also published in the magazine. Deadline: April 1.

Fiction Contest, *Regardie's Magazine*, 1010 Wisconsin Avenue NW, Suite 600, Washington, DC 20007; (202) 342-0410.

Robert F. Kennedy Awards   These awards are given to honor the author or journalist whose work "most faithfully and forcefully reflects Robert F. Kennedy's purposes and beliefs."

• *RFK Book Award*   This award is given for a work of fiction or nonfiction published in the previous calendar year. Deadline: late January.

Frederick Grossberg, Executive Director, RFK Book Awards, 1031 31st Street NW, Washington, DC 20007; (202) 333-1880.

• *RFK Journalism Awards*   These awards are given for accounts about the disadvantaged in the United States. Entries must have been published or broadcast in the year prior to the award, and can be submitted by individuals or their appropriate organization. Deadline: late January.

Director, RFK Journalism Awards, 1031 31st Street NW, Washington, DC 20007; (202) 333-1880.

Towson State University Prize for Literature This annual prize of $1,200 is awarded for an outstanding book or book-length manuscript of fiction, poetry, drama or imaginative nonfiction work by a Maryland writer (40 years old or younger). The work must have either been published in the three years preceding the nomination year, or be scheduled for publication within the nomination year. The author must have been a Maryland resident for at least three years. Deadline: Mid-May.

Annette Chappell, Dean, College of Liberal Arts, Towson State University, Towson, MD 21204; (301) 321-2128.

Washington Independent Writers Awards WIW, long recognized as the nation's largest regional writers' organization, gives out three awards during each calendar year:

• *President's Award* Established in 1989, this honorary award is given each spring to an individual (not necessarily a WIW member) who has contributed significantly to helping writers everywhere—whether by fighting for freedom of expression, by providing assistance to writers or by exemplary writing. Names can be submitted for consideration during the first three months of the year.

• *Philip M. Stern Award* This annual award is presented each spring to recognize the WIW member who, as judged by fellow members, has provided the greatest service to writers and the writing profession during the year. Previous winners include Paul Dickson (1986), Kitty Kelley (1987), Joseph Foote & Barbara Raskin (1988), Dan Moldea (1989), Joel Makower (1990) and Joseph Goulden (1991).

• *Joan G. Sugarman Children's Book Award* Established in 1987 by WIW member Joan G. Sugarman in memory of her late husband, this biannual award honors excellence in fiction or nonfiction writing for children (ages 1–15). Candidates must be residents of the District of Columbia, suburban Virginia or suburban Maryland. Previous winners include Cynthia Voigt (*Tree by Leaf*), Phyllis Naylor (*Beetles, Lightly Toasted*) and Suzanne Fisher Staples (*Shabanu*). The award is administered by WIW's Legal & Educational Fund.

Isolde Chapin, Executive Director, WIW, 733 15th Street NW, Suite 220, Washington, DC 20005; (202) 347-4973.

Washington Journalism Review "Best in Business" Awards Each year, WJR asks its readers—most of whom are people in the news business—to choose the people who have made the most significant contributions in print, radio and TV journalism. The results are announced in the March issue of the magazine. The awards gala, a closely watched affair, is attended by a stellar media crowd.

Suzanne Griggs, Public Relations, Washington Journalism Review, 4716 Pontiac Street, Suite 310, College Park, MD, 20740; (301) 513-0001.

Washington Monthly Political Book Award This annual award is given for a book of fiction or nonfiction that "illuminates a major issue through rigorous reporting, trenchant analysis and literary grace." Previous winners include Taylor Branch, William Greider, Tom Wolfe and Robert Kuttner. Deadline: January 20.

Donne Masaki, Production Manager, Washington Monthly, 1611 Connecticut Avenue NW, Suite 7, Washington, DC 20009; (202) 462-0128.

Washington Post/Children's Book Guild Award For Nonfiction This annual award recognizes a body of nonfiction work aimed at young readers. The winner is selected by a jury of authorities in children's literature and honored at an awards luncheon sponsored by *The Washington Post*. Award: $1,000.

Patricia Markun, Society of Children's Book Writers, 4405 W Street NW, Washington, DC 20007; (202) 965-0403.

The Washington Prize Open to any living American writer except those connected with the sponsor, *The*

Word Works, the prize is given each year to the author of an *unpublished* work of poetry. Entry fee: $10. Award: $1,000 and publication. Deadline: Between February 1 and March 1.

The Word Works, P.O. Box 42164, Washington, DC 20015.

Washingtonian Book Award This award, given each year by *Washingtonian Magazine*, is presented to the author of a work of fiction or nonfiction which best portrays Washington and the way it works. Recent winners include Herman Wouk (*Inside, Outside*), Hedrick Smith (*The Power Game*), Walter Isaacson and Evan Thomas (*The Wise Men*) and Ethan Bronner (*Battle for Justice*). Award: $1,000 donated in the author's name to the book fund of the Martin Luther King, Jr. Memorial Library.

Howard Means, Senior Editor, Washingtonian Magazine, 1828 L Street NW, Washington, DC 20036; (202) 296-3600.

Westinghouse Science Journalism Awards These annual awards, sponsored by the American Association for the Advancement of Science, help to "encourage and recognize outstanding reporting for a general audience on the sciences." Deadline: July 15.

Joan Wrather, Awards Administrator, AAAS Office of Communications, 1333 H Street NW, Washington, DC 20005; (202) 326-6431.

Young Poets Competition These annual awards are given to recognize the literary talents of two area high school students. Honoraria given, along with opportunity to read with established poets during the Joaquin Miller Cabin Summer Poetry Series. Deadline: Mid-March.

The Word Works, P.O. Box 42164, Washington, DC 20015.

BOOK FAIRS & SALES

As every good biblioholic knows, there's nothing like a good book fair or sale to get the acquisitive juices flowing. And why not? Bargains abound during several prominent book fairs and sales held each year in the Washington area. Some events also allow collectors to acquire rare or hard-to-find editions of valued works. Best of all, proceeds are typically used to help support charitable causes, educational programs or organizations committed to improving literacy.

Association of American Foreign Service Women Book Fair   This annual event is held the second or third week of October at the U.S. State Department Building, 2201 C Street NW in Washington, D.C. More than 100,000 books in every conceivable category are offered for sale, at prices ranging from 60 cents on up. Everything is categorized. Proceeds help to support local charities and to sustain academic scholarships for children of employees of the U.S. State Department and the U.S. Foreign Service.

Association of American Foreign Service Women, P.O. Box 70051, Washington, DC 20024; (202) 223-5796.

Brandeis National Women's Committee Used Book Sale   Sponsored by the Greater Washington Chapter of Brandeis University's National Women's Committee, this popular used book sale has grown to such an extent that it is now a *permanent* Washington literary event. To participate, just drop in at the antique shop of the Prevention of Blindness Society's headquarters, located at 3716 Howard Avenue in Kensington, MD. The shop features thousands of used books in all categories; some first editions and autographed books. Unsold books are regularly shipped to federal prisons for their libraries. Days of operation are Tuesday through Saturday.

Estelle Jacobs, National President, Brandeis University National Women's Committee, 5909 Bradley Boulevard, Bethesda, MD 20814; (301) 320-3878.

Celebration of Washington Poetry   The Poetry Committee of the Folger Shakespeare Library, comprised of representatives from many poetry organizations in the Washington area, holds an annual book sale and reading festival in May to celebrate Washington poets.

The Poetry Committee, Folger Shakespeare Library, 201 E. Capitol Street SE, Washington, DC 20003; (202) 544-7077.

Jewish Community Center   The Center sponsors two annual events, both free to the public:

• *Annual Book Fair*   This annual sale, held during November, features the largest selection of books of

Jewish interest available for sale in one place. All books offered at the fair are new, although some are discounted off regular price. Titles include everything from scholarly works to popular fiction. Author appearances are scheduled regularly throughout the eight-day event.

• *Annual Children's Book Fair* This fair features books for children of all ages as well as a large selection of parenting books. Only new books are available for sale, and prominent authors and illustrators are invited to talk and sign copies.

Ms. Tommy Feldman, Director, Literary Arts Department, JCC, 6125 Montrose Avenue, Rockville, MD 20850; (301) 881-0100.

National Press Club Book Fair and Authors' Night Each year, around Thanksgiving, the National Press Club sponsors a unique four-hour public fair for members, guests and the general public. Entries are limited to 75 to 90 titles each year, and authors must agree to appear with their books. All books on sale are written by club members and/or Washington area residents, or are about the Washington area. Proceeds benefit the Resource Center of the National Press Club. Admission is free.

Paul D'Armiento, Chair, National Press Club Book Fair, c/o The National Press Club, 529 14th Street NW, Washington, DC 20045; (202) 822-0604.

Stone Ridge Used Book Sale Each year, since 1968, the Stone Ridge Country Day School has been assembling more than 100,000 used books—many of them rare—for its Spring Used Book Sale. The sale, usually held in April, runs from 8 am to 8 pm on Friday, Saturday and Sunday. After that, on Monday evening, books are half-price from 4 to 8 pm. On Tuesday evening, again from 4 to 8 pm, patrons can fill a grocery bag with books for $5. More than 6,000 people from across the United States attend this popular book sale each year. Proceeds benefit the school's scholarship fund, and there is ample free parking. Admission is free.

Development Office, Stone Ridge Country Day School, 9101 Rockville Pike (at Cedar Lane), Bethesda, MD 20814; (301) 657-4322 (x362 or x372).

University Club's Meet The Authors Night & Book Fair The University Club brings together members, guests and the general public to discuss, buy and have books personalized by some of the nation's leading authors. Usually held in early November, this lively annual event is limited to 50 featured local and national authors who have had books published within the past two years. Admission is free, with all proceeds from book sales used to benefit the University Club's library.

Paul D'Armiento, Chair, University Club Book Fair, c/o The University Club, 1135 16th Street NW, Washington, DC 20036; (202) 862-8800. Peggy Hudgins, Librarian, The University Club.

The Vassar Club Booksale   Each spring, the Vassar Club of Washington sponsors a week-long used book sale at the Departmental Auditorium, Constitution Avenue between 12th and 14th Streets NW in Washington, DC. More than 100,000 general and rare used books are available for sale, along with fine art, collectibles, maps, photos and Washingtoniana. Everything is half-price the last day of the sale.

Vassar Club of Washington Booksale, Book Sorting Center, 2737 Devonshire Place NW, Washington, DC; (301) 299-4855.

Washington Antiquarian Book Fair   Since 1975, this prestigious book fair has featured about 70 antiquarian book dealers from across the country. Some dealers carry general antique or rare books; others are highly specialized. Usually held in early March, the fair is sponsored by Concord Hill School and takes place at the Rosslyn Westpark Hotel in Arlington, Virginia. Proceeds from ticket sales and a silent auction benefit the school. Admission is $12 for the entire fair; $5 per day.

Concord Hill School, 6050 Wisconsin Avenue, Chevy Chase, MD 20815; (301) 654-2626.

WNBA Booksale, Author Autographing Party & Fundraiser   Equal parts party and fundraiser, this popular literary event is held by the local chapter of the Women's National Book Association to benefit local literacy programs. The book sale features author-signed books, along with other recent books in all genres and subjects, at discount prices. Most of the books are donated by local publishers, publishers with local offices, book services, local bookstores and bookstore chains. Proceeds are donated to metropolitan area literacy groups. Held every year in the first week of December.

Diane Ullius, President, WNBA/Washington Chapter, 5621 6th Street South, Arlington, VA 22204; (202) 707-0713.

Women In Communications Book Sale The WIC Book Sale features several thousand new (some autographed) and used books in many categories. Proceeds of this one-day spring event are divided equally among four metropolitan area literacy councils.

Sharon O'Malley, Vice President for Programs, c/o NRECA, 1800 Massachusetts Avenue NW, Washington, DC 20036; (202) 857-9531.

Libraries, Archives & Special Collections

Get your facts first—then you can distort 'em as much as you please.

—MARK TWAIN

In a city where information equals power, one might expect to find a large number of libraries, archives and special collections. But apparently the quest for power in the nation's capital knows no bounds, because the amount of information available here is literally inexhaustible, with all subjects and disciplines well covered.

Fully one-sixth of *all* U.S. library resources can be found in the Washington metropolitan area alone. From the massive Library of Congress to the equally massive National Archives, from seven complete city and county public library systems to 55 outstanding special collections and archives (including the phenomenal resources of the Smithsonian Institution Libraries and Archival Collections) to 53 major U.S. government agency libraries to 35 university and college libraries on 20 campuses, this chapter offers ample proof of just how much information may be gathered by anyone who seeks it here.

And yet, long as it is, this chapter only reflects *a portion* of the vast research holdings which may be found in the nation's capital. To get a more complete picture of the area's library resources, readers are encouraged to consult *Library & Reference Facilities in the Area of the District of Columbia, 12th edition*, published in 1986 by the American Society of Information Science/Knowledge Industry Publications. Currently being revised and updated, this book is the definitive work on which selected listings in this chapter have been based.

While burying one's head in books is the usual purpose of visiting a library, sometimes taking in the surroundings can be just as satisfying as browsing through the stacks. The Thomas Jefferson Building of the Library of Congress, with its rococo lobby and spectacular Main Reading Room, was the most expensive building of its time when completed in 1897 and still commands attention today. The palatial expanse of the Society of the Cincinnati is impressive, while the elegant formal gardens surrounding Dumbarton Oaks can lure anyone to the point of dreamy distraction. So who says research has to be boring?

Most of the libraries, archives and special collections listed in this chapter are free and open to the public. Sometimes, as noted, researchers must seek permission ahead of time and admission fees may be charged. Omitted from the chapter are many small, highly specialized local collections and archives, as well as certain collections which are sometimes open to scholars but *never* open the general public. Although some national association libraries are listed in this chapter, hundreds of others have been omitted because of limited space.

In a time when many American cities are making the mistake of severely curtailing their library resources, the Washington area is still blessed with an abundance of such places. If it's true, as Samuel Johnson once said, that an author "will turn over half a library to make one book," then there should be no lack of books emerging from the nation's capital for years to come.

LIBRARY OF CONGRESS

The Library of Congress ranks alongside the Bibliothèque Nationale in Paris, the British Library in London and the Lenin Library in Moscow as one of the world's truly great libraries. It is also the largest, with more than 100 million items in 470 languages stored on 532 miles of shelving in three magnificent buildings: the Thomas Jefferson Building, the John Adams Building and the James Madison Memorial Building.

Established by the U.S. Congress on April 24, 1800, when $5,000 was set aside for the purchase of "such books as may be necessary for Congress," today's Library is divided into numerous divisions and offices. While each of these divisions and offices is important to the Library's modern role as one of the foremost cultural institutions in the United States, as is the Center for the Book (see page 132), there are 16 which deserve special mention.

African & Middle Eastern Division

The *African Section* covers all countries in Africa south of the Sahara, with the exception of Algeria, Egypt,

Libya, Morocco and Tunisia. Its collections of Africana are among the best in the world, encompassing every major field of study except technical agriculture and clinical medicine (these collections are housed in the National Agricultural Library and the National Library of Medicine).

The *Hebraic Section* offers books in Hebrew (dominant at 120,000 volumes), Yiddish, Aramaic, Syriac, Ethiopic and cognate languages.

The *Near East Section* contains materials in Arabic (dominant holding), Turkish, Persian, Armenian and other languages of the encompassing Afghanistan in the east to Morocco in the west, and Turkey and Central Asia in the north to Sudan in the south, excluding only Israel. The section's Mansuri Collection contains over 5,000 volumes on all phases of Islam and Islamic culture.

John Adams Building, Room 1015, 2nd Street and Independence Avenue, SE, Washington, DC 20540. *African Section*: (202) 707-5528. *Hebraic Section*: (202) 707-5422. *Near East Section*: (702) 207-5421. All sections open to the general public.

American Folklife Center

Created in 1976 with passage of the American Folklife Preservation Act, the AFC has a mandate to "preserve and present American folklife." To this end, the Center engages in a wide range of activities which help to "preserve and present" the many folk cultural traditions of the United States, including research documentation, archival preservation, live presentation, exhibition, publication, dissemination and training.

The AFC has been active in lending field assistance for research and local presentations. Its Archive of Folk Culture serves as the national repository for folk-related recordings, manuscripts and other raw materials. Holdings include 30,000 field recordings (cylinders, discs, wires and tapes) and more than 100,000 sheets of manuscript material.

Thomas Jefferson Building, Ground Floor, 1st Street and Independence Avenue SE, Washington, DC 20540; (202) 707-6590/707–5510. Open to the general public.

Asian Division

The division's *Chinese Collection* contains 525,000 volumes in the Chinese language. In addition, there are several thousand volumes in the Manchu, Mongol, Tibetan, and Moso (Nashi) languages. The Collection is also rich in Chinese local histories (4,000 volumes), works on traditional agriculture and botany and collected writings of individual authors.

The *Korean Collection* contains more than 82,000 volumes and 2,100 current serial titles. The *Japanese Section* contains more than 691,000 volumes covering Japanese history, literature and institutions. The section's holdings are strong in the humanistic and social sciences on Japan, Formosa, Korea and Manchuria and in scientific and technological serials. Its 5,200 reels of microfilm contain the selected archives of the Japanese Foreign Office, Army, Navy and other government agencies from 1868 to 1945.

The *Southern Asia Section* contains more than 500,000 volumes, of which 183,000 volumes are in the languages of the region. The scope of these holdings cover India, Pakistan, Sri Lanka, Bangladesh, Nepal and Bhutan, Burma, Thailand, Laos, Cambodia, Vietnam, Singapore, Malaysia, Brunei, Indonesia and the Philippines.

John Adams Building, 2nd Street and Independence Avenue SE, Washington, DC 20540. *Chinese Collection*: (202) 707-5423/25. *Korean Collection*: (202) 707-5424. *Japanese Section*: (202) 707-5430/31. *Southern Asia Section*: (202) 707-5600/5428. All sections open to the general public.

Children's Literature Center

Mandated to serve "government officials, children's librarians, publishers, writers and illustrators," the CLC publishes an annual annotated list of outstanding children's books as well as guides to children's books at the Library of Congress. The Center also organizes symposia on children's books and related media.

Thomas Jefferson Building, 1st Street and Independence Avenue SE, Washington, DC 20540; (202) 707-5535. Open to the general public.

Copyright Office

The Copyright Office's *Information & Reference Division* maintains records of all works registered for copyright in the United States since 1790, and these records are available for public examination. The division also provides information on how to register a copyright claim. Forms for registration may be obtained by mail or telephone or in person at the division's Public Information Office.

The *Licensing Division* receives and processes royalty fees and statements of account for cable television and satellite carrier licenses semi-annually. Information on these licenses is a matter of public record, and may be obtained by correspondence, phone or personal visit.

James Madison Building, Rooms 401 & 458, 101 Independence Avenue SE, Washington, DC 20559. *Copyright Information Office*: (202) 479-0700. *Licensing Division*: (202) 707-8130. Open to the general public.

European Division

This division maintains the Library's extensive collections related to the social, economic, cultural and political life of Europe (excluding the British Isles, Spain and Portugal). It is also responsible for services and programs which illustrate European influences on the United States and other countries around the world.

John Adams Building, 2nd Street and Independence Avenue SE, Washington, DC 20540; (202) 707-8130. Open to the general public.

Geography & Map Division

This collection is rich in historical material, particularly relating to the United States and other areas of the American continents. It includes about 4 million maps (some dating back six centuries), 50,000 atlases, several hundred globes and a similar number of three-dimensional relief models.

James Madison Building, Room 454, 101 Independence Avenue SE, Washington, DC 20540; (202) 707-6277. Open to the general public.

Hispanic Division

The division serves as a center for studies in Spanish, Portuguese, Brazilian and other Spanish-American cultures. The division's collection of Hispanic and Portuguese materials is among the finest in the world. Representing all major subject areas, its holdings are especially strong in history, literature and the social sciences.

The division also houses the *Archive of Hispanic Literature on Tape*, featuring more than 500 poets and prose writers from Latin America and the Iberian Peninsula reading from their own works.

Thomas Jefferson Building, Room LJ239, 1st Street and Independence Avenue SE, Washington, DC 20540; (202) 707-5397. Open to the general public.

Law Library

Established in 1832, this library now comprises the world's largest and most comprehensive collection of books on foreign, international and comparative law. Covers U.S. and foreign law throughout all historical periods, from ancient law to space law.

The Law Library is divided into five sections: American-British Law, European Law, Hispanic Law, Far Eastern Law and Near Eastern/African Law. There is also a *Rare Book Collection*, comprising more than 25,000 items.

James Madison Building, Second Floor, 101 Independence Avenue SE, Washington, DC 20540; (202) 707-5065. *Reference Desk*: (202) 707-5079. All sections open to the general public.

Manuscript Division

The division has a special reading room where manuscript collections may be consulted under the supervision of reference librarians. These collections contain personal papers of eminent Americans (including those of 23 U.S. Presidents), papers of prominent U.S. government officials from the eighteenth century to the present, records of certain important national organizations and more than 3 million pages of reproductions of manuscripts relating to America in foreign archives and libraries.

Current holdings comprise nearly 40 million items in 10,000 separate collections, including a rough draft of the *Declaration of Independence*, a copy of the Gettysburg Address in Lincoln's handwriting and many other great manuscript treasures of American history and culture.

Manuscripts are open to inspection and copying (although not necessarily photocopying), except where restrictions on access are in effect.

James Madison Building, Room 101, 101 Independence Avenue SE, Washington, DC 20540; (202) 707-5387.

Motion Picture, Broadcasting & Recorded Sound Division

The division has a representative collection of contemporary motion pictures and television programs, dating from 1942 to the present. Its outstanding holdings include the *Mary Pickford* and *George Kleine* collections of early motion pictures, dating from 1900 to 1925, and the *American Film Institute Collection*, covering films made in the 1920s, '30s and '40s; and German, Italian and Japanese features, newsreels and documentary films dating from 1930 to 1945.

The division presently houses nearly 400,000 film reels and videocassettes (about 130,000 titles), along with more than 1.7 million recordings of music and the spoken word dating from the 1890s to the present. Access to film, TV and sound recording materials is arranged through permission of division librarians.

James Madison Building, Rooms 113 & 336, 101 Independence Avenue SE, Washington, DC 20540. *Film & Television*: (202) 707-5840. *Sound Recordings*: (202) 707-7833. Reference library is open to the general public.

Music Division

This division houses the Library's extensive music collection of more than 6 million pieces, including 300,000 books, serials and microforms, as well as printed and manuscript music, letters and other literary manuscripts.

A major part of the collection consists of copyright deposits of music. Holdings also include the largest collection of operatic material in existence: full scores, piano-vocal scores and librettos. Among original manuscripts are holographs of Bach, Handel, Haydn, Mozart, Beethoven, Schubert, Liszt, Brahms, Wagner and Debussy.

The division's extensive musical instrument collections include the *Dayton C. Miller Collection*, containing more than 1,600 flutes and flute-like instruments and five Stradivarius string instruments. The division sponsors chamber music programs, performed for the public in the Library's Coolidge Auditorium.

James Madison Building, Performing Arts Reading Room, 101 Independence Avenue SE, Washington, DC 20540; (202) 707-5503.

Prints & Photographs Division

This division houses the Library's extensive collection of more than 14 million items, including drawings, prints, photographs and photographic negatives, posters and other categories of applied graphic arts. Notable among the division's collection are the *Historic American Buildings Survey* and the *Historic American Engineering Record*, the *Pictorial Archives of Early American Architecture*, the *Carnegie Survey of the Architecture of the South*, a stunning collection of *Civil War Photographs* and master photographs (from daguerreotypes to the present) exemplifying different schools of photography.

Fine prints include the *Hubbard* and *Pennell Collections*, dating from the fifteenth century to the present. Diverse graphic arts collections include political drawings, Art Noveau posters, World War I and II posters, advertising posters and performing arts posters.

Copies of pictures may be purchased from the Library's Photoduplication Service, subject to copyright and other restrictions.

James Madison Building, 101 Independence Avenue SE, Washington, DC 20540; (202) 707-6394. All holdings are open to the public.

Rare Book & Special Collections Division

The division contains more than 500,000 items, including books, pamphlets, periodicals, broadsides, playbills, title pages and a select number of prints, photographs, sheet music, manuscripts, ephemera and memorabilia associated with certain special collections. The holdings in Americana and early imprints dating from pre–1501 are extensive.

Thomas Jefferson Building, 1st Street and Independence Avenue SE, Washington, DC 20540; (202) 707-5434. Open to the public *by permission only*.

Science & Technology Division

The Library's collection in science and technology includes almost 4 million books, nearly 60,000 journal titles and, in the custody of the Science and Technology Division, more than 3 million technical reports, standards and specifications.

Significant among this latter group are the extensive

report series issued by the National Technical Information Service of the Department of Commerce, the Defense Technical Information Center, NASA, the Department of Energy, the Department of Education and the Agency for International Development. Of particular note is the collection of World War II documents issued by the Office of Scientific Research and Development (OSRD) from 1942 to 1953, and the Synthetic Rubber Project during the same period.

The standards and specifications collection includes the documents issued by the American National Standards Institute (ANSI) and members of the ANSI Federation, U.S. federal government and military standards, international standards issued by the International Standards Organization (ISO), the International Electrotechnical Commission (IEC), the Consultative Councils for Radio (CCIR) and for Telephone and Telegraph (CCITT), as well as Soviet and Chinese national standards.

John Adams Building, Science Reading Room, Fifth Floor, 2nd Street and Independence Avenue SE, Washington DC 20540. *Science Reading Room*: (202) 707-5639. *Technical Reports Section*: (202) 707-5655. Open to the general public.

Serial & Government Publications Division

The division contains more than 85,000 current periodical titles and other serials, plus a full depository set of U.S. government publications issued since 1979. Approximately 1,600 domestic and foreign newspapers are currently on file. The division's *Newspaper and Current Periodical Room* is open to the public.

James Madison Building, Room 133, 101 Independence Avenue SE, Washington, DC 20540; (202) 707-5690.

NATIONAL ARCHIVES

Popularly known as the institution which houses originals of America's most cherished national documents (including the Declaration of Independence, the Constitution and the Bill of Rights), the National Archives & Records Service also serves as the repository of official records created throughout the history of the United States.

This massive amount of material, amounting to more than 1.5 million cubic feet of paper and housed in four sites, has been in part provided to the Archives by U.S. Presidents and their staffs, U.S. judges, members of Congress and administrators from each federal agency.

But the Archives' vast holdings also extend beyond the strict accounting of federal affairs. For visitors wanting to trace their family histories, the Archives' pension and census records are exhaustively complete (as are those in the Local History and Genealogy Room at the Library of Congress).

The Archives' extensive records also allow researchers to trace the threads of any significant issue in our nation's history, including western expansion, immigration, agricultural developments, domestic and foreign trade growth, conservation, public health and more. Most archival sources for the study of World War II are also held in the National Archives.

Among the Archives' substantial holdings are: 350,000 books, 1.6 million maps, 54,000 motion picture reels, 69,000 sound recordings (including Nixon's infamous White House tapes during Watergate) and 5 million still pictures (including more than 6,000 of the famous Brady Civil War negatives).

8th Street and Pennsylvania Avenue NW, Washington, DC 20408; (202) 523-3218/86. *Research Information*: (202) 523-3220. All sections are open to the general public, although access to certain classified information may be restricted.

PUBLIC LIBRARIES (MAIN & REGIONAL)

Alexandria Public Libraries   This general public library system features a special collection of Virginiana/ Southern history/ local history comprising 12,000 books, as well as an archive of 7,000 miscellaneous manuscripts, papers, prints, photographs and maps. An on-site Virginiana specialist is available at the system's Lloyd House Branch. Holdings exceed 345,000 volumes. (No regional libraries/3 branch libraries.)

Main Library, 717 Queen Street, Alexandria, VA 22307; (703) 838-4555/4557.

Arlington County Public Libraries   This general public library system has special collections on Virginiana, local history, college and career subjects and an Illustrator's Collection of early children's books. Holdings exceed 560,000 volumes. (No regional libraries/6 branch libraries.)

Central Library, 1015 North Quincy Street, Arlington, VA 22201; (703) 358-5990.

D.C. Public Library System This general public library system features the unique *Washingtoniana Division*, a collection of books and other material that chronicle the history of the District of Columbia. Among the division's holdings is *The Washington Star Collection*, including that now-defunct newspaper's working morgue and photo library. The system's special programs serve the needs of children, young adults, the homebound and the deaf, blind or physically disabled. Holdings exceed 1.4 million volumes. The system has one main library and four regional branch libraries:

• *Martin Luther King, Jr. Public Library (Main)* 901 G Street NW, Washington, DC 20001; (202) 727-1126. *Washingtoniana Division*: (202) 727-1213.

• *Chevy Chase* Connecticut Avenue and McKinley Street NW, Washington, DC 20015; (202) 727-1341.

• *Fort Davis* Alabama Avenue and 37th Street SE, Washington, DC 20020; (202) 727-1349.

• *Georgetown* Wisconsin Avenue and R Street NW, Washington, DC 20007; (202) 727-1353.

• *Woodridge* Rhode Island Avenue and 18th Street NE, Washington, DC 20018; (202) 727-1401.

Falls Church/Mary Riley Styles Public Library In addition to an extensive general book collection, this small city library also has an excellent collection of records, tapes and audio books. Special collections include a local history collection which emphasizes the history of the City of Falls Church. (No regional libraries.)

120 North Virginia Avenue, Falls Church, VA 22046; (703) 241-5030/35.

Fairfax County Public Libraries This general public library system, has special collections on Virginia state and local history, business and technology, records, film and video materials, audiobooks and more. Holdings exceed 2 million volumes. The system has one main library and six regional branch libraries:

• *Fairfax City (Main)* 3915 Chain Bridge Road, Fairfax, VA 22030; (703) 246-2281/246–2741.

• *George Mason* 7001 Little River Turnpike, Annandale, VA 22003; (703) 256-3800.

• *Pohick* 6450 Sydenstricker Road, Burke, VA 22015; (703) 644-7333.

• *Reston* 11925 Bowman Towne Drive, Reston, VA 22090; (703) 689-2700.

• *Sherwood* 2501 Sherwood Hall Lane, Alexandria, VA 22306; (703) 765-3645.

• *Tysons-Pimmit* 7584 Leesburg Pike, Falls Church, VA 22043; (703) 790-8088.

Montgomery County Public Libraries This general public library system includes a *Special Needs Library* in Bethesda that provides braille books, audio books, large-type books and tapes. The system also has a circulating collection of videocassettes and 16mm films. Holdings exceed 1.1 million volumes and 30,000 phonograph records.

The system's Administrative Headquarters are at 99 Maryland Avenue in Rockville, MD (see below). There are also three other regional branch libraries in the system:

• *Bethesda* 7400 Arlington Road, Bethesda, MD 20814; (301) 986-8450.

• *Gaithersburg* 18330 Montgomery Village Avenue, Gaithersburg, MD 20879; (301) 840-2515.

• *Rockville* 99 Maryland Avenue, Rockville, MD 20850; (301) 279-1953.

• *Wheaton* 11701 Georgia Avenue, Wheaton, MD 20902; (301) 949-7710.

Prince George's County Library System This general public library system features major special collections on horse breeding and racing (Bowie Branch), planned communities (Greenbelt Branch), children's books (Hyattsville Branch), local Maryland history (Hyattsville Branch) and African-Americans (Oxon Hill Branch). The system's Talking Book Center is available for readers with visual and/or physical impairments. The system also features numerous monthly book discussion groups for adults at various branches. Holdings exceed 1.1 million volumes. (No regional libraries/branches only.)

Main Library & Administrative Offices, 6532 Adelphi Road, Hyattsville, MD 20782; (301) 699-3500.

SPECIAL COLLECTIONS & ARCHIVES

American Institute of Architects Library The Library contains holdings which emphasize American architecture and practices, urban planning and building technology (22,000 volumes). It also contains a small slide and film collection. Open to the public for reading and reference only.

1735 New York Avenue NW, Washington, DC 20006; (202) 626-7492.

Assassination Archives & Research Center Created in 1984 for the study of political assassinations throughout world history, the Center has holdings with a special focus on post-World War II American assassinations. It maintains a biographical archives and library of several thousand volumes, with bulk of holdings concerning the John F. Kennedy and Martin Luther King, Jr. slayings. It also contains extensive research files. Open to the qualified researchers and the general public for reading and reference.

918 F Street NW, Suite 510, Washington, DC 20004; (202) 393-1917.

Broadcast Pioneers Library The Library is dedicated to the history and preservation of radio and television broadcasting. Holdings include books, scripts, oral histories, photographs and other resources from the beginnings of broadcasting to the present. Open to scholars and the general public by appointment only.

1771 N Street NW, Washington, DC 20036; (202) 223-0088.

Brookings Institution Library This collection, which emphasizes information on politics and the social sciences, is primarily for use by the Brookings Institution staff. It contains 80,000 volumes and 650 periodicals. Open to scholars and the general public by appointment only.

1775 Massachusetts Avenue NW, Washington, DC 20036; (202) 797-6240.

Children's Hospital National Medical Center The Center contains holdings pertaining to pediatrics, hospital administration, nursing, general medicine and dentistry (13,000 volumes and 480 journals). Open to the general public by appointment only; users must be college age or older.

111 Michigan Avenue NW, Washington, DC 20010; (202) 745-3195/96.

Congressional Quarterly/Editorial Research Reports Library A useful collection of information on American political science, history, U.S. government and legislative processes, current events and international relations, the Library contains 10,000 volumes and 20,000 microforms covering all congressional hearings and voting records from 1973 to the present. Open to subscribers by appointment only.

1414 22nd Street NW, Fourth Floor, Washington, DC 20037; (202) 887-8569.

Corcoran Gallery & School of Art Archives The Archives maintains the records of the Corcoran Gallery & School of Art, from the institution's founding in 1869 to the present. Records reflect the Gallery and School's involvement in the development of American art, especially during the nineteenth century. The collection includes exhibition history, catalogues, artist's correspondence, loan records, nineteenth century registrarial records, architectural records and vertical files on American artists. Open to serious scholars by appointment.

17th Street and New York Avenue NW, Washington, DC 20006; (202) 638-3211.

Daughters of the American Revolution Library This collection contains extensive materials on American family history and genealogy, as well as materials on U.S. state and local histories. Librarians also maintain 80,000 research files of unpublished genealogical records drawn from various sources across the nation, and several thousand unpublished volumes written by DAR members. Contains 75,000 volumes. Open to researchers; non-DAR members pay daily entrance fee.

1776 D Street NW, Washington, DC 20006; (202) 628-1776.

Dumbarton Oaks Research Libraries The *Center For Byzantine Studies* is the most extensive library of its kind in the nation, covering history and culture of the Byzantine period and related periods (late classical, Hellenistic, Islamic and medieval East European). Holdings exceed 108,000 volumes and 950 periodicals. Open to qualified researchers by application only.

The *Center for Studies in Landscape Architecture* covers the history of garden design, landscape architecture and horticulture. Contains 13,500 volumes. Open primarily to scholars.

1703 32nd Street NW, Washington, DC 20007; (202) 342-3240.

Environmental Law Institute Library The Library contains 10,000 volumes and 300 periodicals dealing with environmental law and policy, toxic substances, hazardous wastes and land use. Open to the public.

1616 P Street NW, Washington, DC 20036; (202) 328-5150.

Fairfax Law Library The largest county law library in Virginia features 30,000 volumes as well as additional legal materials on microforms, audio books and videocassettes. Open to the public.

4110 Chain Bridge Road, Fairfax, VA 22030; (703) 246-2170.

Folger Shakespeare Library The Library houses the largest collection of early editions of Shakespeare in the world, as well as one of the best collections of materials relating to the English and Continental European Renaissance. The Library's superb Reading Room is open to qualified scholars only, while the Great Hall features year-round exhibits based on the Folger's extensive holdings. The Library also sponsors an Evening Poetry Series and other events which are open to the general public.

201 East Capitol Street SE, Washington, DC 20003; (202) 544-4600.

The Foundation Center Library The Library contains a wealth of information on foundations in America, including annual reports, IRS information returns for more than 30,000 U.S. foundations and a collection of 5,000 books and pamphlets on private American philanthropy. There is also extensive material on fundraising and nonprofit management. Open to the general public, but all materials must be used on the premises.

1001 Connecticut Avenue NW, Suite 938, Washington, DC 20036; (202) 331-1400.

Historical Society of Washington, D.C.   Housed in the magnificent Christian Heurich Mansion near Dupont Circle, the Society's *Library of Washington History* contains 20,000 volumes, 5,000 manuscripts and more than 80,000 prints pertaining to the history and people of Washington. The Library's comprehensive holdings cover all aspects of the city. Open to the general public Wed, Fri and Sat (10 am to 4 pm). An admission fee for nonmembers of the Society may be charged.

1307 New Hampshire Avenue NW, Washington, DC 20036; (202) 785-2068.

Kass Judaic Library   The Library contains more than 6,000 volumes and periodicals of Jewish interest, including materials on American Jewish communities, the Holocaust, Jews in other countries and the nation of Israel. Open to the general public for research. Materials may be checked out by members of the Center only.

Jewish Community Center, 6125 Montrose Road, Rockville, MD 20850; (301) 881-0100.

National Academy of Sciences Library   Archival holdings of the Library comprise publications of the National Academy of Sciences, the National Academy of Engineering, the National Research Council and the Institute of Medicine. The Library also contains about 500 periodicals. Open to the general public by appointment, but all materials must be used in the Library.

2101 Constitution Avenue NW, Washington, DC 20418; (202) 334-2125.

National Center for Standards & Certification Information   The Center contains a reference collection of more than 240,000 standards, specifications, test methods, codes and recommended practices being used in the United States. Open to the public for reference and referral.

National Institute of Standards and Technology, Administration Building (Room A633), Quince Orchard & Clopper Roads, Gaithersburg, MD 20899; (301) 975-4040.

National Civil Rights Library   The Library houses materials devoted to the civil rights and women's rights movements in America. It contains 60,000 volumes on minorities, age, handicapping conditions, economics, education, sociology, employment, housing and population.

1121 Vermont Avenue NW, Room 709, Washington, DC 20425; (202) 376-8114.

National Genealogical Society Library   The Society's Library specializes in American local history and genealogy, with source materials like Bible records, cemetery inscriptions, probate records, vital records and pamphlets. It contains 35 vertical files and 16,000 volumes of unpublished genealogical compilations and source material. Admission is free to members of the Society; $5 per day to nonmembers.

4527 17th Street North, Arlington, VA 22207; (703) 525-0050.

National Geographic Society Library   The Society's holdings span a diversity of subjects which mirror its wide interests, including guidebooks, histories, regional descriptions, reference, general science, geography, cartography, art, natural history, polar exploration, travel and voyages. The Library contains 76,000 volumes, 110,000 maps, 1,500 atlases, 1.5 million clippings and 750 periodical subscriptions. Open to qualified scholars and researchers, with some restrictions.

17th and M Streets NW, Washington, DC 20036; (202) 857-7783.

National Housing Center Library   The Center's Library focuses on all aspects of residential construction and home ownership. It contains 10,000 volumes, 20,000 pamphlets, catalogues, government publications (plus foreign material) and 350 journals. Open to the general public.

National Association of Home Builders, 15th and M Streets NW, Washington, DC 20005; (202) 822-0203.

National Institute of Standards & Technology Research Information Center   The Center provides standards of measurement, quality, performance and the standard physical constants needed in scientific and technical work. It contains 200,000 monographs, bound volumes of journals and publications of international scientific and technical institutions, plus 2,400 journals. The Center also has a fascinating collection of rare books covering the development of the science of measurement.

NIST Administration Building (Room E–106), Quince Orchard & Clopper Roads, Gaithersburg, MD 20899; (301) 975-3052.

National Security Archive The Archive's staff of 30 provides scholars, journalists, librarians, students and other researchers with unclassified and declassified government documents relating to intelligence, espionage, defense, foreign policy and international economics. NSA serves as a nonprofit research institute, library and publisher on these matters. It was founded by former *Washington Post* reporter Scott Armstrong and *New York Times* reporter Ray Bonner. Open to the general public, but call ahead first.

1775 Massachusetts Avenue NW, Washington, DC 20036; (202) 797-0882.

National Trust for Historic Preservation Library The Library's holdings focus on historic preservation, especially relating to archaeology, architecture, building industry, community development and museums. It contains 11,000 volumes, 13,000 vertical files, 500 periodicals, 35,000 slides and black-and-white prints, films and tapes and a special collection of microfiched newspaper clippings. Open to members of the Trust by appointment.

1785 Massachusetts Avenue NW, Washington, DC 20036; (202) 673-4038.

Organization of American States Library The Library's holdings examine all aspects of inter-American relations and the peoples and cultures of the Americas. It contains 310,000 volumes, 4,500 periodicals, more than 200,000 documents and publications of the OAS and 100,000 documents issued by other international organizations and member governments, as well as a collection of more than 5,000 rare books. Open to the general public.

17th Street and Constitution Avenue NW, Washington, DC 20006; (202) 458-3000.

Pan American Health Organization Library This collection of more than 50,000 volumes covers public health in all of the countries of the Americas. Documents and publications of the World Health Organization are also included in holdings. Open to the general public.

525 23rd Street NW, Washington, DC 20037; (202) 861-3200.

St. Elizabeth's Hospital Health Sciences Library The main focus of the hospital's holdings is on psychiatry, psychology, psychoanalysis, neurology, nursing, social work and religion. The Library contains 35,000 volumes, 300 journals and files of bulletins, reports and catalogs. Open to the general public by appointment only.

2700 Martin Luther King, Jr. Avenue SE, Washington, DC 20032; (202) 373-7175.

Smithsonian Institution Libraries & Archival Collections The Libraries and Archival Collections are two separate systems within the gigantic Smithsonian Institution complex, comprising millions of items in a total of 26 local branch and archival locations. Holdings reflect the wide-ranging research interests of the Smithsonian Institution, including aeronautics and astronautics, space, American history and technology, natural history, museology, the history of science and all aspects of culture and the arts.

To use any Smithsonian Institution Archive or Library facility, scholars, serious researchers and the general public *must* call ahead for an appointment. Please note that hours vary at each location and that no location is open on either Saturday or Sunday.

Smithsonian Institution Archives

• *Archives of American Art* Dedicated to the collection, preservation and study of papers and other primary records of the history of visual arts in America, the Archives is the world's single largest source for such information. Comprising more than 8 million items, the Archives includes correspondence, journals, business papers and other documentation of artists, dealers, critics, art historians and art institutions from the eighteenth century to the present. Also included in the Archives are some 3,000 oral history interviews, 300,000 photographs and 25,000 works of art on paper.

National Museum of American Art, 8th and F Streets, NW, Washington, DC 20560; (202) 357-4251.

• *Archives Center* The Center provides research materials for museum staff, scholars, students, writers and other researchers. It is also responsible for the care and use of a growing body of holdings, currently exceeding some 265 collections occupying more than 5,000 cubic feet of space. The holdings are organized in four areas: manuscript collections (personal papers and records of businesses and other organizations), the collection of advertising history, the historical photographs collection and a collection of films, audio tapes and videotapes covering a number of subject areas.

National Museum of American History, 12th Street and Constitution Avenue, NW, Washington, DC 20560; (202) 357-3270.

• *Catalogue of American Portraits* This is a national reference center with files that contain photographs and records of more than 80,000 likenesses of historically important Americans. Arranged alphabetically by subject, the Catalogue's files are extensively cross-referenced by artist.

National Portrait Gallery, 8th and F Streets NW, Washington, DC 20560; (202) 357-2578.

• *Collection Archive* The Archive contains curatorial records of more than 13,000 objects related to the permanent art collection of the Smithsonian's Hirshhorn Museum and Sculpture Garden. All object files include photographs, official records, research notes, correspondence and copies of reference material assembled by the curatorial staff.

Hirshhorn Museum and Sculpture Garden, 8th Street and Independence Avenue SW, Washington, DC 20560; (202) 357-3230.

• *Elliot Elisofon Photographic Archives* The Archives is devoted to the collection, preservation and management of visual resources, while serving as an international clearinghouse for information about African art and cultural history. It houses a rapidly growing permanent collection of 150,000 color slides, 70,000 black-and-white photographs, more than 50 feature films and videotapes and 120,000 feet of unedited film footage. The Archives also maintains a collection of vintage engravings and antique maps dating from the sixteenth to nineteenth centuries.

National Museum of African Art, 950 Independence Avenue SW, Washington, DC 20560; (202) 357-4654.

• *Freer Gallery of Art & Arthur M. Sackler Gallery Library* The collection numbers approximately 45,000 volumes, mostly on Asian and Near Eastern art, with more than half of the holdings in Chinese, Japanese and

Korean. The Library also contains more than 800 volumes of rare books, ranging from the Ming and Qing dynasties in China, to Japanese books of woodblock prints and early travel books on Asia. Holdings also include information on the life and art of James McNeill Whistler and his contemporaries.

Arthur M. Sackler Gallery of Art, 1050 Independence Avenue SW, Washington, DC 20560; (202) 357-2091.

• *Horticulture Research Center* Established to manage the grounds of the Smithsonian museums, the Center has also assembled research archives on horticulture and floriculture, both practical and historic. Holdings include the Burpee Collection of seed trade literature, florist memorabilia and prints and photographs depicting aspects of landscape design.

Office of Horticulture, Arts & Industries Building, 900 Jefferson Drive SW, Washington, DC 20560; (202) 357-1926.

• *Human Studies Film Archives* Established in 1981 to collect and preserve motion picture film and video recordings of western and nonwestern cultures, the Archives consists of more than 3 million feet of ethnographic film and video records of diverse cultures from every major geographical region of the world. The collection includes historic and contemporary, silent and sound and black-and-white and color footage. HFSA also holds supplementary materials related to each film in its collection, including still photographs, sound recordings, annotations, logs, field notes and manuscripts. Researchers must make appointments at least 48 hours in advance.

National Museum of Natural History, 10th Street and Constitution Avenue NW, Washington, DC 20560; (202) 357-3349.

• *Joseph Henry Papers* This division conducts research on the life of Joseph Henry (1797–1878), first secretary of the Smithsonian Institution. It examines the early history of the Smithsonian and the development of American science during the mid-nineteenth century. It also curates the Bell–Henry Library, which contains the scientific library of Alexander Graham Bell and the personal library of Henry. For these purposes, the division has obtained copies of approximately 90,000 manuscripts.

Arts & Industries Building, 900 Jefferson Drive SW, Washington, DC 20560; (202) 357-2787.

• *National Air & Space Archives* Comprising more than 30,000 subject files, the Archives' reference collections contain photographs, pamphlets, clippings, reports, manuscripts, technical manuals and drawings and articles on all aspects of the history and development of aviation and space science and exploration. The Archives contains the U.S. Air Force pre–1954 Still Photograph Collection, comprising 500,000 photographs of aircraft, airships, commercial aircraft, military and aerospace events and activities (available in videodisc). It also contains the Media Resources Unit (more than 4,000 aerospace films) and more than 2 million aircraft engineering drawings from the 1890s to the 1970s, either on microfilm or in print.

National Air & Space Museum, 7th Street and Independence Avenue SW, Washington, DC 20560; (202) 357-3133.

• *National Anthropological Archives* The NAA holds a large collection of historical manuscripts relating 3855/24linguistics, ethnology, archaeology, physical anthropology and history of North American natives. The photograph collection incorporates approximately 150,000 original negatives and prints made by photographers who worked with American Indian subjects.

National Museum of Natural History, 10th Street and Constitution Avenue NW, Washington, DC 20560; (202) 357-1986.

• *National Museum of American Art/National Portrait Gallery Library* The collection includes 60,000 catalogued volumes, principally on American art, history and photography. The Library also contains more than 400 drawers of vertical file material on American artists, art institutions and biography.

National Museum of American Art, 8th and G Streets NW, Washington, DC 20560; (202) 357-1300.

• *Office of Folklife Programs Archive/ Folkways Records Archive* The Archive contains materials documenting hundreds of folk cultures from the United States and many other countries, including 15,000 audio tapes, 300,000 photographs, 500,000 feet of motion picture film, 1,000 videotapes and several hundred research reports and related files. Holdings cover such subjects as occupational folklife, family folklore, American musical traditions and Afro-American and Native American performance traditions.

Office of Folklife Programs, 955 L'Enfant Plaza SW, Suite 2600, Washington, DC 20560; (202) 287-3251.

• *Office of Printing & Photographic Services* The Smithsonian's central photographic facility, the OPPS maintains a library of nearly 1 million negatives and transparencies in an environmentally controlled cold storage room. These materials include the work of Smithsonian photographers dating to the late 1800s, and are continually augmented by those of contemporary photographers.

Office of Printing & Photographic Services, Smithsonian Institution, 14th Street & Constitution Avenue NW, Room CB 054, Washington, DC 20560; (202) 357-1933.

• *Office of Research Support* The ORS maintains seven major research project databases totaling more than 530,000 art data records and 250,000 photographic images. The seven projects are the *Inventory of American Paintings Executed Before 1914*, a computerized index to more than 250,000 paintings in public and private collections; the *Inventory of American Sculpture*, an on-line interactive database containing information on sculpture and outdoor monuments; the *Pre–1877 Art Exhibition Catalogue Index*, recording works of art listed in catalogues and art exhibitions held in the United States and Canada through the centennial Exposition of 1876; the *Smithsonian Art Index*, which lists drawings, prints, paintings and sculptures located in Smithsonian scientific, technical and historical collections; the *Permanent Collection Database*, comprising more than 32,000 objects in the museum's collection; the *Peter A. Juley & Son Collection*, of more than 127,000 photographic negatives documenting American art and artists photographed between 1896 and 1975 by this New York City firm; and the *Slide & Photographic Archives*, a collection of more than 90,000 slides and 200,000 photographs available for study on the premises and 20,000 slides available for public borrowing.

National Museum of American Art, 9th and G Streets NW, Washington, DC 20560; (202) 357-1626.

• *Peale Family Papers* This division's files contain documents, correspondence, diaries, manuscript writings, secondary literature and some photographs which detail and illuminate the work of Charles Willson Peale, portraitist, museum keeper, naturalist and inventor.

National Portrait Gallery, 8th and F Streets NW, Washington, DC 20560; (202) 357-2565.

• *Smithsonian Institution Archives* The Archives was organized in 1967 to collect, preserve and make available the official records of the Smithsonian Institution, the papers of Smithsonian scientists and other staff members and the records of related professional organizations. Automated indices and collection-level descriptions are available to the more than 600 record units in the Archives to assist in reference service and information retrieval.

Arts & Industries Building, 900 Jefferson Drive SW, Washington, DC 20560; (202) 357-1420.

Smithsonian Institution Libraries

• *Central Reference & Loan Services* This division provides library services to the Institution's administrative, financial, publishing and public affairs offices, while coordinating on-line search services, circulation, interlibrary loan and document delivery across the system. It also houses general reference, biographical and interdisciplinary materials, as well as *Smithsoniana*, a special collection pertaining to the Smithsonian Institution.

Natural History Building, Room 27, 10th Street and Constitution Avenue NW, Washington, DC 20560; (202) 357-2139.

• *Dibner Library* The Library includes surviving books from the library of James Smithson, founder of the Institution, as well as 1,800 major holdings in the history of science and technology dating from the fifteenth to the twentieth centuries. It also contains extensive collections in natural history, archaeology, museum catalogues, printing and reproduction methods, almanacs, physical and mathematical sciences and scientific instrumentation.

National Museum of American History, First Floor (West Wing), 14th Street and Constitution Avenue NW, Washington, DC 20560; (202) 357-1568.

• *Museum Reference Center* The Center houses the world's largest known collection of bibliographic and documentary collections concerning all aspects of museology. It also offers museological reference, information and bibliographic services to the museum community worldwide.

Office of Museum Programs, Arts & Industries Building, Room 2235, 900 Jefferson Drive SW, Washington, DC 20560; (202) 786-2271.

• *Museum Support Center Library* The MSC provides information about the conservation of materials and technical aspects of conservation science, including archaeometry, medical entomology, occupational health hazards, taxonomic aspects of marine and estuarine fauna and molecular systematics and molecular evolution.

Museum Support Center, Room C2000, 4210 Silver Hill Road, Suitland, MD 20746; (301) 238-3666.

• *National Air & Space Museum Library* The Library has compiled information on aeronautics, space flight and all other kinds of flight—ballooning, gliding, airplanes and jets, the stratosphere and earth studies. It contains 900,000 photographs of aviation events, 10,000 documentary files (including drawings), 661 reels of microfilm, 210,600 NASA microfiche and a special collection of rare publications on aerospace.

National Air & Space Museum, Room 3100, 6th Street and Independence Avenue SW, Washington, DC 20560; (202) 357-3133.

• *National Museum of African Art Library* The Library's holdings focus on the visual arts of Africa, with supporting collections of African history, archaeology, religion, oral traditions, music, literature, children's books, curriculum materials and general reference books and maps.

National Museum of African Art, Quadrangle, Room 2138, 950 Independence Avenue SW, Washington, DC 20560; (202) 357-4875.

• *National Museum of American History Library* The Library contains 150,000 volumes on American history, the history of science and technology, decorative and graphic arts, numismatics, philately, photography, electricity and the history of musical instruments. It also houses 225,000 trade catalogues in a special collection.

National Museum of American History, Room 5016, 14th Street and Constitution Avenue NW, Washington, DC 20560; (202) 357-2414.

• *National Museum of Natural History Library* The

Library houses a large collection of materials on general biology, geology, evolution and ecology, with 16 smaller subject-based collections in the fields of entomology, invertebrate zoology, mineral sciences, vertebrate zoology, paleontology and others.

National Museum of Natural History, Room 51, 10th Street and Constitution Avenue NW, Washington, DC 20560; (202) 357-1496.

• *National Zoological Park Library* The Library contains books and serials on animal behavior, animal nutrition, care of animals in captivity, conservation and endangered species, horticulture, pathology and veterinary medicine and a special collection of publications from other zoos.

National Zoological Park, Education Building, 3001 Connecticut Avenue NW, Washington, DC 20008; (202) 673-4771.

Society of the Cincinnati Library The Society's magnificent building houses its Library, which contains biographies, vertical files, maps, manuscripts, prints, and microfilms on the history of the American Revolution. The Library, which contains 30,000 volumes, is open to the public.

2118 Massachusetts Avenue NW, Washington, DC 20008; (202) 785-2040.

Textile Museum/Arthur D. Jenkins Library The Library contains 13,000 reference volumes, about 350 periodicals and many auction catalogues and slides on textiles and rugs of the Asian, African, Latin American and Islamic cultures.

2320 S Street NW, Washington, DC 20008; (202) 667-0441.

U.S. GOVERNMENT AGENCY LIBRARIES

Army Corps of Engineers Technical Library This collection includes engineering monographs, technical reports, journals and publications of scientific and technical institutions throughout the world. Primarily for the use of Research Center staff, the Library may also be used by technical personnel of other government agencies upon request. Contains 100,000 items and 500 journals.

Kingman Building, Fort Belvoir, VA 22060; (703) 355-2387/88.

Bureau of the Census Library The Library contains 200,000 volumes on demography, economics, political science, business, education, public health, public administration and data processing, along with 3,000 journals and periodicals. About 85 percent of the Library's materials are government documents, including an extensive historical collection about the U.S. Census which dates from 1790 to the present and includes some 500 photographs. Open to qualified researchers.

Federal Building 3, Silver Hill Road, Room 2455, Suitland, MD 20233; (301) 763-5042.

Commerce Department Libraries The *Main Library* contains 50,000 volumes on business, commerce, foreign trade, economics and related subjects, along with 1,400 periodical titles. The *Law Library* contains 90,000 volumes and 150 journals, including an extensive government document and legislative collection. Both libraries are open to the general public.

• *Main Library* U.S. Department of Commerce Building, 14th Street and Constitution Avenue NW, Room 7046, Washington, DC 20230; (202) 377-2167.

• *Law Library* 14th and E Streets NW, Room 1894, Washington, DC 20030; (202) 377-5517.

Comptroller of the Currency Library The Library contains 40,000 volumes on such closely followed subjects as money, currency, banking, finance, economics and the law. Open to the general public.

Office of Comptroller of the Currency, 490 L'Enfant Plaza East SW, Washington DC 20219; (202) 566-2000.

Congressional Budget Office Library The Library has amassed a large collection of material on the federal budget, how the budget is passed and American economics. It contains 10,000 volumes and 400 periodicals. Open to the general public.

House Office Building (Annex 2), 2nd and D Streets SW, Washington, DC 20515; (202) 226-2635.

Consumer Product Safety Commission Library The Commission's Library contains 15,000 books, 12,000 indexed documents and 500 periodicals relating to consumer product safety, consumer law, business and economics, science and technology. Open to the general public.

5401 Westbard Avenue NW, Washington, DC 20207; (202) 492-6544.

Customs Service Library & Information Center   The Library contains 50,000 volumes, 800 periodicals and an extensive microform collection on U.S. customs duties and tariffs dating from 1789 to the present. Open to the general public.

U.S. Customs Service, 1301 Constitution Avenue NW, Room 3340, Washington, DC 20229; (202) 566-5642.

Drug Enforcement Administration Library   The Library contains a large collection of materials relating to the history, study and control of narcotics and dangerous drugs, especially as related to law enforcement. It contains 10,000 volumes, 225 journals and 24 drawers of vertical files. Open to the general public.

1405 I Street NW, Washington, DC 20537; (202) 633-1369.

Environmental Protection Agency Libraries   The EPA's *Main Library* contains 12,000 volumes, 21,000 government and private documents, 300,000 documents on microfiche (including technical EPA reports) and 800 journals, abstracts, indexes, newsletters and newspapers. The EPA's *Law Library* contains 8,000 volumes and 70 periodicals concentrating on federal law, with special emphasis on administrative and environmental law. Open to the general public by appointment; identification is required to enter the building.

401 M Street SW, Rooms 2902 & 2904, Washington, DC 20460; (202) 382-5919.

Federal Communications Commission Library   This 45,000–volume library contains a wealth of information on broadcasting, common carriers and telecommunications. Open to the general public on weekdays in the afternoon (1 to 4 pm).

1919 M Street NW, Washington, DC 20554; (202) 632-7100.

Federal Deposit Insurance Corporation Library   The Library contains 65,000 volumes in the fields of banking, finance, economics and law, and has current state codes and state bank commission annual reports on file. Open to researchers by appointment.

550 17th Street NW, Washington, DC 20429; (202) 393-8400.

Federal Emergency Management Agency Library Subjects covered in this Library include disaster response plans, civil defense, natural and manmade disasters and nuclear preparedness. It contains 4,000 volumes, 7,500 state emergency plans, 50 periodicals, 500 still photographs, 400 films and 3,000 slides. Open to the general public.

500 C Street SW, Room 123, Washington, DC 20472; (202) 646-3768.

Federal Energy Regulatory Commission Library The Library contains U.S. government documents, technical reports and journals on electric power, natural gas, oil and gas pipelines, utility regulation and federal energy law (30,000 volumes). Open to the general public.

825 North Capitol Street NE, Room 8502, Washington, DC 20426; (202) 357-5479.

Federal Maritime Commission Library The Library contains 10,000 volumes and many other materials relating to the U.S. shipping industry and regulation of common carriers by water. Open to the general public.

1100 L Street NW, Washington, DC 20573; (202) 523-5762.

Federal Trade Commission Library The Library contains 105,000 volumes and 200,000 microforms on legal, business and economic subjects relating to U.S. trade and business. There is a special emphasis on antitrust and consumer protection law and economics. Open to the general public.

6th Street and Pennsylvania Avenue NW, Rm 630, Washington, DC 20580; (202) 326-2395.

Foreign Service Institute Library The Library's holdings cover vital subjects pertinent to all 168 nations of the world, including international relations, politics and government, economics and finance, history and culture, linguistics and communication and social conditions. It contains 35,000 volumes and 500 journals. Open to the general public.

1400 Key Boulevard, Arlington, VA 22209; (703) 235-8727.

General Accounting Office Library The Library contains 75,000 volumes covering areas of program evaluation, policy analysis, energy, accounting, law and civilian and military regulation. The GAO's *Law Library* has a retrospective collection of legislative histories of all public laws. Open to the general public.

441 G Street NW, Washington, DC 20548; (202) 275-2180/275–2585.

General Services Administration Library The Library contains 135,000 volumes and 400 current periodicals on legal, procedures and other matters pertaining to the General Services Administration and its predecessor agencies. Open to the general public for reading and reference only.

18th and F Streets NW, Washington, DC 20405; (202) 501-0788.

Health & Human Services Department Library The Library houses one of the country's outstanding collections in social sciences, public welfare and health sciences. It contains 600,000 books and other publications and 2,500 periodicals. Open to the general public.

330 Independence Avenue SW, Room G–600, Washington, DC 20201; (202) 245-6791.

International Trade Commission Libraries The *Main Library* contains 80,000 volumes and 2,500 periodicals covering tariffs, commercial policy, foreign trade, economic conditions in foreign countries, foreign and domestic statistics, technical and economic problems of industry and various commodities. The *Law Library* contains 10,000 volumes and 75 periodicals on legislative histories of trade and tariff acts. Both libraries are open to the staff of government agencies and serious researchers only.

500 E Street NW, Room 301, Washington, DC 20436; (202) 252-1000.

Interstate Commerce Commission Library The Library contains 93,000 volumes examining administrative law, transportation law, economics and history. Its holdings also comprise legislative histories pertaining to government regulation of transportation agencies. Open to the general public.

12th Street and Constitution Avenue NW, Room 3392, Washington, DC 20423; (202) 275-7328.

Justice Department Libraries The combined libraries contain 300,000 volumes and more than 1 million pieces of microfiche and microfilm on federal and state law, political science, public administration, American history, energy, the environment, business, taxation and the history of the Justice Department. The following divisions are open to the public by appointment:

• *Main Library* Justice Building, Room 5400, (202) 633-3775.

• *Antitrust Library* Justice Building, Room 3310; (202) 633-2431.

• *Civil Library* Justice Building, Room 3344; (202) 633-3523.

• *Civil Rights Library* Justice Building, Room 7618; (202) 633-4098.

• *Criminal Library* Justice Building, Room 100; (202) 724-6934.

• *Land/Natural Resources Library* Justice Building, Room 2333; (202) 633-2768.

• *Tax Library* Justice Building, Room 4335; (202) 633-2819.

Department of Justice Building, 10th Street and Constitution Avenue NW, Washington, DC 20530; (202) 633-2000.

Labor Department Library Housing one of this country's most extensive collections on labor and economics, the Library also carries congressional documents relating to the Department's areas of responsibility. It contains 535,000 books, bound periodicals and pamphlets and 3,000 periodicals. Open to the general public.

200 Constitution Avenue NW, Room N2445, Washington, DC 20210; (202) 523-6992.

Marine Corps Historical Center This collection covers military and Marine Corps history in particular, with an emphasis on amphibious warfare. It contains 30,000 books and documents, 50 journals and Marine Corps unit histories. Historians are available for consultation on Marine Corps history. Open to the general public.

Washington Navy Yard, Building 58, Washington, DC; (202) 433-3447/4253.

Medal of Honor Library   The Library houses comprehensive collections in military science, management and investments. It contains 45,000 books and 2,200 pamphlets, as well as books and cassettes in foreign languages. Open to the public.

Fort George G. Meade, MD Building 8452, Fort Meade, MD 20755; (301) 667-4509.

National Agricultural Library   The Library's mission is to acquire and retain at least one copy of all substantive U.S. publications in the field of agriculture, including botany, chemistry, entomology, forestry, food and nutrition, law, water resources and economics. It contains 1.8 million volumes, 50,000 rare books, 60,000 photographs, 100,000 slides, 13,000 maps, 1,200 posters, 708,000 microfiches and 4,000 microfilm reels. Open to the general public.

U.S. Department of Agriculture, 12th Street and Independence Avenue SW, Washington, DC 20004; (202) 344-3755.

National Defense University Library   The Library's holdings center on foreign affairs, political and social science, government, economics, management, industry, and resource management. It contains 225,000 books, pamphlets, periodicals and government documents in open stacks and 100,000 classified documents in security vault. Those who wish to use the Library must secure advance permission from the Library director.

Fort Lesley J. McNair, 4th and P Streets SW, Washington, DC 20319; (202) 545-6700.

National Endowment for the Arts Library   The Library covers most aspects of American arts in the twentieth century, including arts development, financing, management, organization, preservation and promotion (most titles date from 1971). It contains 6,000 volumes, 125 periodicals and 10 drawers of vertical file material. Open to the public for reference by appointment only.

Old Post Office Building, 12th Street and Pennsylvania Avenue NW, Room 213, Washington, DC 20506; (202) 682-5485.

National Endowment for the Humanities Library The Library is a depository collection of publications resulting from NEH funding, as well as other NEH publications, documents relating to the history of the Endowment and the Jefferson Lecture manuscripts. The collection covers major holdings in all areas of the humanities and selected social science disciplines. Open to the general public by appointment only.

1100 Pennsylvania Avenue NW, Washington, DC 20506; (202) 786-0245.

National Gallery of Art Library The Library's emphasis is on Western European art (Middle Ages to present) and American art (post-Columbian to present). Its special collections, comprising 160,000 monographs and 975 periodicals, include artists' monographs, catalogues (exhibitions, auctions and private collections), early source materials on history of art and photographic archives of European and American art and architecture. Open to visiting scholars, graduate students and advanced readers by permission.

4th Street and Constitution Avenue NW, Washington, DC 20565; (202) 842-6511.

National Institutes of Health Libraries The NIH's *Main Library* contains 85,000 monographs, 165,000 bound periodical volumes, 3,200 current subscriptions, 2,700 monographic serials and 17,000 microforms on all aspects of health, illness, medical science, biology and experimental medicine. The *Division of Computer Research & Technology Library* contains 6,000 monographs and reports and 200 periodicals covering computer science, mathematics, statistics, medical information systems, computer applications in biomedical sciences and information science. Both libraries are open to the general public for reference use only.

National Institutes of Health, Buildings 10 & 12A, 9000 Rockville Pike, Bethesda, MD 20892; (301) 496-2184/1658.

National Labor Relations Board Library The Library's holdings cover the fields of law, labor relations, labor history, economics and political science. It contains 45,000 volumes, including 3,000 bound volumes of NLRB briefs and records in closed cases before the Supreme Court and the U.S. Court of Appeals. Open to the general public.

1717 Pennsylvania Avenue NW, Room 900, Washington, DC 20570; (202) 254-9055.

National Library of Medicine The Library, which has been indexing and cataloguing biomedical literature from around the world for over a century, became part of National Institutes of Health in 1968. It contains 3.5 million books, journals, theses, microforms, audiovisual productions, manuscripts, prints and photographs. Open to the general public.

8600 Rockville Pike, Bethesda MD 20894; (301) 496-4000.

National Oceanic & Atmospheric Administration Libraries The Administration's *Library Service Division* has information on meteorology, climatology, atmospheric physics, geodetic astronomy, nautical and aeronautical cartography, fisheries and fisheries science, ocean engineering, satellite meteorology, oceanography and marine biology. Also featured are fascinating rare book collection of sixteenth- and seventeeth-century scientific treatises. The various libraries of the division contain 800,000 volumes, 9,000 serials, 300,000 reports, meteorological data, synoptic weather maps and atlases. Open to the general public.

6001 Executive Boulevard, Rockville, MD 20852; (301) 443-8330.

National Science Foundation Library The Library, which contains 15,000 volumes and 600 periodicals, places an emphasis on history and philosophy of science, administration of science research and national and international science policy. Open to the general public.

National Science Foundation, 1800 G Street NW, Washington, DC 20550; (202) 357-9859.

Natural Resources Library Housed in the U.S. Department of the Interior, this is the lead library in the Department's *Natural Resources Library and Information System*, comprising more than 400 libraries and information centers across the nation. The Library contains 1 million volumes, including 21,000 serial titles, 250,000 microfiche, 8,000 reels of microfilm and 20,000 doctoral dissertations. Open to the public.

Department of the Interior, 18th and C Streets NW, Washington, DC 20240; (202) 343-3815.

Naval Historical Center Archives The holdings of the Archives cover naval policy, strategy, operations and tactics. Also included are histories of naval commands, documentation on German and Japanese naval operations during World War II and transcripts of oral histories by U.S. Navy personnel. The Archives contains 10,000 feet of manuscript or processed material, dating from 1939 to the present. Most holdings are open to the general public.

Washington Navy Yard, Building 57, Third Floor, 9th and M Streets SE, Washington, DC 20374; (202) 433-4131.

Naval Observatory Library This unique rotunda library contains 65,000 books and journals chiefly on astronomy, but also included are holdings in the fields of mathematics, physics and geophysics. The collection also contains periodicals dating from the seventeenth century, 800 rare books on astronomy published between 1500 and 1800 and a number of star charts and maps. Open to qualified scholars by permission of the librarian.

Massachusetts Avenue and 34th Street NW, Washington, DC 20390; (202) 653-1499.

Nuclear Regulatory Commission Library The holdings of the Library cover nuclear science and engineering, radiation biology, energy, environmental science and management. It contains 20,000 volumes, 1,100 periodicals and 450,000 technical reports on microfiche. Open to the general public by prior appointment.

1717 H Street NW, Washington, DC 20555; (202) 492-7748.

Office of Personnel Management Library The OPM's collection covers personnel management and public administration. It contains 75,000 volumes, including 1,500 volumes comprising a special civil service history.

1900 E Street NW, Washington, DC 20415; (202) 632-7640.

Patent and Trademark Office Scientific Library The Library contains 100,000 volumes and 12 million foreign patent documents covering all aspects of patent grants and filings in the United States and throughout the world. Other materials in the Library cover aspects of applied science and technology. Copies of U.S. patents are available through the Office's photoduplication service. Open to the general public.

U.S. Patent and Trademark Office, 2021 Jefferson Davis Highway, Arlington, VA 20231; (703) 557-2957.

Pentagon Library Formerly known as the *Army Library*, this collection comprises 120,000 volumes, 1 million documents and 1,500 periodicals with an emphasis on military art and science, political and social science, foreign affairs, government, economics, administration, management, computer science, law and legislative materials, Army studies, military unit histories and theses prepared by Army personnel assigned to civilian universities and colleges. Members of the public who have access to the Pentagon may use library materials in nonrestricted areas.

The Pentagon, Room 1A518, Washington, DC 20310; (202) 697-4301.

Performing Arts Library A joint project of the Library of Congress and the John F. Kennedy Center for the Performing Arts, the Library contains 5,000 volumes and 450 periodicals on all aspects of the performing arts. Users may make appointments to listen to any of the Library of Congress' 750,000 recordings. Qualified researchers may arrange to view videos from the collection in the audiovisual area. Open to the general public.

John F. Kennedy Center for the Performing Arts, 2700 F Street NW, Washington, DC 20566; (202) 416-8780/707–6245.

Postal Service Library The Library's holdings, which cover law, social sciences and technology, also include a unique collection of U.S. postal materials. The Library contains 100,000 items, with an emphasis on stamps, reports, clippings, photographs, general postal histories, periodicals of the national postal employee organizations and Universal Postal Union studies. Open to the general public.

475 L'Enfant Plaza SW, Washington, DC 20260; (202) 268-2904.

Securities & Exchange Commission Library The Library's holdings, amounting to 60,000 volumes and 200 periodicals, cover the fields of law, corporate and general finance, economics, accounting, public utilities and stock market activities and control. The Library also contains legislative histories of statutes administered by or affecting the Securities and Exchange Commission. Open to the general public.

450 5th Street NW, Washington, DC 20549; (202) 272-2618.

Small Business Administration Libraries The SBA's *Reference Library* contains 5,000 items and 180 journals covering business management, venture capital, entrepreneurship and research into problems of small business. The *Law Library* focuses on legislation relating to small businesses in America. Open to the general public by prior permission only.

409 3rd Street SW, Washington, DC 20416; (202) 205-6847.

Supreme Court of the United States Library The Library features a collection of 400,000 volumes pertaining to the U.S. legal system, with strong holdings in legislative history and materials about the Court and its justices. Only documents of record are open to the general public.

1 First Street NE, Washington, DC 20543; (202) 479-3000/3175.

Transportation Department Libraries The *Main Library* contains 425,000 volumes, 2,100 periodicals and 585,430 microforms on all aspects of transportation by land, underground and on sea, as well as related technical subjects. The Department's *Coast Guard Law Library* contains items which pertain to laws of the sea and Coast Guard history. Both libraries are open to the general public.

Main Library: 400 7th Street SW, Washington, DC 20590; (202) 366-4000. *Law Library*: 2100 2nd Street SW, Room 4407, Washington, DC 20593; (202) 267-2229.

Treasury Department Library The Library's holdings cover the fields of economics and law, with emphasis on taxation and public finance, money and banking, international law, international economics and domestic economic conditions. Holdings comprise 74,000 volumes, 250,000 microfiche and 8,000 reels of microfilm, including congressional records, reports and documents dating from 1789 to the present. Open to the general public, but identification is required to enter the building.

U.S. Treasury Building, Room 5030, 15th Street and Pennsylvania Avenue NW, Washington, DC 20220; (202) 566-2777.

U.S. Geological Survey Libraries The *Geological Survey Library* has extensive holdings on geology, paleontology, mineralogy, petrology, mineral resources, water resources, surveying and cartography, chemistry and physics, oceanography, soil science, zoology, natural history, remote sensing, environmental science and geothermal energy. It contains 785,000 bound volumes, 269,000 pamphlets, 302,000 maps, 10,000 doctoral dissertations on microfilm and microfiche and 360,000 NTIS reports, Environmental Impact Statements and serial and periodical titles on microfiche.

The *Cartographic Information Center* contains approximately 400,000 sheets of largely geologic and topographic maps dating from the 1850s to the present. Coverage includes general topographic, geological and geophysical features, mineral resources, soil, water and material vegetation. Both libraries are open to the general public.

National Center, 12201 Sunrise Valley Drive, Reston, VA 22092; (703) 648-4302/5555.

U.S. Information Agency Library The USIA, charged with disseminating information about America to the rest of the world, maintains this Library which emphasizes international relations, area studies, political science and Americana. The Library contains 60,000 volumes, 850 current periodicals and an extensive 85–cabinet newspaper morgue. Open to the general public by appointment only.

301 4th Street SW, Room 135, Washington, DC 20547; (202) 485-8947.

Veterans Administration Library The VA's *Central Office Library* contains 13,000 monographs, 900 journal titles, 650 audiovisual titles and a great deal of microfilm and microfiche. Its holdings cover aging, health care planning and administration, herbicides, public administration and military and Veterans Administration history. Open to the general public.

810 Vermont Avenue NW, Room 976, Washington, DC 20420; (202) 233-4000.

Walter Reed Army Medical Center Library The Center's *Main Medical Library* contains 40,000 volumes and 750 periodical titles on clinical medicine, surgery, psychiatry, dentistry, military medicine, nursing and allied health. The Library is completely automated with an integrated library system for cataloguing, circulation, serial control, acquisitions, tracking interlibrary loans and an on-line public access catalogue. Open to qualified researchers and scholars only.

Walter Reed Army Medical Center, Building 2 (Room 2–G), 6825 16th Street NW, Washington, DC 20012; (202) 576-1238.

UNIVERSITY & COLLEGE LIBRARIES

American University Libraries There are three major libraries on AU's campus: the Bender Library (Main), the Washington College of Law Library and the Wesley Theological Seminary Library. All three libraries are open to the general public (subject to some library restrictions), but only AU students may check materials out.

• *Bender Library* With 460,000 books, periodicals, theses and scores, 463,000 microforms and 10,500 non-print media items, this is the main Library on campus. Special collections include the *Artemas Martin Mathematics Library* (devoted chiefly to early works in the field of mathematics), Americana, early works on surveying, the *Charles Nelson Spinks Collection* of rare Japanese materials and the *American Peace Society Library*.

American University, 4400 Massachusetts Avenue NW, Washington, DC 20016; (202) 885-3232.

• *Washington College of Law Library* The Library houses a collection of 121,000 books, periodicals and other materials on the law, including the *Richard Baxter Collection* on international law.

American University, 4400 Massachusetts Avenue NW, Washington, DC 20016; (202) 885-2625.

• *Wesley Theological Seminary Library* The Library contains 112,000 volumes and 550 periodical titles on religion, philosophy, theology and related subjects, including a special collection on the Methodist church and its history.

American University, 4400 Massachusetts Avenue NW, Washington, DC 20016; (202) 885-8691.

Catholic University of America Libraries There are two major libraries on CU's campus: the John K. Mullen Memorial Library (Main) and the Robert J. White Law Library. Both libraries are open to the general public (subject to some library restrictions), but only CU students may check materials out.

• *John K. Mullen Memorial Library* This is the main Library on campus, containing 1 million volumes and 7,000 magazines and other serial publications. Among the Library's most important collections are holdings on anthropology, architecture, archives (papers of nineteenth- and twentieth-century labor leaders), botany, canon law, Celtic philology, chemistry, medieval studies, music, social work, drama and theology. The *Institute of Christian and Oriental Research* also contains important collections.

Catholic University of America, 620 Michigan Avenue NE, Washington, DC 20064; (202) 635-5077/5070.

• *Robert J. White Law Library* The Library contains 140,000 volumes and 500 journal titles covering a wide range of legal subjects, including codes from all 50 U.S. states.

Catholic University of America, 620 Michigan Avenue NE, Washington, DC 20064; (202) 635-5155.

Gallaudet University Library The Library contains 180,000 volumes and 1,500 periodicals concentrating on the liberal arts, including an extensive archive of historical materials on deaf people and deafness. The University, one of America's premier institutions for the education and training of deaf people, also has a special collection of unpublished masters' theses and doctoral dissertations related to deafness and is staffed by information specialists on deafness who are available for consultation. The Library houses the *Baker Collection*, an excellent collection of rare books published from 1526 to the Civil War period. Open to the general public by appointment.

Gallaudet University, 800 Florida Avenue NE, Washington, DC 20002; (202) 651-5212/17.

George Mason University Library The University's main *Fenwick Library* contains 265,000 volumes, 400,000 microforms and 3,200 current periodicals. Among the Library's special collections are the *Federal Theatre Project Collection* of the Library of Congress, the *Mann*

Collection of Early Virginia Maps (dating from 1700), the *American Symphony Orchestra League Archives* and the *Ollie Atkins Photograph Collection.* Open to the general public, but only GMU students may check materials out.

George Mason University, 4400 University Drive, Fairfax, VA 22030; (703) 323-2391.

George Washington University Libraries   There are three major libraries on GWU's campus: the Melvin Gelman Library (Main), the Jacob Burns Law Library and the Medical Center Library. The Gelman and Medical Center Libraries are open to the general public, while the Law Library is open only to qualified scholars or researchers by appointment.

• *Melvin Gelman Library*   This is the main Library on campus, with more than 1 million volumes, 9,000 periodicals, 2,500 university publications and 18,000 theses and dissertations. Holdings include a *Map Collection* of more than 35,000 U.S. Geological Survey maps and 2,500 Defense Mapping Agency maps, microforms of *English Literary Periodicals* from the seventeenth and eighteenth centuries and a collection of *American Periodicals Serials* from the eighteenth and nineteenth centuries.

George Washington University, 2130 H Street NW, Washington, DC 20052; (202) 994-6558.

• *Jacob Burns Law Library*   One of the nation's few depositories for records and briefs of the U.S. Court of Customs and Patent Appeals, the Library contains more than 60,000 volumes, microforms and 1,500 legal and scholarly periodicals.

George Washington University, National Law Center, 716 20th Street NW, Washington, DC 20052; (202) 994-6646/48.

• *Medical Center Library*   Named after Paul Himmelfarb, the Library has substantial holdings related to medicine and health, including 20,000 monographs, 1,400 serials and 1,220 audiovisual items.

George Washington University, 2300 I Street NW, Washington, DC 20052; (202) 676-2850/2962.

Georgetown University Libraries   There are four major libraries on GU's campus: the Lauinger Library (Main), the Edward Bennett Williams Law Library, the Dahlgren Medical Center Library and the National Reference Center for Bioethics Literature. The Lauinger Library's main areas are open to the general public, while the Rare Book Reading Rooms are open to qualified researchers only. The Law Library is open to GU law students, faculty and members of the Bar only. GU's other two libraries are open to the general public.

• *Lauinger Library* Named after Joseph Mark Lauinger, Georgetown University's main Library contains 1.3 million volumes and 706,000 microtext items. The Library also houses 22 superb rare book collections, including an outstanding Dickens collection, the *Shea Collection* (early Americana and American Indians), the *Robert F. Wagner Papers*, the *McCarthy Historical Project Archive* and 55,000 photographs from the photo morgue of *Quigley Publications* (publishers of "Motion Picture Herald" and "Motion Picture Daily").

Georgetown University, 37th & O Streets NW, Washington, DC 20057; (202) 687-7425.

• *Edward Bennett Williams Law Library* The Library contains more than 1.5 million items, including microforms and audiovisuals, with an emphasis on administrative, comparative and international law.

Georgetown University, 111 G Street NW, Washington, DC 20001; (202) 642-9162.

• *Dahlgren Medical Center Library* Named after John Vinton Dahlgren, the Library contains 151,000 volumes, 1,750 journal titles, 11,300 audiovisual programs and 2,000 historic and special collections on medicine, health and medical sciences.

Georgetown University, 3900 Reservoir Road NW, Washington, DC 20007; (202) 687-1266.

• *National Reference Center for Bioethics Literature* The Center features an extensive collection of 15,700 volumes, 80,000 article-length documents and 220 periodicals on bioethics, the systematic study of the social and ethical implications of practices or developments in biology and medicine.

Kennedy Institute of Ethics, Georgetown University, Washington, DC 20057; (202) 687-3885.

Howard University Libraries There are two main libraries on campus: the Undergraduate Library and the Founder's Graduate Library. There are also more specialized collections related to architecture and planning, business and public administration, theater, divinity, health sciences, law, social work and other disciplines in various other HU campus buildings.

• *Undergraduate Library* This general-use Library contains 100,000 volumes, 2,200 serials and 1 million microform items. The *Media Center* houses a phonograph collection, audiovisual software, support equipment and soundproof listening/viewing rooms. Open to the general public, but only HU students may check materials out.

Howard University, 500 Howard Place NW, Washington, DC 20059; (202) 636-5060.

• *Founders Graduate Library* The Library contains 500,000 volumes and 6,000 current periodicals. Special collections include an antislavery collection of documents, English books dating from 1641 to 1700, urban documents and historic papers from the British Parliament. Open to the general public, with the exception of certain special collections.

Howard University, 500 Howard Place NW, Washington, DC 20059; (202) 636-7250/52.

• *Architecture & Planning Library* The Library contains 22,000 volumes, 25,000 slides and 375 current periodicals on architecture, landscape planning and other related subjects. It also houses a special collection of stereophotogrammetric maps of Washington, DC. Open to the general public.

Howard University, 2366 6th Street NW, Washington, DC 20059; (202) 636-7773/74.

• *Business & Public Administration Library* The Library contains 35,000 volumes and 2,100 current serials on business, management and public administration topics. Open to the general public.

Howard University, 2600 6th Street NW, Washington, DC 20059; (202) 636-5161.

• *Channing Pollock Theater Collection* This is a large collection of books, manuscripts, pictures, playbills, posters, broadsides, and memorabilia of the performing arts. Emphasis on nineteenth- and twentieth-century English and American drama and theater. Open to the general public.

Howard University, 500 Howard Place NW, Washington, DC 20059; (202) 636-7259.

• *Divinity Library* The focus of this collection is on

African-American church history, theology, religious education, biblical studies and ministry. There are also complete sets of numerous old journals, many acquired from New York's Auburn Seminary. The Library contains 101,000 volumes and 356 current serials. Open to the general public.

Howard University, 1240 Randolph Street NE, Washington, DC 20017; (202) 636-7282.

• *Health Sciences Library* The Libary contains extensive collections on medicine, dentistry, health and nursing, including many vertical files on prominent African-Americans in these fields. Its holdings comprise 206,000 volumes, 4,000 serials and more than 5,000 audiovisual materials. Open to the general public.

Howard University, 600 W Street NW, Washington, DC 20059; (202) 636-6433/6545.

• *Social Work Library* The Library contains 30,000 volumes and 746 current journals on intervention, direct services, community organization and development and social administration. Open to the general public.

Howard University, 6th Street & Howard Place NW, Washington, DC 20059; (202) 636-7316.

Johns Hopkins University Libraries While the main campus of this prestigious academic institution is in nearby Baltimore, Maryland, JHU also has two notable libraries at its satellite campuses in the Washington area: the R.E. Gibson Library & Information Center and the School of Advanced International Studies Library.

• *R. E. Gibson Library & Information Center* The Applied Physics Laboratory Collection focuses on mathematics, physics, electronics, aeronautics, astronautics, computer sciences and biomedical engineering. The Library contains 60,000 volumes and 1,000 periodicals. Open to the general public.

Johns Hopkins University/Extension Campus, Johns Hopkins Road, Laurel, MD 20707; (301) 953-5151.

• *School of Advanced International Studies Library* Named after Sydney and Elsa Mason, the Library's holdings cover such subjects as diplomacy, international relations, international law and organization, international economics, history, politics and the economics of world geographic areas. It contains 90,000 volumes, 900 periodicals and newspapers. Open to qualified researchers by permission of the librarian only.

Johns Hopkins University/Extension Campus, 1740 Massachusetts Avenue NW, Washington, DC 20036; (202) 785-6805/07.

Montgomery College Library Located on the college's Rockville, Maryland campus, the Library has extensive holdings in most subject areas (especially strong in music and musical scores). It contains 108,000 volumes, 850 periodicals and 7,500 recordings. Open to the general public.

Montgomery College, 51 Mannakee Street, Rockville, MD 20850; (301) 279-5067.

Mount Vernon College Library The College's main Eckles Library has especially strong holdings in women's studies, fine arts, interior design and the decorative arts. It contains 60,000 books and other publications. Open to the general public.

Mount Vernon College, 2100 Foxhall Road NW, Washington, DC 20007; (202) 331-3544.

Northern Virginia Community College Libraries Each of NOVA's five campuses in the Washington metropolitan area has a library which is available for use by its students as well as the general public. Only NOVA students may check materials out of the libraries listed below.

• *Alexandria* The Library contains 77,000 volumes and 370 periodicals.

3001 North Beauregard Street, Alexandria, VA 22311; (703) 845-6231.

• *Annandale* The Library contains 94,000 volumes and 520 periodicals.

8333 Little River Turnpike, Annandale, VA 22003; (703) 323-3128.

• *Loudoun* The Library contains 36,000 volumes and 375 periodicals.

1000 Harry Flood Byrd Highway, Sterling, VA 22170; (703) 450-2567.

• *Manassas* The Library contains 35,000 volumes and 200 periodicals.

6901 Sudley Road, Manassas, VA 22110; (703) 257-6640.

• *Woodbridge* The Library contains 34,000 volumes and 259 periodicals.

15200 Neabsco Mills Road, Woodbridge, VA 22191; (703) 878-5733.

Prince George's Community College Library This general-use Library contains 75,000 volumes, 483 periodicals, microfilm backfiles and videocassettes, 12,000 slides, 3,000 audiotapes and 5,700 phonorecords. It also has special collections of books and periodicals on "The Film as Art" and on "Nursing in America." Listening and viewing facilities are provided. Open to the general public.

Prince George's Community College, 301 Largo Road, Largo, MD 20772; (301) 322-0105.

University of District of Columbia Library UDC's main library facility covers eight major subject areas: business, education, human ecology, life sciences, physical sciences, engineering, technology, and liberal and fine arts. Special collections include *Human Relations Area Files*, the *Afro-Hispanic-American Media Collection*, the *Nichols Collection of American History* and the *Slave Narrative & Source Materials Collection*. Open to the general public.

University of the District of Columbia, Main Campus (Van Ness), 4200 Connecticut Avenue NW, Washington, DC 20008; (202) 282-7501.

University of Maryland Libraries The university's main Library is the *Theodore R. McKeldin Library*, containing reference works, periodicals, circulating books and other materials in all fields. The Library's branches include the *Hornbake Undergraduate Library*, the *Engineering & Physical Sciences Library*, the *Music Library*, the *Architecture Library*, the *Art Library* and the *Chemistry Library*. Total holdings comprise 1.7 million volumes, 2.4 million microform units, newspapers, and periodicals and a wealth of government documents, phonograph records, films and filmstrips. Open to the general public.

University of Maryland, College Park, MD 20742; (301) 405-5704/37.

Virginia Theological Seminary Library The Library's main collection emphasizes biblical studies, theology, Anglicanism, systematic theology and church history. Total holdings comprise more than 100,000 volumes. Open to the general public.

3737 Seminary Road, Alexandria, VA 22304; (703) 370-6602.

Bookstores & Book Dealers

Where is human nature so weak as in a bookstore?
—HENRY WARD BEECHER

Lord! When you sell a man a book you don't sell him just twelve ounces of paper and ink and glue—you sell him a whole new life. Love and friendship and humour and ships at sea by night —there's all heaven and earth in a book, a real book.

—CHRISTOPHER MORLEY

U pon entering a bookstore—a real bookstore, as Christopher Morley might say—the biblioholic is seized with a passion not unlike that of the explorer, the archaeologist or the deep sea diver. It is the thrill of the hunt, the keen expectation of discovering treasures which can be savored and enjoyed for a lifetime.

After spending many happy hours browsing through bookstores here in the United States and in Europe, my chief observation is that each store is a reflection of the habits, thinking and tastes of its owner/s. Get to know all the nooks and crannies of a favorite bookstore, and you'll have learned a lot about its owner/s as well.

Like other retail ventures, a bookstore's real measure is in the quality and quantity of merchandise you see. When someone has carefully considered which titles the store should carry, there will be a discernible pattern of acquisition reflected in the bookstore's inventory. And when this pattern of acquisition is further matched by a sufficient quantity of books—organized and arranged in interesting, compelling ways—the urge to buy can become overwhelming.

If you ever feel this way in a bookstore, whether you break down and make a purchase or not, take a moment to let the owner or manager know. He or she will be delighted to hear that the hundreds of decisions made each day to build inventory, display merchandise and anticipate reader interests have paid off.

In 1989, this chapter listed some 450 "bookstores and

223

newsstands in the District of Columbia, suburban
Maryland and suburban Virginia, along with information on private book dealers and specialized mail order
book operations." In this edition, the number of entries
in this chapter remains approximately the same (442),
but the chapter is no longer subdivided geographically
due to many convincing letters from readers who argued
against doing so. "In this metropolitan area," wrote one
reader, "a well-stocked specialty bookstore carrying
what one wants yet located some miles away is still
worth the drive." The chapter has been changed accord-
ingly.

The "General Interest" section of this chapter begins
with "Independent Bookstores," a category comprising
24 independent local bookstores and 2 local bookstore
chains (totaling 8 locations) which carry a large selection
of new books in all categories of interest. When a
bookstore in this section has developed a reputation for
carrying a plentiful selection of certain books (e.g.
religion, arts, literature), the information is duly noted.

The section also lists "National Chain Bookstores" in
the region, including a detailed listing of all local store
locations for B. Dalton Bookseller (18), Benjamin Books
(2), Borders (1), Brentano's (7), Crown Books (62),
Doubleday's (2), Scribner's (1) and Waldenbooks (20).
Addresses and hours are noted throughout the section,
but it is recommended you call ahead to confirm information listed.

Under "Specialty Interest," readers will find listings
for 265 independent local bookstores and 34 private
book dealers specializing in certain kinds of books,
including used, rare and out-of-print books or books in
various genres (e.g., mysteries, science fiction & fantasy). While these bookstores or dealers may also sell
other books or printed material, they have chosen to
concentrate *the bulk* of their inventories in specific
ways. If you are having trouble finding a certain book
in a "general interest" bookstore, you might try giving
a "specialty interest" bookstore or private book dealer a
call. Again, it is recommended you call ahead to confirm
information listed.

One final note: many of the private book dealers
listed in this section serve the public by mail or by
appointment *only*. Please be courteous, and write ahead
or call during regular business hours. Do not show up
unannounced on a private book dealer's doorstep. If

your passion lies in hunting down rare or hard-to-find books, you must be willing to play by the rules.

Otherwise, there are no rules. May the one who has bought, begged, borrowed or stolen the most books in a lifetime be declared the winner, and may the rest of us hope to outlive that person long enough to go to the estate sale.

GENERAL INTEREST

Independent Bookstores

Bick's Books   This inviting neighborhood bookstore in Adams Morgan features an amazing variety of books (30,000 +) on all subjects and topics. Bick's is especially strong in poetry, literature, Eastern and Western philosophy, politics, women's studies, Black and African history and art titles. There are *hundreds* of magazines for sale. Bick's hosts frequent book signings and regular poetry readings, and handles special/mail orders.

2309 18th Street NW, Washington, DC 20009; (202) 328-2356. *Hours*: Mon-Thurs, 10 am to 11 pm; Fri & Sat, 10 am to 12 midnight; Sun, 12 noon to 8 pm.

Bookland of Greenbelt   Bookland carries a large selection of books in all categories at sale prices, with an emphasis on bestsellers, children's books, business titles (taxes, career guides, computer books). The store also stocks a variety of national magazines.

Beltway Plaza Shopping Center, 6064 Greenbelt Road, Greenbelt, MD 20770; (301) 474-0033. *Hours*: Mon-Sat, 10 am to 9:30 pm; Sun, 12 noon to 8 pm.

Books Unlimited   Books Unlimited emphasizes literature, Judaica and children's and parenting books (40 percent of the store is devoted to children's books and there is a children's play area). The store also features a large selection of mystery, science fiction, history and biography titles. Books Unlimited stocks greeting cards and stationery, publishes a free newsletter and handles special orders.

2729 Wilson Boulevard, Arlington, VA 22201; (703) 525-0550. *Hours*: Mon, Wed & Fri, 10 am to 9 pm; Tues, Thurs & Sat, 10 am to 6 pm.

The Bookstall   This cozy bookstore emphasizes contemporary literature, poetry, travel (literature and guides) and children's books. It also carries a large selection of books on the Washington area, plus diaries, dictionaries in various languages and gardening books. Special orders are accepted.

10144 River Road, Potomac, MD 20854; (301) 469-7800. *Hours*: Mon-Thurs, 10 am to 7 pm; Fri & Sat 10 am to 8 pm; Sun, 12 noon to 5 pm.

Bowes Books   Bowes features a large selection of science fiction and romance titles. It also carries some used books, office and art supplies, gifts, cake decorating supplies and even handles custom framing. Special orders are accepted.

718 Great Mills Road, Lexington Park, MD 20653; (301) 863-6200. *Hours*: Mon-Sat, 9 am to 6 pm.

Bridge Street Books   Bridge Street specializes in politics, literature, philosophy, history, Judaica and film titles. Mail, phone and special orders are accepted.

2814 Pennsylvania Avenue NW, Washington, DC 20007; (202) 965-5200. *Hours*: Mon-Thurs, 10 am to 7 pm; Fri & Sat, 10 am to 10 pm; Sun, 1 pm to 6 pm.

Calliope Bookshop   Calliope is strong in the humanities—literature, poetry, philosophy, mythology, history, criticism, music, fine art and photography. It also has a number of travel books, children's titles, remainders, calendars and little-known fiction titles for sale. Special orders are accepted.

3424 Connecticut Avenue NW, Washington, DC 20008; (202) 364-0111. *Hours*: Mon-Sat, 10 am to 10 pm; Sun, 12 noon to 9 pm.

Chapters: A Literary Bookstore   A book lover's haven, this well-stocked store has doubled its shelf space by moving to larger skylit quarters. Specializing in literature, poetry, criticism and small/university press titles, Chapters also has extensive selections in many other areas (e.g. children's, gardening, travel). The store stocks a wonderful variety of literary postcards. Regular author readings and book signings, along with Friday afternoon teas, are part of the fun. Five calendars of "Literary & Other To-Do's" are issued yearly. Chapters offers a frequent buyer plan, gift wrapping is provided at no extra charge and mail, phone and special orders are accepted. Autographed books may also be reserved.

1512 K Street NW, Washington, DC 20005; (202)

347-5495. *Hours*: Mon-Fri, 10 am to 6:30 pm; Sat, 11 am to 5 pm.

Charing Cross Books & Cards Charing Cross has more than half of its titles devoted to nonfiction, with a selection that emphasizes regional, history and travel books. The store carries many mysteries, Penguins and books on music. There are small but growing sections of large-print books and books in French. The store also carries cards and stationery. Special, mail and phone orders are accepted.

88 Maryland Avenue, Annapolis, MD 21401; (301) 268-1440. *Hours*: Mon-Sat, 9:30 am to 9 pm; Sun, 9 am to 5 pm (shorter hours in winter).

Chuck & Dave's Books Etcetera A casual, friendly atmosphere permeates this full-service bookstore, with large sections devoted to children's books, contemporary literature and new age/psychology books. The store also stocks a large selection of museum quality greeting cards, children's educational materials and games. Special orders are accepted, and worldwide shipping is available.

7001 Carroll Avenue, Takoma Park, MD 20912; (301) 891-2665. *Hours*: Mon-Fri, 11 am to 8 pm; Sat, 10 am to 7 pm; Sun, 10 am to 5 pm.

Cleveland Park Bookshop Located in the heart of Cleveland Park, this full-service neighborhood bookstore offers an extensive selection of quality fiction and nonfiction books. Greeting and holiday cards are in plentiful supply. Special and mail orders are accepted.

3706 Macomb Street NW, Washington, DC 20016; (202) 363-1112. *Hours*: Mon-Wed, 10 am to 6 pm; Thurs-Sat, 10 am to 9 pm; Sun, 12 noon to 5 pm.

Corsica Bookshop Corsica specializes in books on Maryland, as well as cookbooks, children's books and some used books. A search service is offered, and special orders are accepted.

101 S. Commerce Street, Centreville, MD 21617; (301) 758-1453. *Hours*: Mon-Sat, 9 am to 5 pm.

Cover To Cover Bookstore & Cafe Cover to Cover emphasizes women's issues, spiritual and new age books, psychology, health, children's, parenting and science. It also carries new age music cassettes, audiobooks, calendars and cards. Special and mail orders (on both new and out-of-print books) are accepted. The Cafe provides sustenance after a busy day of browsing and/or buying.

7284 Cradlerock Way, Columbia, MD 21045; (301) 381-9200. *Hours*: Mon-Thurs, 9 am to 9 pm; Fri & Sat, 9 am to 10 pm; Sun, 10 am to 8 pm.

Crest Books Village Crest Books carries a large selection of books for children and teens, as well as art, cooking, fiction, reference, self-help, travel, computer science and music titles. The store also rents and sells musical instruments and accessories, including sheet music and instructional materials for music teachers.

46590 Community Plaza, Sterling, VA 22170; (703) 450-4200. *Hours*: Mon-Sat, 9:30 am to 9:30 pm; Sun, 10:30 am to 5:30 pm.

Cricket Bookshop Cricket emphasizes children's books, cookbooks, mysteries, and fantasy/science fiction titles. It also carries many gardening, outdoors and regional books, and stocks cards, stationery and gifts. Discounts of 35 percent off list price of hardcover bestsellers (*The Washington Post* and *The New York Times*) are available. Special, mail and phone orders are accepted.

17800 New Hampshire Avenue, Ashton, MD 20861; (301) 774-4242. *Hours*: Mon-Fri, 10 am to 7 pm (Thurs until 8 pm); Sat, 10 am to 6 pm; Sun, 12 noon to 5 pm.

Francis Scott Key Bookshop A Washington institution, this charming rowhouse has served as both a bookstore and Georgetown meeting place since the 1930s. The store is strong in biography, art, travel, English literature, political science and gardening titles, and carries a large selection of children's books. Special orders are accepted, and local delivery is available.

28th and O Streets NW, Washington, DC 20007; (202) 337-4144. *Hours*: Mon-Sat, 9:30 am to 6 pm; Sun, 12 noon to 5 pm.

Gilpin House Bookshop Gilpin House is a general interest bookstore, with an emphasis on politics, history and biography. It also carries a large selection of gardening books, cookbooks and travel books, stocks unusual gifts from around the world and features a large selection of magazines and newspapers. The store opens early on Sundays for neighborhood "coffee klatches," in which locally prominent people join other residents for lively conversations over doughnuts, coffee and *The New York Times*. Special, mail and phone orders are accepted.

208 King Street, Alexandria, VA 22314; (703) 549-1880. *Hours*: Mon-Thurs, 10 am to 10 pm; Fri, 10 am to 11 pm; Sat, 9 am to 11 pm; Sun, 8:30 am to 10 pm.

Kramerbooks & Afterwords While this comfortable bookstore/cafe has something for everyone, it is particularly strong in history, biography, literature, art, travel and non-North American fiction. The store stocks many magazines and some newspapers. Kramerbooks hosts regular book signings, and offers a full range of customer services. Afterwords Cafe is a place to eat and sip espresso after feeding your mind.

1517 Connecticut Avenue NW, Washington, DC 20036; (202) 387-1400. *Hours*: Sun-Thurs, 7:30 am to 1 am; Fri & Sat, 24 hours.

Maryland Book Exchange The MBE has a huge stock of general titles (80,000+) and technical and professional books (20,000+), plus a full line of textbooks and school, office, art, engineering and business supplies for University of Maryland students. The store's general book section includes titles in every category, with largest selections in science, literature, fiction, science fiction and children's books. The professional/ reference section emphasizes computer sciences, engineering, math, physics and industrial education.

4500 College Avenue, College Park, MD 20740; (301) 927-2510. *Hours*: Mon-Fri, 9 am to 6 pm; Sat, 9 am to 5 pm; Sun, 12 noon to 5 pm.

New Leaf Bookstore This general interest bookstore places an emphasis on literature, philosophy, religion, psychology, reference, metaphysics, and books on cooking, diet and health. It also carries local authors' works, plus audio and video cassettes and globes. A search service is available.

36 Main Street, Warrenton, VA 22116; (703) 347-7323. *Hours*: Mon & Wed, 10 am to 6 pm; Tues, Thurs & Sat, 9 am to 6 pm; Fri, 9 am to 7:30 pm; Sun, 12 noon to 4 pm.

Olsson's Books & Records This dynamic local chain of 5 well-stocked bookstores offers an extensive selection of quality fiction and nonfiction in a broad range of categories. Audio books, calendars, postcards and a full line of CDs and tapes are also on sale at each store location. Book signings and author readings are regular occurrences at all stores. All *Washington Post* hardcover bestsellers are sold at a discount of 25 percent off list price, and the chain's "Penguin Book Club" allows members to enjoy further discounts. Mail, phone and special orders are available. Interstore transfers are available upon request.

• *Alexandria* This location is strong in books about travel, history, regional titles, small press books and remainders. 106 South Union Street, Old Town Alexandria, VA 22314; (703) 684-0077. *Hours*: Mon-Thurs, 10 am to 10 pm; Fri & Sat, 10 am to 12 midnight; Sun, 11 am to 6 pm.

• *Bethesda* This location is strong in science, psychology, theater, children's books and remainders. Woodmont Center, 7647 Old Georgetown Road, Bethesda, MD 20814; (301) 652-3336. *Hours*: Mon-Sat, 10 am to 10 pm, Sun, 11 am to 7 pm.

• *Downtown/Dupont Circle* This location is strong in fiction, science fiction, mystery, travel literature, mythology, writer's reference books and foreign languages. 1307 19th Street NW, Washington, DC 20036; (202) 785-1133. *Hours*: Mon-Sat, 10 am to 9 pm; Sun, 12 noon to 6 pm.

• *Downtown/Metro Center* This location is strong in African-American studies, law, fiction, military intelligence and mystery. 1200 F Street NW, Washington, DC 20004; (202) 347-3686. *Hours*: Mon-Sat, 10 am to 7 pm; Sun, 12 noon to 6 pm.

• *Georgetown* This location is strong in history, fiction, poetry, regional studies university press titles and philosophy. 1239 Wisconsin Avenue NW, Washington, DC 20007; (202) 338-9544. *Hours*: Mon-Thurs, 10 am to 10:45 pm; Fri & Sat, 10 am to 12 midnight; Sun, 12 noon to 7 pm.

Politics & Prose Bookstore A full-service bookstore, Politics & Prose features large sections devoted to fiction, biography, psychology, Penguin Classics, Vintage Contemporaries, health books, cookbooks and children's books. Many author readings and book signings are described in the store's free bimonthly calendar of literary events. Politics & Prose also sells and rents audio tapes, and stocks greeting cards, bookmarks, wrapping paper and gifts. Special orders are accepted.

5015 Connecticut Avenue NW, Washington, DC 20008; (202) 364-1919. *Hours*: Mon-Sat, 10 am to 10 pm; Sun, 11 am to 6 pm.

Reprint Book Shop   Despite its name, this is a general interest bookstore which carries some 30,000 new books on every subject. It also stocks audio books, postcards and maps. Special, phone and mail orders are accepted.

456 L'Enfant Plaza SW, Washington, DC 20024; (202) 554-5070. *Hours*: Mon-Fri, 9 am to 6 pm; Sat, 10 am to 5 pm.

Sidney Kramer Books   This inviting store carries a large and varied selection of books, with a strong emphasis on business and professional titles in such subjects as political science, economics, business, management, computer sciences, foreign affairs, military history, science and technology. It also features a fine selection of fiction, travel and children's titles, and hosts frequent author signings and receptions. Phone, special and mail orders are accepted, and worldwide shipping is available. A free catalogue is mailed upon request.

1825 I Street NW, Washington, DC 20006; (202) 293-2685/ (800) 423-2665. *Hours*: Mon-Fri, 9 am to 6:30 pm; Sat, 10 am to 5 pm.

Trover Shops   This local chain of 3 well-situated stores offers a large selection of hardcover bestsellers, travel guides, children's books and cookbooks. All Trover stores carry Bibles, greeting cards, maps, magazines and newspapers. The Capitol Hill store has a large selection of political books. Special orders are accepted.

• *Capitol Hill*   221 Pennsylvania Avenue SE, Washington, DC 20003; (202) 547-2665. *Hours*: Mon-Fri, 7 am to 9 pm; Sat, 7 am to 7 pm; Sun, 7 am to 3 pm.

• *Downtown/Farragut Square*   1031 Connecticut Avenue NW, Washington, DC 20032; (202) 659-8138. *Hours*: Mon-Fri, 8 am to 6:30 pm; Sat, 9 am to 5 pm.

• *Downtown/McPherson Square*   800 15th Street NW, Washington, DC 20056; (202) 347-2177. *Hours*: Mon-Fri, 8 am to 5:45 pm.

Vertigo Books   This full-service bookstore has large sections devoted to politics, literature, media studies and the humanities from a global perspective, as well as many children's books. Vertigo sponsors author readings and book signings, and stocks greeting cards and calendars. Special orders are accepted, and worldwide shipping is available.

1337 Connecticut Avenue NW, Washington, DC 20036; (202) 429-9272. Hours: Mon-Sat, 11 am to 7 pm; Sun, 12 noon to 5 pm.

National Chain Bookstores

B. Dalton Bookseller All 18 local B. Dalton Bookseller stores carry a full selection of fiction and nonfiction titles in every major category, including large sections devoted to reference, history, biography, computers, psychology, mystery, romance and children's ("B. Dalton Junior"). Some stores also have separate computer book/software stores within them (Software, Etc.). Patrons will find a full range of magazines and newspapers in stock, as well as remainders. National hardcover bestsellers are typically discounted at 25 percent or more off list price.

• *Annapolis* 147 Annapolis Mall, Annapolis, MD 21401; (301) 266-6370. *Hours*: Mon-Sat, 10 am to 9:30 pm; Sun, 12 noon to 5 pm.

• *Arlington I* Ballston Common Mall, 4238 Wilson Boulevard, Arlington, VA 22203; (703) 522-8822. *Hours*: Mon-Sat, 10 am to 9:30 pm; Sun, 12 noon to 5 pm.

• *Arlington II* Crystal Underground, 1661 Crystal Square Arcade, Arlington, VA 22202; (703) 553-9558. *Hours*: Mon-Wed & Fri, 10 am to 7 pm, Thurs, 10 am to 9 pm; Sat, 10 am to 6 pm.

• *Arlington III* 2117 Crystal Plaza Shops, Arlington, VA 22202; (703) 415-0333. *Hours*: Mon-Sat, 10 am to 9 pm; Sun, 12 noon to 5 pm.

• *Chevy Chase* Mazza Gallerie, 5335 Wisconsin Avenue NW, Washington, DC 20015; (202) 362-7055. *Hours*: Mon-Fri, 10 am to 8 pm; Sat & Sun, 12 noon to 5 pm.

• *Columbia* 1059 Columbia Mall, 10300 Little Patuxent Parkway, Columbia, MD 21044; (301) 997-7744. *Hours*: Mon-Sat, 10 am to 9:30 pm; Sun, 12 noon to 6 pm.

• *Downtown/K Street*   1776 K Street NW, Washington, DC 20006; (202) 872-0863. *Hours*: Mon-Fri, 9 am to 8 pm; Sat, 11 am to 6 pm.

• *Downtown/Pennsylvania Avenue*   The Shops at National Place, 1331 Pennsylvania Avenue NW, Washington, DC 20004; (202) 393-1468. *Hours*: Mon-Fri, 10 am to 9 pm; Sat, 10 am to 7 pm; Sun, 12 noon to 5 pm.

• *Falls Church I*   Seven Corners Shopping Mall, 6201 Arlington Boulevard, Falls Church, VA 22044; (703) 241-7505. *Hours*: Mon-Sat, 10 am to 9 pm; Sun, 12 noon to 5 pm.

• *Falls Church II*   Skyline Plaza Mall, 5155 Leesburg Pike, Falls Church, VA 22041; (703) 820-4250. *Hours*: Mon-Sat, 10 am to 9 pm; Sun, 12 noon to 5 pm.

• *Gaithersburg*   Lake Forest Mall, 701 Russell Avenue, Gaithersburg, MD 20877; (301) 926-6443. *Hours*: Mon-Sat, 10 am to 9:30 pm; Sun, 12 noon to 6 pm.

• *Glen Burnie*   Marley Station, Glen Burnie, MD 21601; (301) 760-0177. *Hours*: Mon-Sat, 10 am to 9:30 pm; Sun, 12 noon to 6 pm.

• *Hyattsville*   Prince George's Plaza, 3500 East-West Highway, Hyattsville, MD 20782; (301) 559-9779. *Hours*: Mon-Sat, 10 am to 9:30 pm; Sun, 12 noon to 5 pm.

• *Kensington*   White Flint Mall, 11301 Rockville Pike, Kensington, MD 20895; (301) 984-3730. *Hours*: Mon-Sat, 10 am to 9:30 pm; Sun, 12 noon to 6 pm.

• *Laurel*   Laurel Centre, 1139 Washington Boulevard, Laurel, MD 20707; (301) 490-7400. *Hours*: Mon-Sat, 10 am to 9:30 pm; Sun, 12 noon to 5 pm.

• *McLean*   The Galleria at Tyson's II, 1711 International Drive, McLean, VA 22102; (703) 821-2041. *Hours*: Mon-Sat, 10 am to 9:30 pm; Sun, 12 noon to 6 pm.

• *Springfield*   Springfield Mall, 6712 Franconia Road, Springfield, VA 22150; (703) 971-7010. *Hours*: Mon-Thurs, 10 am to 9:30 pm; Fri & Sat, 10 am to 10 pm; Sun, 12 noon to 5 pm.

• *Union Station*   50 Massachusetts Avenue NE, Washington, DC 20002; (202) 289-1724. *Hours*: Mon-Sat, 10 am to 9 pm; Sun, 12 noon to 6 pm.

Benjamin Books   What better way to await a delayed flight at National or Dulles Airports than to browse through these well-stocked bookstores? Offering greater depth and selection than one usually expects to find in an airport store, both Benjamin Books locations carry many hardcover bestsellers and mass market paperbacks at reasonable prices. There is an emphasis on travel, history, mystery, adventure, children's and business books. Both stores, part of a 20–store chain of airport bookstores based in Linden, NJ, also carry greeting cards, audio books, bookmarks and a good selection of local and national maps.

• *Dulles International Airport* Fairfax, VA; (703) 661-8941. *Hours*: Daily, 7 am to 10 pm.

• *Washington National Airport* Alexandria, VA; (703) 549-1941. *Hours*: Daily, 7 am to 9:30 pm.

Borders Book Shop One of the newest and largest additions to Washington's literary scene, Borders Book Shop beckons the book lover out to Rockville, MD with an extensive title base (over 100,000 in 30 sections) and spacious, comfortable surroundings. Part of a Michigan-based national chain of 16 stores, Borders is especially strong in history, literature, cooking and social sciences. It carries thousands of university and small press titles, as well as a large selection of national and international newspapers, magazines and journals. The store also owns Borders Book Shop for Kids next door (see listing under "Children's & Juvenile").

11500 Rockville Pike, Rockville, MD 20852; (301) 816-1067/ FAX (301) 816-8940. *Hours*: Mon-Sat, 9 am to 11 pm; Sun, 11 am to 8 pm.

Brentano's All seven local Brentano's stores carry a full selection of general interest titles, with an emphasis on quality fiction, history, sociology, business, travel (literature and guides), cookbooks, children's and art books. The stores also carry Mont Blanc pens, Crane stationery, desk calendars, magazines and newspapers. Special, mail and phone orders are accepted, and each store hosts frequent book signings.

• *Alexandria* Landmark Center, 5801 Duke Street, Alexandria, VA 22304; (703) 914-0254. *Hours*: Mon-Sat, 10 am to 9:30 pm; Sun, 12 noon to 6 pm.

• *Arlington* Fashion Centre at Pentagon City, 1100 S. Hayes Street, Arlington, VA 22202; (703) 415-4010.

Hours: Mon-Sat, 10 am to 9:30 pm; Sun, 12 noon to 6 pm.

• *Chevy Chase* Mazza Gallerie, 5335 Wisconsin Avenue NW, Washington, DC 20015; (202) 364-2289. *Hours*: Mon-Sat, 10 am to 9:30 pm; Sun, 12 noon to 6 pm.

• *Fairfax* Fair Oaks Mall, Fairfax, VA 22030; (703) 591-8985. *Hours*: Mon-Sat, 10 am to 9:30 pm; Sun, 12 noon to 6 pm.

• *McLean* Tyson's Corner Center, McLean, VA (703) 760-8956. *Hours*: Mon-Sat, 10 am to 9:30 pm; Sun, 12 noon to 6 pm.

• *Reston* Reston Town Center, 11904 Market Street, Reston, VA 22090; (703) 709-6312. *Hours*: Mon-Sat, 10 am to 9:30 pm; Sun, 12 noon to 6 pm.

• *Springfield* Springfield Mall, 6712 Franconia Road, Springfield, VA 22150; (703) 719-5669. *Hours*: Mon-Sat, 10 am to 9:30 pm; Sun, 12 noon to 6 pm.

Crown Books All 62 local Crown stores offer a broad selection of bestselling fiction and nonfiction books— many deeply discounted — including reference, health, history, biography, mystery and detective, art and many other titles. Adult and children's books, magazines, newspapers, audiotapes and some videocassettes are all in stock. Discounts range from 25 to 40 percent off *New York Times* bestsellers; 20 to 50 percent off hardcover art, cook and reference books; 10 percent off paperbacks and magazines; and 25 percent off computer books. Most stores have large shelves of remainders, many for $2 or less.

Six Crown stores are designated in the following listings as "Super Crowns," which means they have access to inventory of 80,000 + titles in all categories. Super Crowns offer the same discounted prices as other Crown stores, but patrons enjoy a larger selection of books, not all of which are current bestsellers. Super Crowns will also special order books for customers upon request.

• *Alexandria I* 6244 Little River Turnpike, Alexandria, Va 22312; (703) 750-3553. *Hours*: Mon-Sat, 10 am to 9:30 pm; Sun, 10 am to 6 pm. [*Super Crown*]

• *Alexandria II* 1716 Duke Street, Alexandria, VA

22314; (703) 548-9548. *Hours*: Mon-Sat, 9 am to 7 pm; Sun, 11 am to 5 pm.

• *Alexandria III* 3676 King Street, Alexandria, VA 22302; (703) 379-0944. *Hours*: Mon-Sat, 10 am to 9 pm; Sun, 11 am to 5 pm.

• *Alexandria IV* 500 King Street, Alexandria, VA 22314; (703) 548-3432. *Hours*: Mon-Sat, 10 am to 10 pm; Sun, 10 am to 6 pm.

• *Alexandria V* 6140A Rose Hill Drive, Alexandria, VA 22310; (703) 922-4672. *Hours*: Mon-Sat, 11 am to 8 pm; Sun, 11 am to 5 pm.

• *Alexandria VI* 6244 North King's Highway, Alexandria, VA 22303; (703) 765-1858. *Hours*: Mon-Sat, 10 am to 9 pm; Sun, 11 am to 5 pm.

• *Annandale I* 7428 Little River Turnpike, Annandale, VA 22003; (703) 941-7318. *Hours*: Mon-Sat, 10 am to 9 pm; Sun, 11 am to 5 pm.

• *Annandale II* 6914 Braddock Road, Annandale, VA 22003; (703) 941-1458. *Hours*: Mon-Sat, 10 am to 9 pm; Sun, 11 am to 5 pm.

• *Annapolis I* 176 Main Street, Annapolis, MD 21401; (301) 261-1939. *Hours*: Mon-Sat, 10 am to 9 pm; Sun, 11 am to 5 pm.

• *Annapolis II* 150Q Jennifer Road, Annapolis, MD 21401; (301) 266-3353. *Hours*: Mon-Sat, 11 am to 9 pm; Sun, 11 am to 5 pm.

• *Arlington I* 4017 S. 28th Street, A–210, Arlington, VA 22206; (703) 931-6949. *Hours*: Mon-Sat, 10 am to 9 pm; Sun, 11 am to 5 pm.

• *Arlington II* 3533 S. Jefferson Street, Bailey's Crossroads, VA 22041; (703) 998-3102. *Hours*: Mon-Sat, 10 am to 9 pm; Sun, 11 am to 5 pm.

• *Bethesda I* 4601A East-West Highway, Bethesda, MD 20814; (301) 656-5775. *Hours*: Mon-Sat, 10 am to 9:30 pm; Sun, 10 am to 6 pm.

• *Bethesda II* 5438 Westbard Avenue, Bethesda, MD 20816; (301) 986-0091. *Hours*: Mon-Sat, 10 am to 8 pm; Sun, 11 am to 5 pm.

• *Bowie* 3232 Superior Lane, Bowie, MD 20715;

(301) 262-4101. *Hours*: Mon-Sat, 10 am to 9 pm; Sun, 11 am to 5 pm.

• *Burke I* 9246 Old Keene Mill Road, Burke, VA 22015; (703) 451-0350. *Hours*: Mon-Sat, 10 am to 9 pm; Sun, 11 am to 5 pm.

• *Burke II* 6025 E Burke Center Parkway, Burke, VA 22015; (703) 239-0566. *Hours*: Mon-Sat, 10 am to 9 pm; Sun, 11 am to 5 pm.

• *Centreville* 14215 E. Centreville Square Road, Centreville, VA 22020; (703) 968-6577. *Hours*: Mon-Sat, 10 am to 9 pm; Sun, 11 am to 5 pm.

• *Chantilly* 13936 Lee Jackson Memorial Highway, Chantilly, VA 22021; (703) 378-2052. *Hours*: Mon-Sat, 11 am to 9 pm; Sun, 11 am to 5 pm.

• *Cleveland Park* 3335 Connecticut Avenue NW, Washington, DC 20008; (202) 966-7232. *Hours*: Mon-Sat, 10 am to 9 pm; Sun, 11 am to 6 pm.

• *College Park* 7410 Baltimore Avenue, College Park, MD 20740; (301) 927-6511. *Hours*: Mon-Sat, 11 am to 9 pm; Sun, 11 am to 6 pm.

• *Columbia* 6435 Dobbin Road, Columbia, MD 21045; (301) 730-3099. *Hours*: Mon-Sat, 10 am to 9 pm; Sun, 11 am to 5 pm.

• *Crofton* 1153 Maryland Route 3 North, Gambrills, MD 21054; (301) 721-9355. *Hours*: Mon-Sat, 10 am to 9 pm; Sun, 11 am to 5 pm.

• *Downtown/Farragut North* 1155 19th Street NW, Washington, DC 20036; (202) 659-4172. *Hours*: Mon-Sat, 9 am to 9 pm; Sun, 11 am to 6 pm.

• *Downtown/Franklin Square* 1275 K Street NW, Washington, DC 20005; (202) 298-7170. *Hours*: Mon-Fri, 10 am to 7 pm; Sat, 10 am to 6 pm; Sun, 11 am to 5 pm.

• *Downtown/K Street* 2020 K Street NW, Washington, DC 20006; (202) 659-2030. *Hours*: Mon-Fri, 9 am to 8 pm; Sat & Sun, 10 am to 6 pm.

• *Downtown/Lafayette Square* 1710 G Street NW, Washington, DC 20006; (202) 789-2277. *Hours*: Mon-Fri, 9 am to 7 pm; Sat, 10 am to 6 pm.

• *Downtown/West End* 1200 New Hampshire Avenue NW, Washington, DC 20036; (202) 822-8331. *Hours*: Mon-Sat, 9 am to 8 pm; Sun, 11 am to 5 pm.

• *Ellicott City* 4725 E. Dorsey Hall Drive, Ellicott City, MD 21043; (301) 740-8343. *Hours*: Mon-Sat, 10 am to 9 pm; Sun, 11 am to 5 pm.

• *Fairfax I* 9508 Main Street, Fairfax, VA 22031; (703) 425-9188. *Hours*: Mon-Sat, 10 am to 10 pm; Sun, 10 am to 8 pm. [*Super Crown*]

• *Fairfax II* 5620B Ox Road, Fairfax, VA 22039; (703) 425-2363. *Hours*: Mon-Sat, 10 am to 9 pm; Sun, 11 am to 5 pm.

• *Falls Church I* 6112EF Arlington Boulevard, Falls Church, VA 22044; (703) 534-4830. *Hours*: Mon-Sat, 10 am to 9 pm; Sun, 11 am to 5 pm.

• *Falls Church II* Loehman's Plaza, 7271A Arlington Boulevard, Falls Church, VA 22042; (703) 573-3500. Hours: Mon-Sat, 10 am to 9:30 pm; Sun, 10 am to 6 pm.

• *Friendship Heights* Jenifer Mall, 4400 Jenifer Street NW, Washington, DC 20015; (202) 966-8784. *Hours*: Mon-Sat, 10 am to 9 pm; Sun, 10 am to 6 pm.

• *Gaithersburg I* 632 Quince Orchard Road, Gaithersburg, MD 20878; (301) 258-9330. *Hours*: Mon-Sat, 10 am to 9 pm; Sun, 11 am to 5 pm.

• *Gaithersburg II* 9645 Lost Knife Road, Gaithersburg, MD 20879; (301) 869-1636. *Hours*: Mon-Sat, 10 am to 9 pm; Sun, 11 am to 5 pm.

• *Georgetown* 3131 M Street NW, Washington, DC 20007; (202) 333-4493. *Hours*: Mon-Thurs, 11 am to 11 pm; Fri & Sat, 11 am to 12 pm; Sun, 11 am to 8 pm.

• *Germantown* 13004 Middlebrook Road, Germantown, MD 20874; (301) 540-8799. *Hours*: Mon-Sat, 11 am to 9 pm; Sun, 11 am to 5 pm.

• *Greenbelt* Greenway Shopping Center, 7495 Greenbelt Road, Greenbelt, MD 20770; (301) 441-8220. Hours: Mon-Sat, 10 am to 9 pm; Sun, 11 am to 5 pm. [*Super Crown*]

• *Kensington* White Flint Plaza, 5108 Nicholson Lane, Kensington, MD 20895; (301) 770-6729. *Hours*: Mon-Sat, 10 am to 10 pm; Sun, 10 am to 7 pm. [*Super Crown*]

• *Laurel* 352 Domer Avenue, Laurel, MD 20707; (301) 953-9663. *Hours*: Mon-Sat, 10 am to 9 pm; Sun, 11 am to 5 pm.

• *Leesburg* 59B Catoctin Circle NE, Leesburg, VA 22075; (703) 771-2585. *Hours*: Mon-Sat, 10 am to 9 pm; Sun, 11 am to 5 pm.

• *Manassas* 8389 Sudley Road, Manassas, VA 22110; (703) 631-0409. *Hours*: Mon-Sat, 10 am to 9 pm; Sun, 11 am to 5 pm. [*Super Crown*]

• *McLean* 1457 Chain Bridge Road, McLean, VA 22101; (703) 893-7640. *Hours*: Mon-Fri, 10 am to 9:30 pm; Sat, 9 am to 9:30 pm; Sun, 10 am to 6 pm. [*Super Crown*]

• *Oakton* 2924 Chain Bridge Road, Oakton, VA 22124; (703) 281-0820. *Hours*: Mon-Sat, 10 am to 9 pm; Sun, 11 am to 5 pm.

• *Olney* 18153–5 Village Mart Drive, Olney, MD 20832; (301) 774-3917. *Hours*: Mon-Sat, 10 am to 9 pm; Sun, 11 am to 5 pm.

• *Potomac* 7727 Tuckerman Lane, Potomac, MD 20854; (301) 299-4104. *Hours*: Mon-Sat, 10 am to 9 pm; Sun, 11 am to 5 pm.

• *Reston* 11160H South Lake Drive, Reston, VA 22091; (703) 620-6560. *Hours*: Mon-Sat, 10 am to 9 pm; Sun, 11 am to 5 pm.

• *Rockville I* 15130 Frederick Road, Rockville, MD 20850; (301) 424-1676. *Hours*: Mon-Sat, 10 am to 9 pm; Sun, 11 am to 6 pm.

• *Rockville II* 1677 Rockville Pike, Rockville, MD 20850; (301) 468-2912. *Hours*: Mon-Sat, 10 am to 9 pm; Sun, 11 am to 5 pm.

• *Silver Spring I* 13826 Outlet Drive, Silver Spring, MD 20905; (301) 890-6177. *Hours*: Mon-Sat, 10 am to 9 pm; Sun, 11 am to 5 pm.

• *Silver Spring II* 13663 Georgia Avenue, Silver Spring, MD 20906; (301) 949-6636. *Hours*: Mon-Sat, 10 am to 9 pm; Sun, 11 am to 5 pm.

• *Silver Spring III* 11231 New Hampshire Avenue, Silver Spring, MD 20904; (301) 593-2599. *Hours*: Mon-Sat, 10 am to 9 pm; Sun, 11 am to 5 pm.

- *Springfield*   6435 Springfield Plaza, Springfield, VA 22150; (703) 569-6666. *Hours*: Mon-Sat, 10 am to 9:30 pm; Sun, 10 am to 6 pm.

- *Sterling*   21800 TownCenter Plaza, Sterling, VA 22170; (703) 450-6889. *Hours*: Mon-Sat, 10 am to 9 pm; Sun, 11 am to 5 pm.

- *Upper Marlboro*   5775A Crain Highway, Upper Marlboro, MD 20772; (301) 627-8500. *Hours*: Mon-Sat, 10 am to 8 pm; Sun, 11 am to 5 pm.

- *Van Ness/UDC*   4301 Connecticut Avenue NW, Washington, DC 20008; (202) 966-2576. *Hours*: Mon-Sat, 10 am to 9 pm; Sun, 11 am to 5 pm.

- *Vienna*   8365E Leesburg Pike, Vienna, VA 22180; (703) 442-0133. *Hours*: Mon-Sat, 10 am to 9 pm; Sun, 11 am to 5 pm.

- *Waldorf*   Waldorf Shopper's World, Route 301, Waldorf, MD 20603; (301) 645-3922. *Hours*: Mon-Sat, 10 am to 9 pm; Sun, 11 am to 5 pm.

- *Wheaton*   11181 Viers Mill Road, Wheaton, MD 20902; (301) 942-7995. *Hours*: Mon-Sat, 10 am to 9:30 pm; Sun, 10 am to 6 pm.

- *Woodbridge I*   14567A Jefferson Davis Highway, Woodbridge, VA 22191; (703) 491-2144. *Hours*: Mon-Sat, 10 am to 9 pm; Sun, 11 am to 5 pm.

- *Woodbridge II*   12492 Dillingham Square, Woodbridge, VA 22192; (703) 878-2550. *Hours*: Mon-Sat, 10 am to 9 pm; Sun, 11 am to 5 pm.

Doubleday Book Shops   An American tradition for 80 years, the Doubleday bookstore in New York is now duplicated in name (and, to some extent, in style) in the form of these two jewel-like stores in Washington, DC's suburbs. Both stores have hundreds of titles in all categories, fiction and non-fiction. Both locations offer many special services, including free gift wrapping with a gift card, gift certificates and worldwide shipping. Special, phone and fax orders are accepted. Corporate accounts are welcome.

- *Fairfax*   Fair Oaks Mall, 11828–L Fair Oaks, Fairfax, VA 22033; (703) 273-1258. *Hours*: Mon-Sat, 10 am–9:30 pm; Sun, 12 noon to 6 pm.

- *Gaithersburg*   Lake Forest Mall, 201 Russell Avenue, Gaithersburg, MD 20877; (301) 258-9398. *Hours*: Mon-Sat, 10 am to 9:30 pm; Sun, 12 noon to 6 pm.

Scribner's Bookstore Those who mourn the passing of the famous New York City Scribner's Bookstore on Fifth Avenue should make plans to visit this new incarnation of the store in Arlington. Now owned by Barnes & Noble, Scribner's has thousands of general-interest books on display, divided by archways into what the store calls "book boutiques." Each "boutique" is dedicated to a major category (such as history, literature, business, etc.), which is then further subdivided into "special sections" of various kinds. Carrying everything from hard and softcover editions of best-sellers to hard-to-find literary works, Scribner's is especially strong in the fine arts, sports, photography and the performing arts. Services include special ordering, mail order and gift wrapping.

Fashion Centre at Pentagon City, 1100 S. Hayes Street, Arlington, VA 22202; (703) 415-2005. *Hours*: Mon-Sat, 10 am to 9:30 pm; Sun, 11 am to 6 pm.

Waldenbooks All 20 local Waldenbooks stores feature a large variety of fiction and nonfiction titles in all categories, including adult and children's books, magazines, tapes (audio and video) and computer books. Discounts off list price are offered on all hardcover best-sellers. All stores also offer "Preferred Reader" memberships, which entitle members to additional 10 percent discounts on merchandise. Stores will handle special orders, and regular guides are sent by mail. There is a special toll-free ordering number available.

• *Alexandria* Landmark Center, 5001 Duke Street, Alexandria, VA 22304; (703) 658-9576. *Hours*: Mon-Sat, 10 am to 9:30 pm; Sun, 12:30 pm to 6 pm.

• *Annapolis* 136 Annapolis Mall, Annapolis, MD; (301) 266-6065. *Hours*: Mon-Sat, 10 am to 9:30 pm; Sun, 12 noon to 5 pm.

• *Arlington* Ballston Commons Mall, 4238 Wilson Boulevard, Arlington, VA 22203; (703) 527-2442. *Hours*: Mon-Sat, 10 am to 9:30 pm; Sun, 12 noon to 5 pm.

• *Bethesda* 143 Montgomery Mall, 7101 Democracy Blvd, Bethesda, MD 20817; (301) 469-8810. Hours: Mon-Sat, 10 am to 9:30 pm; Sun, 12 noon to 5 pm.

- *Columbia*   The Mall at Columbia, 10300 Little Patuxent Parkway, Columbia, MD 21044; (301) 730-6990. *Hours*: Mon-Sat, 10 am to 9:30 pm; Sun, 12 noon to 5 pm.

- *Downtown/Pennsylvania Avenue*   Formerly the Globe Bookstore, this store carries regular Waldenbooks stock and much of what Globe was best known for—language books, international tapes and periodicals, world travel and political affairs books. 1700 Pennsylvania Avenue NW, Washington, DC 20006; (202) 393-1490. *Hours*: Mon-Fri, 9:30 am to 6 pm; Sat, 10 am to 6 pm.

- *Forestville*   Forest Village Park Mall, 3325 Donnell Drive, Forestville, MD 20746; (301) 568-6911. *Hours*: Mon-Sat, 10 am to 9:30 pm; Sun, 12 noon to 5 pm.

- *Friendship Heights*   Spring Valley Shopping Center, 4845 Massachusetts Avenue NW, Washington, DC 20016; (202) 362-6329. *Hours*: Mon-Fri, 9:30 am to 7 pm; Sat, 9:30 am to 6 pm; Sun, 10:30 am to 3:30 pm.

- *Gaithersburg*   Lake Forest Shopping Center, 701 Russell Avenue, Gaithersburg, MD 20877; (301) 921-9248. *Hours*: Mon-Sat, 10 am to 9:30 pm; Sun, 12 noon to 6 pm.

- *Georgetown*   Georgetown Park, 3222 M Street NW, Washington, DC 20007; (202) 333-8033. *Hours*: Mon-Fri, 10 am to 9 pm; Sat, 10 am to 7 pm; Sun, 12 noon to 6 pm.

- *Glen Burnie I*   258 Harundale Center, 7700 Ritchie Highway, Glen Burnie, MD 21061; (301) 761-1976. *Hours*: Mon-Sat, 10 am to 9:30 pm; Sun, 12 noon to 5 pm.

- *Glen Burnie II*   Glen Burnie Mall, 6711 Ritchie Highway, Glen Burnie, MD 21061; (301) 760-1233. *Hours*: Mon-Sat, 10 am to 9:30 pm; Sun, 12 noon to 5 pm.

- *Glen Burnie III*   Marley Station, 7900 Ritchie Highway, Glen Burnie, MD 21061; (301) 760-5733. Hours: Mon-Sat, 10 am to 9:30 pm; Sun, 12 noon to 5 pm.

- *Landover*   Landover Mall, 2223 Brightseat Road, Landover, MD 20785; (301) 322-9220. *Hours*: Mon-Sat, 10 am to 9:30 pm; Sun, 12 noon to 5 pm.

• *Laurel* Laurel Center, 1139 Washington Blvd, Laurel, MD 20707; (301) 953-3807. Hours: Mon-Sat, 10 am to 9:30 pm; Sun, 12 noon to 5 pm.

• *Manassas* 181 Manassas Mall, 8300 Sudley Road, Manassas, VA 22110; (703) 368-8366. *Hours*: Mon-Sat, 10 am to 9:30 pm; Sun, 12 noon to 6 pm.

• *McLean* Tysons Corner Center, McLean, VA 22102; (703) 893-4208. *Hours*: Mon-Sat, 10 am to 9:30 pm; Sun, 12 noon to 6 pm.

• *Springfield* 6725 Springfield Mall, Springfield, VA 22150; (703) 971-9443. *Hours*: Mon-Sat, 10 am to 9:30 pm; Sun, 12 noon to 5 pm.

• *Waldorf* St. Charles Town Centre, #5000 Highway 301 South, Waldorf, MD 20603; (301) 645-0770. *Hours*: Mon-Sat, 10 am to 9:30 pm; Sun 11 am to 5 pm.

• *Wheaton* Wheaton Plaza, Wheaton, MD 20902; (301) 946-0202. *Hours*: Mon-Sat, 10 am to 9:30 pm; Sun, 12 noon to 5 pm.

SPECIALTY INTEREST

African-American

Pyramid Bookstores All three stores carry books by and about people of African descent, including titles on Islam, Black politics, the Caribbean, the arts, nutrition and metaphysics. The stores also stock children's books, video and audio cassettes, greeting cards, periodicals, posters, dolls and games.

• *House of Knowledge* 2849 Georgia Avenue NW, Washington, DC 20001; (202) 328-0190. *Hours*: Mon-Sat, 11 am to 7 pm; Sun, 12 noon to 5 pm.

• *House of Understanding* Hechinger Mall, 1548 Benning Road NE, Washington, DC 20002; (202) 396-1100. *Hours*: Mon-Sat, 10 am to 8 pm; Sun, 12 noon to 5 pm.

• *Prince Georges Plaza* 3500 East-West Highway, Hyattsville, MD 20782; (301) 559-5200. *Hours*: Mon-Sat, 10 am to 9:30 pm; Sun, 12 noon to 5 pm.

Arts & Architecture

American Institute of Architects Bookstore Located in the AIA's main headquarters building, the store features architectural city guides, children's books on architecture, posters, calendars, T-shirts, games, stationery, greeting cards and gifts. Mail order, special and phone orders are accepted.

1735 New York Avenue NW, Washington, DC 20006; (202) 626-7475. *Hours*: Mon-Fri, 8:30 am to 5 pm.

Backstage   Backstage specializes in books on the performing arts: scripts, theater, acting, film/television, musicals, opera and dance. It also carries stage makeup, dance gear, costumes (sale and rental), posters and gifts. Special and mail orders are accepted, and a newsletter is available by mail.

2101 P Street NW, Washington, DC 20037; (202) 775-1488. *Hours*: Mon-Sat, 10 am to 6 pm (except Thurs, 10 am to 8 pm).

Bird In Hand Bookstore & Gallery   The bookstore features books on art, architecture, archaeology and photography. The gallery sells fine prints, small paintings and photography, mostly by local artists.

323 7th Street SE, Washington, DC 20003; (202) 543-0744. *Hours*: Tues-Sun, 11 am to 5 pm.

Bookworks   This bookstore of The Washington Project for the Arts carries books by and about local, national and international artists, plus literature, art theory, children's and architecture titles. It also stocks cards, magazines and new music, and rents videotapes.

400 7th Street NW, Washington, DC 20004; (202) 347-4590. *Hours*: Mon-Fri, 11 am to 6 pm; Sat & Sun, 11 am to 5 pm.

Decatur House Bookshop   Owned and operated by the National Trust for Historic Preservation, this bookshop carries many Preservation Press titles, plus a selection of books on Americana, antiques, architecture, arts and crafts and cooking. It also sells fine gifts and jewelry.

1600 H Street NW, Washington, DC 20006; (202) 842-1856. *Hours*: Mon-Fri, 10 am to 5:30 pm; Sat, 10 am to 4 pm.

Franz Bader Bookstore   The store carries a large selection of books on the visual arts, including many imports. Subjects covered include art and art history, architecture and design, graphic arts, photography and crafts. One corner of the store is devoted to German books—mostly classic and contemporary literature. Many calendars and periodicals are also available. Services include worldwide shipping, and mail, phone and special orders.

1911 I Street NW, Washington, DC 20006; (202) 337-5440. *Hours*: Mon-Sat, 10 am to 6 pm.

Children's & Juvenile

A Happy Thought Children's Bookstore   This happy store carries a large selection of books for children and young teens, including many picture books. Book-related stuffed animals, records, audio books and music cassettes, selected toys, videos and art supplies are also on sale. The store sponsors regular workshops (mostly on art), puppet shows, concerts and author talks and book signings. Services include special and mail orders. School accounts are welcomed.

4836 MacArthur Boulevard NW, Washington, DC 20007; (202) 337-8300. *Hours*: Mon-Sat, 10 am to 5:30 pm.

A Likely Story Children's Bookstore   Here's a complete bookstore for kids and their parents, with lots of classics and how-to's for kids and early teens and even adult books on parenting and other topics. Stocked from floor to ceiling with plush animals, cassettes, cards and gift wrapping, A Likely Story features a delightful children's play and reading area and a "storyhour" each weekend for kids. Mail, phone and special orders are accepted, and school accounts are welcomed. There is a regular newsletter available upon request.

1555 King Street, Alexandria, VA 22314; (703) 836-2498. *Hours*: Mon-Sat, 10 am to 6 pm; Sun, 1 pm to 5 pm.

The Book Nook: A Children's Bookstore   This children's bookstore carries a wide range of quality literature for children, parents and teachers, along with book-related puppets, posters, bookplates, kidstamps and stuffed animals. A separate in-store "Teacher's Nook" offers an extensive selection of professional educational books. Special mail and phone orders are accepted, and gift wrapping is provided at no extra charge.

10312 Main Street, Fairfax, VA 22030; (703) 591-6545. *Hours*: Mon-Sat, 10 am to 6 pm; Thurs, 10 am to 8 pm. Open Sundays during fall months.

Borders Book Shop for Kids   Located next door to Borders Book Shop in Rockville, MD, this lively stand-alone store features carpeted play tiers, toys and room for kids and their parents to spread out on the floor and enjoy a favorite book together. With nearly 18,000 children's titles, Borders Book Shop for Kids carries a full selection of fiction and nonfiction for children and teens, as well as gifts and other items. A store newsletter lists a full calendar of readings, signings, book discussions and special programs for children. Mail, phone and fax for special orders (any book in print) are accepted. The store will also reserve and ship books, and provides free gift wrapping.

11500 Rockville Pike, Rockville, MD 20852; (301) 816-1067/ FAX (301) 816-8940. *Hours*: Mon-Sat, 9 am to 11 pm; Sun, 11 am to 8 pm.

Building Blocks, A Children's Bookshop   This store features a complete line of children's books for ages pre-K up to junior high, with classics for older teens. It also carries foreign language books for children, parent and teacher resource books, audio books, music and videos for children and greeting cards. Special orders are accepted, and school accounts are welcomed.

69 Maryland Avenue, Annapolis, MD 21401; (301) 268-6848. *Hours*: Mon-Sat, 10 am to 5 pm; Sun, 1 pm to 5 pm.

The Cheshire Cat Book Store   The Cheshire Cat carries all kinds of books for and about children (pre-K to early teens), including a large selection of picture books, audio books, music cassettes, posters and calendars. The store publishes an events newsletter (5 times p/year), and hosts book signings and special events. Services include gift wrapping and mailing. Special and phone orders are accepted.

5512 Connecticut Avenue NW, Washington, DC 20015; (202) 244-3956. *Hours*: Mon-Sat, 9:30 am to 5:30 pm (except Thurs, 9:30 am to 8 pm).

Fairy Godmother   This store carries books for children under age 12 on all subjects, including a large selection of picture books. There are some books for young teens and a limited stock of books for adults (especially about music and architecture). Audio books, music cassettes, toys, cards and book-related stuffed animals are also on sale. Gift wrapping and mailing are available; special orders are accepted.

319 7th Street SE, Washington, DC 20003; (202) 547-5474. *Hours*: Mon-Fri, 11 am to 6 pm; Sat, 10 am to 5:30 pm.

Imagination Station   Here's a bookstore for children of all ages, with a special focus on the earliest years. Imagination Station carries adventure books, classics, science fiction, religious books and novels for teens. A fine selection of books for children in French, German and Spanish is also available, along with foreign language dictionaries. There is a large inventory of audio books and book/cassette combinations for sale, as well as videos for sale and rent. The store publishes a free newsletter three times a year, which features book reviews and upcoming events and programs (author readings, story telling and other special events). Special orders are accepted.

4530 Lee Highway, Arlington, VA 22207; (703) 522-2047. *Hours*: Mon-Sat, 10 am to 6 pm; Sun, 11 am to 4 pm.

John Davy Toys   This toy store has a substantial children's book section. It carries books in English, French, German and Spanish for all ages and in all genres—from classics and nursery rhymes to novels for teens.

301 Cameron Street, Alexandria, VA 22314; (703) 683-0079. *Hours*: Mon-Sat, 10 am to 5:30 pm; Sun, 11 am to 5 pm.

Junior Editions   Books for infants through teens in all subjects are on sale here, including classic picture books, fiction for older children, nonfiction, poetry, biography and reference. Junior Editions also carries children's music cassettes, videos, audio books and plush animals. Book club and special orders are accepted.

Columbia Mall, Columbia, MD 21044; (301) 730-2665. *Hours*: Mon-Sat, 10 am to 9:30 pm; Sun, 12 noon to 5 pm.

Lowen's Book Department   This toy store has a substantial number of books on sale for children of all ages, as well as a small section of classics, mysteries and books on parenting for adults. All categories are represented, including fiction, picture books, poetry, Newberry winners and anthologies.

7201 Wisconsin Avenue, Bethesda, MD 20814; (301) 652-1289. *Hours*: Mon-Sat, 9:30 am to 6 pm (open Thurs until 9 pm).

Stories Unlimited   Stories Unlimited carries books and gifts for kids and early teens, with an emphasis on fiction. There is a large selection of poetry and problem-solving books, as well as video and audio cassettes, stationery, book-related stuffed animals, posters and toys.

Market Station, Loudon Street, Ste 112D, Leesburg, VA 22075; (703) 777-6995. *Hours*: Mon-Sat, 10 am to 6 pm; Sun, 12 noon to 5 pm.

Storybook Palace   The store carries books for children from pre-K through mid-teens, including a large selection of first books, books on parenting and nonfiction. It also carries audio books, music tapes, book-related stuffed animals, select videos and puppets. Storybook Palace offers parent workshops, author and book character appearances, puppet shows and story times. Special and mail orders are accepted, and school accounts are welcomed. A free newsletter and gift certificates are available.

Burke Town Plaza, 9538 Old Keene Mill Road, Burke, VA 22015; (703) 644-2300. *Hours*: Mon-Fri, 10 am to 6 pm (open Thurs until 8 pm); Sat, 10 am to 6 pm.

Travelling Talesman   This "portable" children's bookstore allows you and your friends to shop for children's books at home. Operating on the same principle as Tupperware parties, The Travelling Talesman brings a broad selection of commercially published (and age-appropriate) children's books to your home. You simply bring a group of parents and children together and let the Talesman know the age level and subjects you're interested in. A free catalogue is available.

JFA Enterprises, P.O. Box 12267, Arlington, VA 22209; (703) 528-2474.

Toys Etc.   This toy store has an entire wing devoted to children's books on many subjects, including classics and science, biography and history. There are also some books for adults (bestsellers, classics in paperback and mysteries).

Cabin John Mall, 11325 Seven Locks Road, Potomac, MD 20854; (301) 299-8300. *Hours*: Mon-Fri, 10 am to 7:45 pm; Sat, 10 am to 6 pm; Sun, 12 noon to 5 pm.

Comic Books & Collectibles

Aftertime Comics   Aftertime features new and back-issue comics, both mainstream and independent. It also carries autographs, library collections, literary magazines, cards, art, posters and reproductions. A search service is available, and the store offers a free subscription service.

1304 King Street, Alexandria, VA 22314; (703) 548-5030. *Hours*: Mon-Sat, 11 am to 7 pm; Sun, 12 noon to 6 pm.

Another World   In Another World, new and old comic books and comic book paraphernalia (Batman hats, etc.) may be found. Comics for young children, fantasy and science fiction paperbacks, T-shirts, posters, paraphernalia, toys, miniatures and role-playing adventure games are also available.

1504 Wisconsin Avenue NW, Washington, DC 20007; (202) 333-8650. *Hours*: Mon-Thurs, 10 am to 9 pm; Fri & Sat, 10 am to 10 pm; Sun, 11 am to 7 pm.

Anything Collectible   This store carries comics, baseball cards, antique prints, paperbacks, many collectibles and rare books on various subjects.

969 Ritchie Highway, Severna Park, MD 21146; (301) 647-5222. *Hours*: Tues-Fri, 12 noon to 6:30 pm; Sat, 10 am to 6 pm.

Big Planet Comics   At Big Planet, patrons can find new comics from every comic book publisher, plus a large selection of back issues (even collectors' items). Posters and T-shirts are also sold here, and a free subscription service is available.

4908 Fairmont Avenue, Bethesda, MD 20814; (301) 654-6856. *Hours*: Mon-Sat, 11 am to 6 pm (open Fri until 8 pm); Sun, 12 noon to 5 pm.

Blue Beetle Comics & Baseball Cards   Both Blue Beetle locations carry a large selection of comic books and baseball cards, along with many other collectibles.

• *Camp Springs*   5814 Allentown Way, Camp

Springs, MD 20748; (301) 449-3307. *Hours*: Mon-Fri, 12 noon to 8 pm, Sat, 10 am to 6 pm; Sun, noon to 5 pm.

• *Waldorf* 4815–C Festival Way, Waldorf, MD 20601; (301) 843-1434. *Hours*: Mon-Fri, 10:30 am to 8 pm; Sat, 10 am to 9 pm; Sun, 12 noon to 5 pm.

Book & Comic Outlet   The Outlet carries comics from all publishers, plus selected paperbacks in the romance, science fiction, horror, adventure and western genres. It also carries magazines, posters, T-shirts and toys.

Carrollton Mall, 7736 Riverdale Road, New Carrollton, MD 20784; (301) 731-5851. *Hours*: Mon-Sat, 10 am to 10 pm; Sun, 12 noon to 6 pm.

Capital Comics Center & Book Niche   This store's inventory is about 60% comic books and 40% new and used books. Book subjects include biography, films and filmmaking, history, horticulture, mystery and detective, nature and the environment, science fiction and fantasy, comedy, metaphysics and the occult, art, music and the classics. The Niche also carries trading cards, posters and novelties.

2008 Mount Vernon Avenue, Alexandria, VA 22301; (703) 548-3466. *Hours*: Mon-Sat, 12 noon to 7 pm (open Fri until 8 pm).

Closet of Comics   In the Closet, one can find new and back issues of comics from a wide variety of comic book publishers, including DC, Marvel and "lesser known's."

7319 Baltimore Avenue, College Park, MD 20740; (301) 699-0498. *Hours*: Daily, 11 am to 6 pm (except Fri, 12 noon to 7 pm).

Collector's Choice   This store carries comic books, sports cards and related memorabilia from the 1800s to the present. It also carries many first editions (mystery and science fiction).

Laurel Shopping Center, Laurel, MD 20707; (301) 725-0887. *Hours*: Mon-Fri, 12 noon to 8 pm; Sat, 11 am to 7 pm; Sun, 12 noon to 4 pm.

Collector's World   The World carries a large selection of collectible books and records. Beyond books, it also acquires and sells many kinds of gum and tobacco cards, from the 1800s to the present.

612 Quince Orchard Road, Gaithersburg, MD 20878;

(301) 840-0520. *Hours*: Mon-Fri, 11 am to 8 pm; Sat &
Sun, 11 am to 4 pm.

Comic Classics In addition to comic books and baseball cards, Comic Classics also sells used paperbacks
(science fiction, horror, romance and mystery).
365 Main Street, Laurel, MD 20707; (301) 490-9811.
Hours: Mon-Fri, 12 noon to 8 pm.

Fantasy Five & Dime The Five & Dime specializes in
comic books and other collectibles.
1113 West Church Road, Sterling, VA 22170; (703)
444-9222. *Hours*: Mon & Fri, 12 noon to 9 pm; Sat, 10
am to 8 pm; Sun, 12 noon to 6 pm. Closed Tues-Thurs.

Geppi's Comic World of Silver Spring Geppi's carries a
large selection of comic books, cards, posters and other
collectibles. The store also offers a call-in "Comic Hotline," which helps patrons understand more about the
latest titles available.
8317 Fenton Street, Silver Spring, MD 20910; (301)
588-2545/ 792-2754. *Hours*: Mon-Fri, 11 am to 6 pm;
Sat, 10 am to 6 pm; Sun, 12 noon to 5 pm.

Foreign

Alfa Books (Interlingua Communications) Alfa carries
many foreign language books for adults and children. It
also sells or rents foreign-language audio books and
videos.
2615 Columbia Pike, Arlington, VA 22204; (703) 920-
6644. *Hours*: Tues-Fri, 10 am to 6 pm; Sat, 8 am to 4
pm.

The He Bookstore This store carries Vietnamese books
in various categories, plus Vietnamese music on cassettes, records and CDs.
6763A Wilson Boulevard, Falls Church, VA 22034;
(703) 532-7890. *Hours*: Daily, 11 am to 8 pm.

Iran Books This store specializes in books in Persian
about Iran. Mail order only.
8014 Old Georgetown Road, Bethesda, MD 20814;
(301) 986-0079.

Lado International Institute Bookshop Lado specializes
in instructional texts to help learn and understand En-

glish. Foreign language materials, dictionaries and office supplies are also available. Special and phone orders are accepted.

2233 Wisconsin Avenue NW, Washington, DC 20007; (202) 338-3133. *Hours*: Mon-Fri, 9 am to 7:30 pm; Sat, 9 am to 2 pm.

Latin American Books An entire warehouse houses a large selection of new, used, out-of-print and rare books on Latin America, the Caribbean, Spain and Portugal (and their former African and Asian colonies) and the Hispanic U.S. in all languages and disciplines. Subject collections are also built to order. The owners can send requested titles/subject matter to your home, office or hotel for inspection. Mail order, gift wrap and dispatch services are available.

P.O. Box 39090, Washington, DC 20016; 244-4173. *Hours*: Daily by appointment.

Media Bookstore Korean books and music, including CDs, are on sale here.

3536 Carlin Spring Road, Bailey's Crossroads, VA 22041; (703) 931-1212. *Hours*: Mon-Sat, 10:30 am to 6:30 pm.

Modern Language Bookstore This store specializes in French, German and Spanish imports, including best-sellers, classics, criticism and dictionaries. It also carries learning tapes, language study aids in all languages, children's books, audio books, greeting cards, posters, travel guides and maps.

3160 O Street NW, Washington, DC 20007; (202) 338-8963. *Hours*: Tues-Sat, 10 am to 7 pm; Sun, 12 noon to 6 pm.

Sakura Books & Foods Japanese books, magazines, gifts and food are on sale in this unusual store.

15809 S. Frederick Road, Rockville, MD 20850; (301) 948-5112. *Hours*: Tues-Sun, 10 am to 7 pm.

Saludos This store carries Spanish-language books in many categories, including fiction, children's, bestsellers, dictionaries and other reference works. It also carries music instruction books, videos, records, tapes and CDs, all in Spanish. Saludos stocks greeting cards, magazines and newspapers.

3811I South George Mason Drive, Bailey's Crossroads, VA 22041; (703) 820-5550. *Hours*: Mon-Sat, 10:30 am to 9 pm; Sun, 10:30 am to 7 pm.

Scottish Merchant   The Merchant carries books, audio books and videotapes dealing with Scottish history, literature, folklore, music, art, travel, genealogy, dress and other aspects of the Scottish culture. Special collections of Nigel Tranter and Robert Burns are available, as are Scottish clothing, jewelry and gifts.

215 King Street, Alexandria, VA 22314; (703) 548-2900/739–2302. *Hours*: Mon-Sat, 11 am to 9 pm; Sun, 12 noon to 8 pm.

Universal Chinese Bookstore   This store carries Chinese books in various subject areas, as well as Chinese records and tapes.

6763 Wilson Boulevard, Falls Church, VA 22034; (703) 241-7070. Hours: Daily, 11 am to 7 pm.

Victor Kamkin Bookstore   This store carries Russian language books on all subjects. Mail order service is available.

4956 Bolling Brook Plaza, Rockville, MD 20852; (301) 881-5973. *Hours*: Mon-Sat, 9 am to 5 pm.

Gay & Lesbian

Lambda Rising   Lambda Rising specializes in books for gay men and lesbians and their families and friends. It also carries greeting cards, videos, T-shirts, games, gifts, jewelry, calendars, newspapers and magazines. Mail order services are available.

1625 Connecticut Avenue NW, Washington, DC 20009; (202) 462-6969. *Hours*: Daily, 10 am to 12 midnight.

Hobbies & Diversions

G Street Fabrics Bookstore   This store carries many books on fabric, fashion, costume, sewing, textiles, needle arts and quilting. It also features greeting cards, calendars, magazines, posters, newsletter, notebooks and period costume patterns. Special orders, mail and phone orders are accepted, and the store also offers a search service.

11854 Rockville Pike, Rockville, MD 20852; (301) 231-8998. *Hours*: Mon-Fri, 10 am to 9 pm; Sat, 10 am to 6 pm; Sun, 12 noon to 5 pm.

Museums, Historic Sites & Art Galleries

Corcoran Gallery Shop   This bookstore in the Corcoran Gallery of Art specializes in art and photography, and also carries greeting cards, games, jewelry, periodicals, art reproductions and toys.

17th Street & New York Avenue NW, Washington, DC 20006; (202) 638-3211. *Hours*: Tues-Sun, 10 am to 4:30 pm (except Thurs, 10 am to 9 pm).

Folger Shakespeare Library Museum Shop   The Folger's museum shop sells many books about the English Renaissance, but it also stocks books on the late Medieval and post-Renaissance periods. The store carries books on English herbs, gardening and tea, plays-on-tape, posters, original etchings, jewelry, scarves, T-shirts and totes—all related to the Renaissance or Elizabethan periods.

201 East Capitol Street SE, Washington, DC 20003; (202) 544-4600. *Hours*: Mon-Sat, 10 am to 4 pm.

Hillwood Museum Shop   In a museum which specializes in Russian and French decorative arts, this shop features Russian art books and literature (in English). Children's books, gifts and reproductions are also for sale.

4155 Linnean Avenue NW, Washington, DC 20008; (202) 686-8510. *Hours*: Tues-Sat, 10 am to 5 pm.

National Archives Museum Store   This store has a large book section specializing in American history. It also carries posters, crafts, jewelry, historic campaign buttons, postcards, calendars and gifts related to U.S. history.

Pennsylvania Avenue between 7th & 9th Streets NW, Washington, DC 20408; (202) 523-1514. *Hours*: Daily, 10 am to 5:30 pm (except April 1 through Labor Day, 10 am to 9 pm).

National Gallery of Art Museum Stores   Both stores feature a large selection of books on all the fine arts, from ancient Greece and Rome to the present. Subjects include painting, sculpture and some decorative arts, art theory and criticism, photography/film and architecture. Exhibit catalogues and books related to special exhibits or permanent collection are also on sale. The stores carry many reproductions (from cards to posters) of works in the Gallery. The West Building store emphasizes ancient art up to eighteenth-century French salon painting, while the East Building store starts with French Impressionism and continues through contemporary art.

Constitution Avenue between 4th & 6th Streets NW, Washington, DC 20565; (202) 842-6466. *Hours*: Mon-Sat, 10 am to 5 pm; Sun, 11 am to 6 pm.

National Museum of Women in the Arts Museum Shop This shop carries books on art history, exhibition catalogs and literature by women artists. It also stocks video tapes about women artists, cards, posters and jewelry.

1250 New York Avenue NW, Washington, DC 20005; (202) 783-5000. *Hours*: Tues-Sat, 10 am to 5 pm; Sun, 12 noon to 5 pm.

Parks & History Association Bookshops All eighteen shops of the Association, located at major National Park Service (NPS) monuments and memorials throughout the region, carry specialty books and materials (gifts, maps, posters) highlighting appropriate subjects for each location. Please call (202) 472-3083 for hours and specific information for the store(s) you plan to visit.

• *Antietam National Battlefield Bookshop* Civil War buffs will find a plentiful selection of books on Antietam and other Civil War battles. There are many titles on Maryland history. Highway 65 North, Sharpsburg, MD 21782; (301) 432-4329.

• *Arlington House, Robert E. Lee Memorial Bookstore* New and remaindered books for adults and children on the Civil War, Robert E. Lee and Southern culture (including cookbooks) are on sale. The store also stocks postcards, films and historic reproductions. Arlington National Cemetery, Arlington, VA 22101; (703) 557-3156.

• *Arlington Visitors Center Bookshop* Books on military history, including the Civil War, WWI and WWII and Vietnam, are on sale here. The shop also carries books and videos about the Washington area, including guidebooks. Arlington Cemetery, Arlington, VA 22101; (703) 557-1713.

• *C & O Canal Bookshop* Books on the C & O Canal, nature and children's subjects are sold here. 11710 MacArthur Boulevard, Potomac, MD 20854.

• *Clara Barton House Bookshop* Books on the Civil War and the history of nursing are sold here. 5801 Oxford Road, Glen Echo, MD 20812; (301) 492-6245.

• *Ford's Theatre & Lincoln Museum Bookshop* Civil War books and Americana, along with many books and materials about Lincoln, may be found in this landmark theatre. Ford's Theatre, 511 10th Street NW, Washington, DC 20004; (202) 426-6927.

• *Fort Washington Park Bookshop* Civil War books and books about military history are sold here. Fort Washington Park, Fort Washington, MD; (202) 763-4600.

• *Frederick Douglass Home Bookshop* The bookshop features all of the writings and biographies of Frederick Douglass, as well as many books on African-American history. Frederick Douglass Home, 1411 W Street SE, Washington, DC 20020; (202) 426–5960.

• *Glen Echo Gallery* The Gallery sells carousel books and memorabilia. It also handles consignment art and sponsors regular exhibits. Glen Echo Park, MacArthur Blvd, Glen Echo, MD 20812; (301) 492-6282.

• *Great Falls Park Bookshop* The shop sells books on nature, the environment, geology and the outdoors, with a focus on Great Falls Park. It also carries historical books about the C & O Canal.
9200 Old Dominion Drive, Great Falls, VA 22066; (703) 235-1194.

• *Jefferson Memorial Bookshop* The shop sells books and other materials related to the Revolutionary War, Jefferson's history and early American biography. Jefferson Memorial, Haines Point, Washington, DC 20042; (202) 426-2177.

• *Kenilworth Aquatic Gardens Bookshop* Books on aquatic plants and gardens and general nature topics are featured in this shop. Route 295/Anacostia Freeway, Washington, DC; (202) 426-6905.

• *Lincoln Memorial Bookshop*   Civil War books and Americana, along with many books and materials about Lincoln, are in plentiful supply in this shop. Lincoln Memorial, 23rd and Lincoln Memorial Circle NW, Washington, DC 20242; (202) 653-9088.

• *Pierce Mill Bookshop*   Books on milling and historic subjects are for sale here, along with many books on the history of the Washington area. 2375 Tilden Street NW, Washington, DC 20008; (202) 426-6908.

• *Prince William Forest Park Bookshop*   The shop carries books on the park, nature topics and children's subjects. Triangle, VA 22172; (703) 221-2104.

• *Rock Creek Park Bookshop*   The shop carries books on nature, astronomy and the environment. Rock Creek Park, 1800 Beach Drive, Washington, DC 20015; (202) 426-6829.

• *Tower Bookshop*   The shop carries books on historic Washington, as well as general books on historic preservation. The Pavilion-Old Post Office Building, 12th Street and Pennsylvania Avenue NW, Washington, DC 20004; (202) 523-5695.

• *Washington Monument Bookshop*   The shop features the writings and biographies of George Washington, as well as books on the Washington area. Washington Monument, 15th Street & Constitution Avenue NW, Washington, DC 20242; (202) 472-6419.

Manassas National Battlefield Park Bookstore   This well-stocked bookstore carries many historical books and videos about the Civil War, along with certain titles about Manassas. Owned and operated by the Eastern National Park and Monument Association Bookstore in Philadelphia, PA.

6511 Sudley Road, Manassas, Va 22110; (703) 754-7107. *Hours*: Daily, dawn to dusk.

Phillips Collection Museum Shop   The shop carries books on the arts, including titles on architecture, art history, painting, sculpture, interior design and gardens. Museum publications and monographs on artists are also for sale. The shop also carries a large collection of posters, reproductions and postcards, journals, calendars, paper goods, jewelry, mobiles, educational games for children and art supplies. Special orders are accepted.

1600 21st Street NW, Washington, DC 20009; (202) 667-6106. *Hours*: Tues-Sat, 10 am to 5 pm; Sun, 2 to 7 pm.

Smithsonian Institution Museum Shops   Each of the major museums of the Smithsonian Institution has its own shop, with books, posters, cards, jewelry and other gift items relating to the museum's holdings on sale. All shops open each day from 10 am to 5:30 pm, and even later during summer months. For general information, call (202) 287-3563.

• *Arts & Industries Building*   The shop carries books on nineteenth-century American crafts and customs, as well as cards, jewelry and an extensive collection of Victoriana. 900 Jefferson Drive SW, Washington, DC 20560; (202) 357-1368/9.

• *Freer Gallery of Art*   Books on Oriental and early twentieth-century American art are available in the shop, as well as postcards, notecards, desk sets, slides, prints, ceramics, jewelry and needlepoint kits. 12th Street & Jefferson Drive SW, Washington, DC 20560; (202) 357-2104.

• *Hirshhorn Museum & Sculpture Garden*   The shop features books on twentieth-century art and sculpture, as well as postcards, posters and jewelry. Independence Avenue & 8th Street SW, Washington, DC 20560; (202) 357-4405.

• *National Air & Space Museum*   Both shops carry numerous books on aeronautics, astronautics and the history of human flight. The shop on the lower level carries postcards, models, slides, posters and freeze-dried ice cream. The Spacearium shop on the upper level carries books, posters and first-day stamp covers. 6th and Independence Avenue SW, Washington, DC 20560; (202) 357-1387.

• *National Museum of African Art*   The shop carries books on African art, designs and crafts, as well as postcards, jewelry, textiles, baskets and carvings. 950 Independence Avenue SW, Washington, DC 20560; (202) 786-2147.

• *National Museum of American Art*   Books on art (especially by American artists) are available in the shop, as well as exhibition catalogues, slides, postcards and reproductions. 8th & G Streets NW, Washington, DC 20560; (202) 357-1545.

• *National Museum of American History* The shop carries books on American history and related subjects, as well as audio and video tape cassettes, posters, prints, toys, games, dolls, jewelry and other gift items. 14th Street & Constitution Avenue NW, Washington, DC 20560; (202) 357-1527/28.

• *National Museum of Natural History* The shop carries books on natural history, anthropology and many dinosaur books and toys. Also available are postcards, posters, jewelry and original crafts. 10th Street & Constitution Avenue NW, Washington, DC 20560; (202) 357-1535/36.

• *National Portrait Gallery* The shop carries books on American history and art, as well as exhibition catalogues, slides, postcards, posters, reproductions, jewelry, scarves, china and silver. 8th & F Streets NW, Washington, DC 20560; (202) 357-1447.

• *Renwick Gallery* The shop carries books on American crafts and design, as well as many quality crafts, jewelry and objects relating to museum exhibitions. Pennsylvania Avenue & 17th Street NW, Washington, DC 20560; (202) 357-1445.

• *Arthur M. Sackler Gallery of Art* The shop carries an extensive selection of books on Near and Far Eastern art, as well as gifts, cards, posters and reproductions. 1050 Independence Avenue SW, Washington, DC 20560; (202) 786-2088.

Textile Museum Shop The shop carries many general interest books about textiles, with a focus on Oriental carpets and how-to books on knitting, embroidering and lacemaking. Books, museum publications and other items relating to current exhibits are also on sale, as well as jewelry (contemporary and ethnographic), baskets and many special textiles (including handpainted and imported ties and silk scarves).

2320 S Street NW, Washington, DC 20008; (202) 667-0441. *Hours*: Mon-Sat, 10 am to 5; Sun, 1 to 5 pm.

Mystery

Mystery Bookshop Billed as the "Home of Masterpiece Murder and Collectible Crime," Mystery Bookshop carries a large selection of new mysteries, detective fiction, espionage, true crime, thrillers, suspense, reference and children's mysteries. The store also features many used books in these categories, plus mystery audio and video cassettes for sale. Mystery Bookshop holds book signings, readings and writers' symposia by local and national mystery authors and sponsors a local chapter of Mystery Readers International.

7700 Old Georgetown Road, Bethesda, MD 20814; (301) 657-2665. *Hours*: Mon-Sat, 10 am to 7 pm; Sun, 12 noon to 5 pm.

MysteryBooks Relax in comfortable wing chairs and peruse one the area's largest selections of detective, suspense and spy fiction at MysteryBooks. A great place to find mystery audio books, large-print books, anthologies, horror, reference and hard-to-find British titles, the store also features its exclusive "Crime and Nourishment" Gift Baskets, combining specially selected books and gourmet foods. Other mystery-related gifts are also on sale, including puzzles, games, mugs and T-shirts. The store offers a free 72–page mail order catalogue, and hosts frequent book signings by best-selling local and national mystery authors. Items are shipped "with pleasure."

1715 Connecticut Avenue NW, Washington, DC 20009; (202) 483-1600/ (800) 955-2279. *Hours*: Mon-Fri, 11 am to 7 pm; Sat, 10 am to 6 pm; Sun, 12 noon to 5 pm.

Nature & The Outdoors

Friends of the National Zoo Bookstore The FONZ Bookstore features books on the animal world and wildlife, including nature-related fiction for teens & adults and Audubon books. Nature films and videos (including National Geographic specials), bird feeders and birdseed, minerals, rocks, fossils, posters, gifts and cards are also on sale.

3001 Connecticut Avenue NW, Washington, DC 20008; (202) 673-4800. *Hours*: Mon-Fri, 10 am to 4:30 pm; Sat & Sun, 10 am to 5:30 pm.

Habitat Owned and operated by the National Wildlife Federation, these book and gift shops carry titles on nature, wildlife and the environment and many reference books (including those published by the Federation).

Books and other items for children, gifts, greeting cards, T-shirts and posters are also on sale.

• *Scott Circle*   1400 16th Street NW, Washington, DC 20036; (202) 797-6644. *Hours*: Mon-Fri, 10 am to 5:30 pm.

• *Vienna*   8925 Leesburg Pike, Vienna, VA 22184; (703) 790-4456. *Hours*: Mon-Fri, 8:30 am to 4 pm.

National Geographic Society Bookstore   Books for children and adults published by the Society are sold here exclusively, along with Geographic Society postcards, atlases, maps and globes.

17th & M Streets NW, Washington, DC 20036; (202) 921-1200. *Hours*: Mon-Sat, 9 am to 5 pm; Sun, 10 am to 5 pm.

The Nature Company   This national chain of stores, devoted to the "observation, appreciation and understanding of nature," has five area locations that feature a large selection of books on nature and the natural world. Subjects include plants and animals (including dinosaurs), science, the body and nature commentary. Each store also features large children's book sections.

• *Annapolis*   134 Main Street, Annapolis, MD 21404; (301) 268-3909. *Hours*: Mon-Sat, 10 am to 9:30 pm; Sun, 11 am to 6 pm.

• *Arlington*   Fashion Centre at Pentagon City, 1100 S. Hayes Street, Arlington, VA 22202; (703) 415-3700. *Hours*: Mon-Sat, 10 am to 9:30 pm; Sun, 11 am to 6 pm.

• *Georgetown*   1323 Wisconsin Avenue NW, Washington, DC 20007; (202) 333-4100. *Hours*: Mon-Fri, 10 am to 9 pm; Sat, 10 am to 10 pm; Sun, 12 noon to 6 pm.

• *McLean*   Tyson's Corner Center, McLean, VA 22102; (703) 760-8930. *Hours*: Mon-Sat, 10 am to 9:30 pm; Sun, 12 noon to 5 pm.

• *Union Station*   50 Massachusetts Avenue NE, Washington, DC 20002; (202) 842-3700. *Hours*: Mon-Sat, 10 am to 9 pm; Sun, noon to 6.

One Good Tern   This store specializes in nature books, including books published by the Sierra Club and Audubon Society, field guides by Roger Tory Peterson and other naturalists, travel guides and children's nature books. It also carries binoculars, bird feeders and spotting scopes. A birding booklist is available upon request.

1710 Fern Street, Alexandria, VA 22302; (703) 820-8376/ (800) 432-8376. *Hours*: Mon-Fri, 10 am to 6 pm (open Tues and Thurs until 8 pm); Sat, 9 am to 6 pm; Sun, 12 noon to 5 pm.

Wild Bird Centers   Each store location of this chain offers a large selection of books on birds, nature and the environment, as well as bird feeders and houses, field guides, binoculars, scopes, clothing and gifts.

• *Annapolis*   101 Annapolis Street, Annapolis, MD 21401; (301) 280-0033. *Hours*: Mon-Fri, 11 am to 6 pm; Sat, 10 am to 6 pm; Sun, 12 noon to 5 pm.

• *Cabin John*   7687 MacArthur Boulevard, Cabin John, MD 20818; (301) 229-3141. *Hours*: Daily, 10 am to 6 pm.

• *Gaithersburg*   420 E. Diamond Avenue, Gaithersburg, MD 20877; (301) 330-9453. *Hours*: Daily, 10 am to 6 pm.

Wild Bird Company   Each store location carries an excellent selection of books and other items on local and national birdwatching. Also available are feeders, houses and seed for backyard birdwatchers, videos (for sale and rent), audio cassettes, CDs, T-shirts, binoculars and scopes (for sale and rent), gifts and cards. The stores offer free newsletters and catalogues, will handle special, mail and phone orders and provide worldwide shipping.

• *Frederick*   45 Waverly Drive, Frederick, MD 21702; (301) 698-2545. *Hours*: Mon-Sat, 10 am to 6 pm (open Thurs & Fri until 7 pm); Sun, 12 noon to 5 pm.

• *Rockville*   617 Hungerford Drive, Rockville, MD 20852; (301) 279-0079. *Hours*: Mon-Sat, 10 am to 6 pm (open Wed until 8 pm); Sun, 12 noon to 5 pm.

Nautical

Fawcett Boat Supplies Book Department   Fawcett's offers a large selection of books on sailing and power boating, including many titles on rigging, splicing and repairing. It also carries books about the Chesapeake Bay and Annapolis.

110 Compromise Street, Annapolis, MD 21401; (301)

267-8681. *Hours*: Mon-Sat, 8:30 am to 5 pm; Sun, 11 am to 4 pm.

New Age & Metaphysical

Beautiful Day Bookstore This natural food store carries books on homeopathy, organic agriculture, nutrition, health, and organic and natural cooking.

5010 Berwyn Road, College Park, MD 20740; (301) 345-2121. *Hours*: Mon-Sat, 9 am to 7:30 pm; Sun, 10 am to 4 pm.

Blue Nile Trading Company Blue Nile carries metaphysical and health books on many subjects, including vegetarianism, vitamins and macrobiotics.

2826 Georgia Avenue NW, Washington, DC 20001; (202) 232-3535. *Hours*: Mon-Sat, 11 am to 7 pm.

Divine Science Metaphysical Bookstore Metaphysical books, Marian Heath cards, pamphlets and sermons-on-tape are all available in this bookstore.

2025 35th Street NW, Washington, DC 20007; (202) 333-7631. *Hours*: Mon-Fri, 10 am to 3 pm.

Sun & Moon Sun & Moon features a large selection of New Age, metaphysical and holistic health books, as well as meditation tapes, music tapes and various gifts from 28 countries.

203 Harrison Street, Leesburg, VA 22075; (703) 777-2466. *Hours*: Mon-Sat, 10 am to 6 pm; Sun, 12 noon to 5 pm.

Yes! Bookshop Yes! carries books on inner development, New Age, travel, Asian studies, ancient history, astrology, healing, body work, spirituality, meditation, mythology, psychology, philosophy, religion and more. It also stocks new age music (cassettes, records and CDs), computer astrology charts and greeting cards. Special, phone and mail orders are accepted, and worldwide delivery is available.

1035 31st Street NW, Washington, DC 20007; (202) 338-7874/Video Department, 1303 N. Fillmore Street, Arlington, Virginia; (703) 276-9522. *Hours*: Mon-Sat, 10 am to 10 pm; Sun, noon to 6 pm.

Newsstands

B & B News Stand Billing itself as "one of the world's largest newsstands," B & B carries a vast selection of U.S. and foreign newspapers and magazines. It also stocks some paperback books, sundries and other items.

2621 Connecticut Avenue NW, Washington, DC 20008; (202) 234-0494. *Hours*: Mon-Fri, 9 am to 12 midnight; Sat & Sun, 7 am to 12 midnight.

Book 'N Card This newsstand and bookstore emphasizes literature, science fiction and history (especially the Civil War), and features a large selection of magazines and newspapers.

8110 Arlington Blvd, Falls Church, VA 22042; (703) 560-6999. *Hours*: Mon-Fri, 9 am to 10 pm; Sat, 9 am to 9 pm; Sun, 9 am to 6 pm.

Faber, Coe & Gregg Newsstands Located in historic Union Station, these two newsstands (both on the Lower Level) carry a wide range of local and national newspapers and magazines, a good selection of mass market paperbacks, some gifts and various sundries.

Historic Union Station, 50 Massachusetts Avenue NE, Washington, DC 20002; (202) 789-0100.

Key Bridge Newsstand Disguised as a convenience store, this small newsstand carries many U.S. and foreign newspapers and magazines, along with sundries and other items.

3326 M Street NW, Washington, DC 20007; (202) 338-2626. *Hours*: Daily, 8 am to 8 pm.

Max Wonder This store carries a large selection of newspapers, magazines and videotapes, as well as a small selection of used books.

11236 Georgia Avenue, Wheaton, MD 20902; (301) 942-4119. *Hours*: Mon-Sat, 9 am to 10 pm; Sun, 9 am to 9 pm.

The News Room The News Room features a large assortment of newspapers, journals and U.S. and foreign magazines on every subject, including many collector's editions and significant back issues. It also carries a sizeable selection of paperback books, literary and academic journals, computer books, cards, T-shirts, sundries and more.

1753 Connecticut Avenue NW, Washington, DC 20009; (202) 332-1489. *Hours*: Mon-Fri, 7 am to 10 pm; Sat, 7 am to midnight; Sun, 7 am to 10 pm.

Political Thought

Brookings Institution Bookstore   The bookstore of this prestigious think tank carries its own books and other publications on governmental studies, economic studies and foreign policy.

1775 Massachusetts Avenue NW, Washington, DC 20036; (202) 797-6258. *Hours*: Mon-Fri, 9 am to 4:30 pm.

Revolution Books   Revolution Books carries a large selection of books on economics, history, science and technology, revolutionary internationalism, political theory, radical politics and current events.

1815 Adams Mill Road NW, Washington, DC 20009; (202) 265-1969. *Hours*: Mon-Fri, 12 noon to 7 pm; Sat, 11 am to 7 pm; Sun, 12 noon to 5 pm.

Private Book Dealers (Mail Order/By Appointment)

Agribookstore   Operated by Winrock International, a nonprofit institute for agricultural development in the Third World, this dealer carries American and foreign books on agriculture, forestry, the environment, natural resources and development. It also sells maps, computer software and slide sets. Mail order only.

1611 North Kent Street, Arlington, VA 22209; (703) 525-9455.

American Book Centres   ABC carries a large selection of scholarly and collectible used, rare and new books in all price ranges. It specializes in: area studies (all continents and languages), history, military, archeology, travel, anthropology, art & architecture, photography, music, entertainment, literature and more. First editions and fine bindings are available. Subject collections are on hand or built to order. ABC features custom in-home or office service at no extra cost, as well as gift wrapping and dispatch. Mail order and/or by appointment.

P.O. Box 39090, Washington, DC 20016; (202) 244-4173.

Antiquarian Tobacciana   This dealer specializes in books on tobacco and smoking, including facsimile, first and limited editions, used, imported, rare and out-of-print titles. Antiquarian Tobacciana also tracks foreign language editions and remainders. Mail order only.

11505 Turnbridge Lane, Reston, VA 22094; no phone listed.

Arlington Book Company   Books imported from England, France and Germany about clocks and watches are the focus of this dealer. Mail order only.

2706 Elsmore Street, Fairfax, VA 22031; (703) 280-2005.

Ashe & Deane   A & D offers a selection of rare and out-of-print books from the eighteenth and nineteenth centuries. Some earlier works are also available. A search service is available. Mail order and/or by appointment.

P.O. Box 15601, Chevy Chase, MD 20825; (301) 588-9590.

Audubon Prints and Books   This dealer specializes in new and used books by or about John James Audubon. Original prints and reproductions are also available. Mail order and/or by appointment.

9720 Spring Ridge Lane, Vienna, VA 22182; (703) 759-5567.

Bartleby's   This dealer specializes in general interest and antiquarian books on America. Mail order and/or by appointment.

4823 Fairmont Avenue, Bethesda, MD 20814; (301) 654-4373.

Steven C. Bernard First Editions   This dealer specializes in modern first editions, including science fiction and mysteries. A catalogue is available. Mail order only.

15011 Plainfield Lane, Darnestown, MD 20874; (301) 948-8423.

Bickerstaff & Barclay   Used, out-of-print and rare photography books are available from this dealer. Mail order only.

P. O. Box 46259, Washington, D.C. 20050–6259; no phone listed.

Books of Colonial America   Used, rare and out-of-print books on America, history, Marylandiana, New Yorkiana, Pennsylvaniana, meteorology and climatology are the focus of this dealer. A search service is available. Mail order only.

3611 Janet Road, Wheaton, MD 20906; (301) 946-6490.

Culpepper, Hughes & Head This dealer specializes in new, used, rare and out-of-print books on Africa, black studies and Caribbean history. It also offers remainders. A free catalogue is available. Mail order only.

9770 Basket Ring Road, Columbia, MD 21045; (301) 730-1484.

Q.M. Dabney & Co This dealer specializes in books on military history, especially U.S. and British military history. It also sells books on American history, European history, the Wild West, music, law and the social sciences. Used, rare, illustrated and out-of-print books are available, as well as remainders, first, facsimile and limited editions. A catalogue is available. Mail order only.

11910 Parklawn Drive, Rockville, MD 20852; (301) 881-1470.

Frazier's Americana Frazier's orders and shows books on the Civil War, history, American presidents and the presidency. New, used, old and rare books are available, as well as first, limited and facsimile editions. It also sells maps, posters, sheet music, autographs and manuscripts. A search service is available. Mail order only.

10509 Walter Point Way, Mitchellville, MD 20721; (301) 336-3616.

Doris Frohnsdorf This dealer specializes in illustrated and children's books. Mail order and/or by appointment.

P.O. Box 2306, Gaithersburg, MD 20886; (301) 869-1256.

John Gach Books John Gach carries a large inventory (30,000 +) of second-hand, out-of-print and rare books on the history of ideas, philosophy, psychiatry, psychology and psychoanalysis. It also features many current books on these subjects. Free catalogues are available (4–6 per year). Mail order and/or by appointment.

5620 Waterloo Road, Columbia, MD 21045; (301) 465-9023.

Garden Variety A variety of garden books, plus cards and gifts about gardening, may be acquired from this dealer. Mail order only.

P.O. Box 40721, Washington, DC 20016; (202) 686-1229.

Mrs. Duff Gilfond Fugitive Books Intercepted This is a search service exclusively for out-of-print books on any subject. Mail order and/or by appointment

1722 19th Street NW, Suite 811, Washington, DC 20009; (202) 387-1418.

Joshua Heller Rare Books, Inc. Specializing in press and illustrated books, as well as artist's books, this dealer also offers fine bindings. A catalogue is available. Mail order and/or by appointment.

P.O. Box 39114, Washington, DC 20016; (202) 966-9411.

Hirschtritt's "1712" History of Books Hirschtritt's specializes in rare and out-of-print books on Americana, Orientalia and golf. It also carries a general stock of out-of-print books. First and limited editions, as well as illustrated books, are available. A search service is offered. Mail and phone orders only.

1712 Republic Road, Silver Spring, MD 20902; (301) 649-5393.

Jennie's Book Nook Jennie's specializes in old, rare and out-of-print titles in biography, fiction, history, poetry and Virginiana. It also publishes and sells books on genealogy. A search service is available. Mail order only.

15 West Howell Avenue, Alexandria, VA 22301; (703) 683-0694.

Frank & Laurese Katen The Katens specialize in books on numismatics (coins and currency). Modern, rare, out-of-print, old and imported books are available. Mail orders and/or by appointment.

P.O. Box 4047, Silver Spring, MD 20914; (301) 384-9444/9449.

John W. Knott, Jr. This dealer specializes in science fiction, fantasy and horror titles. It sells limited editions, British firsts, specialty press and new small press books. Mail order and/or by appointment.

8453 Early Bud Way, Laurel, MD 20723; (301) 725-7537.

Peter Koffsky Koffsky specializes in out-of-print books on history, plus maps and ephemera. Mail order only.

1708 Glenkarney Place, Silver Spring, MD 20902; (301) 649-6105.

Robert A. Madle Books This dealer offers new, used, rare and out-of-print science fiction/fantasy and related material, including science fiction magazines and pulps. A catalogue is available, and search service is provided. Mail order and/or by appointment.

4406 Bestor Drive, Rockville, MD 20853; (301) 460-4712.

National Intelligence Book Center NIBC specializes in nonfiction books on espionage, including how-to's of counter-intelligence, wire tapping, surveillance and physical security, trade craft (cover identities, mail drops, letter opening and explosives), history of intelligence agencies. It offers current and out-of-print books, and also imports foreign books in all languages on these subjects. A special NIBC section may be found at Olsson's Books & Records at Dupont Circle. The dealer offers a subscription catalogue (6 times per year). Mail order and/or by appointment.

1700 K Street NW, Suite 607, Washington, DC 20006; (202) 797-1234.

O'Boyle Books This dealer offers general interest rare, out-of-print, first-edition and modern books. O'Boyle exhibits regularly at book fairs. Mail order and/or by appointment.

14605 Pebblestone Drive, Silver Spring, MD 20905; (301) 384-9346.

William B. O'Neill Books on modern Greece, Cyprus, Turkey, Armenia and the Middle East are available from this dealer, as well as Baedeker Travel Guides. An annual catalogue is available by subscription ($7.50 per year). Mail order and/or by appointment.

P.O. Box 2275, Reston, VA 22090; (703) 860-0782.

Old Hickory Bookshop Ltd. Old Hickory specializes in rare and out-of-print medical, dentistry, science and technology books. Mail order and/or by appointment.

20225 New Hampshire Avenue, Brinklow, MD 20862; (301) 924-2225.

Old World Mail Auctions   Old World specializes in rare travel books, such as accounts by Europeans of U.S. travel, books with plates of U.S. views, nineteenth-century atlases, maps, prints and old newspapers. Five mail auctions are held annually, and a catalogue is available. Mail order and/or by appointment.

5614 Northfield Road, Bethesda, MD 20817; (301) 657-9074.

Quill & Brush   Q & B features nineteenth- and twentieth-century first editions of collectible authors, principally literature. It also publishes an excellent series of "Author Price Guides," which are looseleaf bibliographies of twentieth-century authors (115 available). A catalogue is available. Mail order and/or by appointment.

P.O. Box 5365, Rockville, MD 20851; (301) 460-3700.

Bacon Race Books   Bacon Race specializes in new, used and rare books on the American Civil War. Mail order only.

3717 Pleasant Ridge Road, Annandale, VA 22003; (703) 560-7376.

John C. Rather   This dealer specializes in illustrated, rare and out-of-print books on chess, photography, magic/conjuring, art history and mountaineering. Mail order only.

P.O. Box 273, Kensington, MD 20895; (301) 942-0515.

Jo Ann Reisler Ltd.   Jo Ann sells only rare children's and illustrated books, principally from the late eighteenth-through early twentieth-centuries. She also sells original illustrative art (primarily from children's books). Mail order and/or by appointment.

360 Glyndon Street NE, Vienna, VA 22180; (703) 938-2237.

Oscar Shapiro   This dealer specializes in out-of-print, old and rare books on chess, music and the violin. He also sells autographs, manuscripts, lithographs and engravings on music. An annual catalogue is provided.

3726 Connecticut Avenue NW, Washington, DC 20008; no phone listed.

Thistle & Shamrock Books   Thistle & Shamrock offers adult and children's books on Scottish and Irish history, literature and culture. Foreign language, imports, remainders and used books are available. Mail order only.
P.O. Box 42, Alexandria, VA 22313; (703) 548-2207.

Ron Van Sickle Military Books   This dealer specializes in used, out-of-print and some new books on military history emphasizing the American Civil War. A catalogue is available. Mail order and/or by appointment.
P.O. Box 2419, Gaithersburg, MD 20886; (301) 330-2400.

Voyages Books & Art   Voyages specializes in used, old and rare books of twentieth-century literature. First editions, illustrated and limited editions, paperbacks and fine bindings on all subjects are available. Mail order only.
4705 Buttersworth Place NW, Washington, DC 20016 or c/o Washington Antique center, 209 Madison, Alexandria, VA; (202) 364-0378.

Yak & Yeti Books   Yak & Yeti specializes in used, in-print and rare books on the Himalayas, Central Asia and Tibet. A free book list is available. Mail order and/or by appointment.
P.O. Box 5736, Rockville, MD 20855; (301) 977-7285.

Professional, Academic & Business

Anderson Brothers Bookstore   This well-stocked store carries a full line of textbooks for nearby George Mason University. Its general interest section also features best-sellers, reference (general and nursing) and children's books, clothing, office and school supplies and novelty items.
10661 Braddock Road, Fairfax, VA 22032; (703) 352-8008. *Hours*: Mon-Sat, 10 am to 6 pm.

Hammett's Learning World   These educational stores carry workbooks, reference books, teaching supplies and other materials for students, teachers and parents. Most items are geared for children at the elementary school level.

• *Oakton* 2914 Chain Bridge Road, Oakton, VA 22124; (703) 938-0047. *Hours*: Mon-Thurs, 10 am to 9 pm; Fri & Sat, 10 am to 5 pm.

• *Springfield* Springfield Tower Mall, 6420 Brandon Avenue, Springfield, VA 22150; (703) 569-2303. *Hours*: Mon-Fri, 10 am to 6 pm; Sat, 9 am to 5 pm.

Reiter's Scientific & Professional Books Reiter's carries a large selection on books about business, computer science, architecture, economics, mathematics, engineering, physics, chemistry, business, biology, medicine, philosophy, psychology, physics and statistics. Special orders are accepted, and worldwide shipping is available.

2021 K Street NW, Washington, DC 20006; (202) 223-3327. *Hours*: Mon-Fri, 9 am to 7:30 pm; Sat, 9:30 am to 6 pm; Sun, 12 noon to 5 pm.

Tools of the Trade: Books for Communicators This comfortable, well-stocked bookstore specializes in books for writers, editors, typographers, graphic designers, publishers (classic and desktop) and scientific and business communicators. It carries new hardcover, trade paper and some text and professional books on public relations, advertising, consulting and successfully running a small business. A catalogue is available, and mail or special orders are welcome.

Roundhouse Square, 1434–B Duke Street, Alexandria, VA 22314; (703) 683-4186/ FAX (703) 683-5837. *Hours*: Mon-Fri, 10 am to 5 pm. Also open the first Saturday of each month, 10 am to 5 pm.

Washington Law Book Company WLBC carries many law books and other textbooks (international trade, accounting, finance, etc.) for students of George Washington University Law School. It also carries non-textbooks on law and other subjects.

1900 G Street NW, Washington, DC 20006; (202) 371-6667. *Hours*: Mon-Fri, 9:30 am to 6 pm; Sat, 10 am to 5 pm.

Writer's Center Book Gallery A bookstore for writers and readers, this cozy place carries small press fiction and poetry, books on writing and more than 100 literary magazines. The store is owned and operated by The Writer's Center, which sponsors readings, workshops and special conferences and publishes *Poet Lore* and *Carousel*. At the Book Gallery, Center members receive a 10% discount and may display books on consignment.

7815 Old Georgetown Road, Bethesda, MD 20814; (301) 654-8664. *Hours*: Mon-Thurs, 10 am to 8 pm; Fri & Sat, 10 am to 5 pm; Sun, 1 pm to 5 pm.

Religious

Agape Bookstore   Agape carries Christian books, bibles, music tapes, comics, posters and greeting cards.

1001 Connecticut Avenue NW, Washington, DC 20036; (202) 223-3282. *Hours*: Mon-Fri, 10:30 am to 6:30 pm.

Ark & Dove   Christian books and supplies, bibles, candles, song and choral books, tapes, church supplies, cards and gifts are available in this store.

6122 Rose Hill Drive, Alexandria, VA 22310; (703) 971-7000. *Hours*: Mon-Sat, 10 am to 6 pm (open Tues & Thurs until 8 pm).

Baptist Bookstore   This book and supply store carries many items for children and adults, including bibles and music, with an emphasis on Baptist theology.

7259 Commerce Street, Springfield, VA 22150; (703) 569-0067. *Hours*: Mon-Sat, 10 am to 6 pm (open Tues & Thurs until 8 pm).

Battle's Religious Bookstore   Battle's carries religious books, sheet music, pulpit furniture and communion wear.

4311 Sheriff Road NE, Washington, DC 20019; (202) 399-2366. *Hours*: Mon-Sat, 9 am to 5 pm.

Buddhist Vihara Society Bookstore   This bookstore features many titles on Buddhism and meditation.

5017 16th Street NW, Washington, DC 20011; (202) 723-0773. *Hours*: Daily, 9 am to 9 pm.

Catholic Book Store   Catholic books and a full line of church supplies are available in this store.

11272 Georgia Avenue, Wheaton, MD; (301) 942-4700. *Hours*: Mon-Sat, 9 am to 5:45 pm.

Chesapeake Book & Health Food Center   This store features religious books for children and adults, with an emphasis on Adventism. It also carries books on health, music, nature and the environment, as well as vitamins, health food, magazines, gifts, greeting cards, records, videos, art, greeting cards and college and church supplies.

6600 Martin Road, Columbia, MD 21044; (301) 995-1913. *Hours*: Mon-Thurs, 8:30 am to 5:30 pm (open Thur until 8 pm); Fri, 8:30 am to 1 pm; Sun, 9 am to 3 pm. Closed Saturday.

Choice Books　Choice features Christian inspirational books, bibles and bible study materials.

11923 Lee Highway, Fairfax, VA 22030; (703) 830-2800. *Hours*: Mon-Fri, 8:30 am to 5:30 pm.

Christian Bookshop　This store carries religious books, church supplies, recorded music, gifts and greeting cards.

35 Parole Plaza, Annapolis, MD 21401; (301) 266-8360. *Hours*: Mon-Sat, 9 am to 9 pm.

Evangel Bookstore　Numerous Christian books, bibles, gifts, cards, tapes, records, cassettes, songbooks and gifts are available in this store.

5900 Old Branch Avenue, Camp Springs, MD 20748; (301) 899-5940. *Hours*: Mon-Fri, 10 am to 5 pm.

Evangel Temple Bookstore　The store of this church features religious books and bibles.

616 Rhode Island Avenue NE, Washington, DC 20002; (202) 636-3615. *Hours*: Mon-Fri, 11 am to 7 pm; Sat, 11 am to 4 pm.

Evangelical Used Books　This private dealer sells used and out-of-print books on religion, with an emphasis on theology and evangelical Christianity.

1815 N. Nelson Street, Arlington, VA 22207; (703) 522-0596. *Hours*: By appointment only.

Gospel Bookstore　Gospel sells Christian books for adults and children, bibles, reference books, music, church supplies, gifts, greeting cards, toys, reproductions and videocassettes.

337 Hospital Drive, Ste A–2, Glen Burnie, MD 21061; (301) 761-3845. *Hours*: Mon-Fri, 10 am to 9 pm; Sat, 10 am to 6 pm.

Grace Christian Bookstore   In addition to being a full-service print shop, Grace Christian sells religious books, bibles, tapes and videos.

1102 West Church Road, Sterling, VA 22170; (703) 450-4121. *Hours*: Mon-Fri, 9 am to 6 pm; Sat, 9 am to 4 pm.

The Great Commission   This store sells Christian books, cards, prints, sheet music, tapes and gifts.

2107 North Pollard Street, Arlington, VA 22205; (703) 525-0222. *Hours*: Mon-Sat, 10 am to 7 pm.

His Presence   His Presence sells religious books for adults and children, bibles, cassettes, CDs, gifts, cards and figurines.

3238 Old Pickett Road, Fairfax, VA 22030; (703) 273-6234. *Hours*: Mon-Sat, 10 am to 7 pm. Later hours by appointment.

Hope & Hesed—A Celebrate New Life Store   This store carries Christian books for adults and children, gifts, tapes and greeting cards.

9017 Gaithers Road, Gaithersburg, MD 20877; (301) 840-1540. *Hours*: Mon-Sat, 9:30 am to 6 pm.

Jacob's Well Christian Books   Books, gifts, sermons-on-tape, music tapes, videos and jewelry are available at Jacob's Well.

170 Great Mills Road, Lexington Park, MD 20653; (301) 863-6388. *Hours*: Mon-Fri, 10 am to 6:30 pm; Sat, 10 am to 5 pm.

Jesus Bookstores   The three stores in this local chain each carry religious books for children and adults, bibles, records, tapes, videocassettes, jewelry, gifts, cards and church supplies.

• *Alexandria*   7700 Richmond Highway, Alexandria, VA 22306; 780-3200. *Hours*: Mon, Wed & Fri, 10 am to 9 pm; Tues, Thurs & Sat, 10 am to 6 pm.

• *Dale City*   14214 Smoketown Road, Dale City;

690-4777. *Hours*: Mon, Wed & Fri, 10 am to 9 pm; Tues, Thurs & Sat, 10 am to 6 pm.

• *Woodbridge* 13426 Jefferson Davis Highway, Woodbridge; 690-3161. *Hours*: Mon-Sat, 10 am to 6 pm (open Tues & Thurs until 8 pm).

Jewish Bookstore of Greater Washington Featuring a full line of fiction and nonfiction books about Judaism and Judaica, this store covers such subjects as religion, philosophy, music, children, cooking, law, holidays, prayer and travel. It also carries gifts, records and tapes.

11250 Georgia Avenue, Wheaton, MD 20902; (301) 942-2237. *Hours*: Mon-Thurs, 10 am to 6 pm; Fri, 10 am to 2 pm; Sun, 10 am to 5 pm. Closed Saturday.

Let There Be Praise A varied selection of religious books for adults and children is available here, as well as bibles, church supplies, gifts, greeting cards, videos and tapes.

9 Catoctin Circle SE, Leesburg, VA 22075; (703) 777-6311. *Hours*: Mon-Sat, 9:30 am to 6 pm; Fri, 9:30 am to 8 pm.

Libson's Hebrew Books & Gifts Libson's carries a full line of books about Judaism and Judaica, as well as gifts and 14–carat jewelry. The store will also produce invitations for weddings, bar mitzvahs, etc.

2305 University Boulevard West, Wheaton, MD 20902; (301) 933-1800. *Hours*: Mon-Thurs, 9:30 am to 6 pm (open Wed until 7 pm & Thurs until 8 pm; Fri, 9:30 am to 2 pm; Sun, 9:30 am to 5 pm. Closed Saturday.

Maranatha Christian Bookstore This store carries religious books, bibles, cards, gifts, music and jewelry.

1607 Commonwealth Avenue, Alexandria, VA 22301; (703) 548-2895. *Hours*: Mon-Fri, 10 am to 6 pm; Thurs, 10 am to 8 pm; Sat, 10 am to 5 pm.

Mustard Seed The two local Mustard Seed stores carry inspirational books, bibles, tapes and gifts, as well as greeting cards and gift wrap.

• *Arlington* 2401 Columbia Pike, Arlington, VA 22204; (703) 979-3549. *Hours*: Mon-Sat, 10 am to 6 pm; Thurs, 10 am to 8 pm.

• *Manassas* 7851 Sudley Road, Manassas, VA 22110; (703) 361-1125. *Hours*: Mon-Sat, 10 am to 9 pm.

National Presbyterian Church Books & Gifts This store carries religious books for adults and children (primarily Presbyterian), as well as bibles, sermons-on-tape, gifts and greeting cards.

4101 Nebraska Avenue NW, Washington, DC 20016; (202) 537-0800. *Hours*: Tues-Fri, 9 am to 4 pm; Sun, 8 am to 1 pm.

Newman Book Store of Washington Owned by Paulist Press, this store carries religious books of interest to Catholics and mainstream Protestants, plus textbooks for the theology and religion students at Catholic University and Howard University Divinity School.

3329 8th Street NE, Washington, DC 20017; (202) 526-1036. *Hours*: Mon-Sat, 9 am to 5 pm.

The Olive Branch Both store locations carry bibles, books, records, tapes, music, gifts, cards and church supplies.

• *Rockville* 765 Rockville Pike, Rockville, MD 20852; (301) 340-1129. *Hours*: Mon & Wed, 9:30 am to 6 pm; Tues, Thurs and Fri, 9:30 am to 9 pm; Sat, 9 am to 4:30 pm.

• *Silver Spring* 15426 New Hampshire Avenue, Silver Spring, MD 20904; (301) 384-9303. *Hours*: Mon-Wed, 9 am to 6 pm; Thurs & Fri, 9:30 am to 8 pm; Sat, 9:30 am to 4:30 pm.

Potomac Adventist Book & Health Food Center A large selection of religious books for children and adults is available at this store, with an emphasis on Adventism. The store also carries books on health, music, nature and the environment, plus vitamins, health food, magazines, gifts, greeting cards, records, videos, art, and college and church supplies.

8400 Carroll Avenue, Takoma Park, MD 20912; (301) 439-0700. *Hours*: Mon-Wed, 9 am to 5:30 pm; Thurs, 9 am to 9 pm; Fri, 9 am to 2:30 pm.

Pursell's Church Supplies Pursell's stocks many religious books and church supplies.

Waterside Mall, 401 M Street SW, Washington, DC

20024; (202) 484-9563. *Hours*: Mon-Fri, 10 am to 6 pm; Sat, 10 am to 2 pm.

Rock Uniform and Christian Bookstore   This store stocks religious books, greeting cards, games, records and tapes and sheet music.

1104 H Street NE, Washington, DC 20002; (202) 398-3333. *Hours*: Mon & Wed, 10 am to 5 pm; Tues & Thurs-Sat, 10 am to 6 pm.

St. Paul Catholic Book & Media Center   Featuring a large selection of Catholic books for all ages, St. Paul also carries family and religious instruction videos, cassettes and cards.

1025 King Street, Alexandria, VA 22314; (703) 549-3806. *Hours*: Mon-Fri, 9:30 am to 5:30 pm; Sat, 9:30 am to 5 pm.

Seminary Book Service   This service specializes in academic religious books, including treatises and commentaries about the Bible, liturgical reference works, theology and the Episcopal church and spiritual classics. It also sells religious supplies and gifts, and primarily serves Virginia Theological Seminary. Mail order service is available.

900 Quaker Lane, Alexandria, VA 22304; (703) 370-6161/(800) 368-3756. *Hours*: Mon-Sat, 10 am to 5 pm.

This Is The Place Bookstore   A full selection of Mormon Church books and supplies may be found here, as well as books and other materials on biblical and women's studies.

10408 Montgomery Avenue, Kensington, MD 20895; (301) 933-1943. *Hours*: Mon, 10 am to 4 pm; Wed, Thurs & Sat, 10 am to 6 pm; Tues & Fri, 10 am to 9 pm.

Truro Church Bookstore   Located within historic Truro Church, this store carries religious books for children and adults, as well as a selection of greeting cards, jewelry, videocassettes, tapes, records, CDs and songbooks.

10520 Main Street, Fairfax, VA 22030; (703) 273-8686. Hours: Mon-Fri, 9:30 am to 4:30 pm; Sat, 10 am to 2 pm; Sun, 9 am to 2 pm.

Washington Bible College Bookstore   Selling more to the general public than to students of the college, this store carries a large selection of religious books, including sections on theology, bible commentaries, Christian living, biography, great Christian leaders, counseling, fiction, family, books on women, men and health and social and ethical issues (all by Christian authors). It also carries Christian videos, tapes, CDs and choral music.

6511 Princess Garden Parkway, Lanham, MD 20706; (301) 552-1400. Hours: Mon-Sat, 9 am to 8:30 pm; Sat, 10 am to 5 pm.

Washington National Cathedral Museum & Bookshop Located below the magnificent Cathedral, this store carries many books on religion, theology, art and architecture. Bibles, crafts, gifts, greeting cards, jewelry, posters, religious goods and stationery are also on sale.

Wisconsin Avenue & Massachusetts Avenue NW, Washington, DC 20016; (202) 537-6267. *Hours*: Daily, 9:30 am to 5 pm (extended hours May-August).

Way of the Cross Ministry Way of the Cross carries religious books, bibles, cassettes, gifts, greeting cards and church supplies.

3466 14th Street NW, Washington, DC 20001; (202) 265-0908. *Hours*: Mon-Sat, 10 am to 6 pm.

Whosoever Will Church of God Christian & Religious Books This store sells books, tapes and records. Its health department carries books on the body, healing herbs, diet products and skin lotions.

3847 34th Street, Mount Ranier, MD; (301) 699-5008. *Hours*: Mon-Wed, 10 am to 6 pm; Thurs & Sat, 10 am to 7 pm.

Words of Wisdom Books & Gifts Words of Wisdom features a fine selection of Christian books and bibles, along with gifts, jewelry, greeting cards, religious goods, church supplies, tapes, CDs and videocassettes. Bible monogramming is available. The store also carries books on current political and social issues from a Christian perspective.

4209 Annandale Center Drive, Annandale, VA 22003; (703) 256-3005. *Hours*: Mon-Sat, 9:30 am to 5:30 pm (open Thurs until 7 pm).

Zondervan Family Bookstore Zondervan carries a large selection of religious books, Bibles, tapes, CDs, songbooks, gifts, cards and church supplies.

Fair Oaks Mall, Fairfax, VA 22033; (703) 352-1489. *Hours*: Mon-Sat, 10 am to 9:30 pm.

Remainder Services

Daedalus Books   A national mail order service which chooses from among thousands of remainders each year "those books which are of lasting value," Daedalus tries to find a good mix between books offered by commercial publishers and those offered by university presses which are of general interest. The company is especially strong in fiction, history, philosophy, science and art. Special orders are accepted, and Daedalus will mail free catalogues (6 per year).

P.O. Box 9132, Hyattsville, MD 20781–0932; (301) 779-4224/ (800) 395-2665.

Science Fiction & Fantasy

Barbarian Books   This general-interest used bookstore specializes in science fiction books, but it also has a varied general stock which includes comics, literature, children's books and bibliographies.

11254 Triangle Lane, Wheaton, MD 20902; (301) 946-4184. *Hours*: Tues-Sat, 12 noon to 6 pm; Sun, 1 pm to 6 pm.

Dream Wizards   Dream Wizards carries mostly nonfiction books on mysticism, magic, folklore, tarot, conjuring and strange phenomena. The store also sells games, greeting cards, posters, toys and computer software.

17 Rockville Pike/Rear, Rockville, MD 20852; (301) 881-3530. *Hours*: Mon & Tues, 11 am to 6 pm, Wed-Fri, 11 am to 8 pm; Sat, 10 am to 6 pm; Sun, 12 noon to 5 pm.

Hole In The Wall Books   This used bookstore carries a large and varied selection of science fiction and fantasy titles. It also features horror, mystery and detective fiction and comics, plus some new books and literary/historical fiction.

905 West Broad Street, Falls Church, VA 22046; (703) 536-2511. *Hours*: Mon-Fri, 10 am to 9 pm; Sat & Sun, 10 am to 6 pm.

The Magic Page   This used bookstore carries many science fiction and some general interest titles. Its broad stock also includes comic books, literature, children's books and bibliographies. It is owned by Barbarian Books (see above).

7416 Laurel-Bowie Road, Bowie, MD 20715; (301) 262-4735. *Hours*: Tues-Thurs, 3 pm to 5 pm; Fri, 3 pm to 8 pm; Sat, 12 noon to 6 pm.

Sports

Baseball Corner The Baseball Corner specializes in hard-to-find baseball books and publications. It also carries sports cards and paper sports collectibles.

5224 Port Royal Road, Springfield, VA 22150; (703) 524-8640. *Hours*: Mon-Fri, 10 am to 8 pm; Sat, 10 am to 6 pm; Sun, 12 noon to 5 pm.

Sports Books Etc.   Sports fans will find a large selection of new books on all sports here, plus an extensive collection of sports videos, magazines, calendars, posters and trading cards. This store shares space with *The Baseball Corner* (see above). Special and mail orders are accepted.

5224 Port Royal Road, Springfield, VA 22151; (703) 321-8660. *Hours*: Mon-Fri, 10 am to 8 pm; Sat, 10 am to 6 pm; Sun, 12 noon to 5 pm.

Travel & Tourism

The Map Store   This colorful store features hundreds of maps for the general buyer and the specialist, including nautical and aeronautical maps. The Map Store carries a full selection of domestic and foreign travel guidebooks, atlases, globes, map pins and markers, geographic reference material, antique map reproductions and celestial charts. A map mounting and framing service is available, and mail orders are accepted.

1636 I Street NW, Washington, DC 20006; (202) 628-2608. *Hours*: Mon-Fri, 9 am to 5:30 pm; Sat, 10 am to 4 pm.

National Map Gallery & Travel Center   Offering a complete selection of local, regional, national and international maps, this store also carries a number of travel guidebooks, atlases, globes, geographic software and business books. Mounting and laminating service is available, and mail orders are accepted.

Historic Union Station, 50 Massachusetts Avenue NE,

Washington, DC 20002; (202) 789-0100. *Hours*: Mon-Sat, 10 am to 9 pm; Sun, 12 noon to 6 pm.

Travel Books Unlimited & Language Center   This well-stocked travel bookstore carries a comprehensive selection of foreign language books, materials and cassette courses in more than 90 languages. It also carries a full selection of maps, travel guides and diaries, atlases, histories, dictionaries, grammars, travel videos, audio books and phrase books. Special and mail orders are accepted, and a free catalogue is available.

4931 Cordell Avenue, Bethesda, MD 20814; (301) 951-8533. *Hours*: Mon-Sat, 10 am to 9 pm; Sun, 12 noon to 5 pm.

Travel Merchandise Mart   The TMM offers a full selection of travel books, guides, language books and tapes, maps and other travel items (such as electrical outlet converters).

1425 K Street NW, Washington, DC 20005; (202) 371-6656. *Hours*: Mon-Fri, 9 am to 5 pm.

Universities & Colleges

American University Campus Store   AU's store sells general trade books, plus textbooks and remainders. It also has gifts, cards, college supplies, posters, computer software and sundries for sale.

American University, Massachusetts & Nebraska Avenues NW, Washington, DC 20016; (202) 885-6300. *Hours*: Mon-Fri, 9 am to 6 pm; Sat, 11 am to 3 pm.

Capitol College Bookstore   The CC store sells textbooks and some trade books in the areas of electronics, computers and engineering. It also carries clothing and school supplies.

11301 Springfield Road, Laurel, MD 20708; (301) 953-7561. *Hours*: Mon & Tues, 9 am to 6 pm; Wed & Thurs, 9 am to 5 pm; Fri, 9 am to 2 pm.

Catholic University of America Bookstore   CU's store carries general trade books, plus textbooks, school paraphernalia (sweat shirts, hats, etc.) and school supplies.

Catholic University of America, 620 Michigan Avenue NE, Washington, DC 20064; (202) 635-5232. *Hours*: Mon-Tues, 9 am to 6:30 pm; Wed-Thurs, 9 am to 5:30 pm; Fri, 9 am to 4 pm; Sat, 10 am to 1 pm.

Columbia Union College Bookstore   CUC's store carries textbooks and some trade books, plus art and college supplies, greeting cards, reproductions, computer software, video cassettes, sporting goods and calculators.

7600 Flower Avenue, Takoma Park, MD 20912; (301) 891-4096. *Hours*: Mon-Thurs, 9 am to 7 pm; Fri, 9 am to 2 pm.

Gallaudet University Bookstore   The store at the nation's leading school for deaf education carries many textbooks, with an emphasis on the liberal arts and deafness. A full selection of titles on sign language, hearing loss and other issues is available, as are many books written by deaf authors. Also on sale are some trade books, as well as clothes, school supplies, gifts and devices for the deaf (wake-up devices, TV decoders, telephone devices, etc.).

Gallaudet University, 800 Florida Avenue NE, Washington, DC 20002; (202) 651-5271/(800) 451-1073. *Hours*: Mon-Fri, 9 am to 4:30 am.

Georgetown University Bookstore   GU's bookstore sells general trade books, plus textbooks, school supplies and gifts.

Georgetown University, Lauinger Building, 3800 Reservoir Road, Washington, DC 20057; (202) 687-7482. *Hours*: Mon-Fri, 9 am to 8 pm; Sat & Sun, 11 am to 5 pm.

George Mason University Bookstore   GMU's bookstore carries textbooks and general interest books in a full range of categories, from computers to literature. The store also stocks study aids, soft goods, clothes, school supplies, sundries, greeting cards and jewelry.

GMU Student Union, 4400 University Avenue, Fairfax, VA 22030; (703) 425-3991. *Hours*: Mon-Thurs, 8 am to 7:30 pm; Fri, 8 am to 4 pm; Sat, 10 am to 3 pm.

George Washington University Bookstore   GWU's store carries textbooks, technical books and general trade books (even some children's books). It also stocks a full line of art, school and technical supplies, as well as remainders, greeting cards, posters, reproductions, snacks, gifts and magazines (U.S. and foreign). Special orders are accepted.

George Washington University, Marvin Center, 800 21st Street NW, Washington, DC 20052; (202) 994-6870.

Hours: Mon-Thurs, 9 am to 7 pm; Fri, 9 am to 5 pm; Sat, 11 am to 4 pm.

Howard Community College Bookstore   This store carries mostly textbooks and some trade books emphasizing self-help, as well as paperback bestsellers, cookbooks, reference and children's books. HCC's store also stocks greeting cards, gifts, magazines, school supplies, sportswear and sundries.

Little Patuxent Parkway, Columbia, MD 21044; (301) 992-4816. *Hours*: Mon-Fri, 8:30 am to 3:30 pm; Mon-Thurs, 5 pm to 8 pm.

Howard University Bookstore   The store carries new and used textbooks for Howard University classes, including the Dental-Medical School. Subject areas include African-American studies, health, dentistry, medicine and nursing. The store also carries some trade, medical reference and African-American heritage books, as well as college supplies.

Howard University, 2401 4th Street NW, Washington, DC 20059; (202) 636-6657. *Hours*: Mon-Fri, 9 am to 4:45 pm.

Marymount College Bookstore   The college's store carries textbooks and general interest books in many categories, including fiction and reference. It also stocks clothing, art and college supplies, greeting cards, posters and gifts.

2807 North Glebe Road, Arlington, VA 22207; (703) 284-1614. *Hours*: Mon, Tues & Thurs, 9 am to 4:30 pm; Wed, 9 am to 6 pm; Fri, 9 am to 2 pm.

Montgomery College Bookstores   The college's three bookstores carry textbooks, trade books (mostly study aids, computer and reference books), greeting cards, clothes, school and art supplies and sundries.

• *Germantown Campus*   20200 Observation Drive, Germantown, MD 20874; (301) 972-2388. *Hours*: Mon-Thurs, 8:30 am to 1:30 pm/ 4 pm to 7 pm.

• *Rockville Campus*   Campus Center, North Campus Drive, Rockville, MD 20850; (301) 279-5302. *Hours*: Mon-Thurs, 8:30 am to 1:30 pm/ 4 pm to 7 pm.

• *Takoma Park Campus*   New York & Takoma Avenues, Takoma Park, MD 20912; (301) 587-6243. *Hours*: Mon-Thurs, 8:30 am to 1:30 pm/ 4 pm to 7 pm.

Northern Virginia Community College Bookstores   All four NOVA Community College bookstores carry a large selection of books, as well as college supplies, gifts and sundries.

• *Alexandria Campus*   The store carries new and used textbooks, with a small supply of general interest books. 3101 North Beauregard Street, Alexandria, VA 22311; (703) 671-0043. *Hours*: Mon & Tues, 9 am to 8 pm; Wed & Thurs, 9 am to 5 pm; Fri, 8 am to 1 pm.

• *Annandale Campus*   The store carries new and used textbooks, plus a good selection of general interest books and many business and accounting titles. 8333 Little River Turnpike, Annandale, VA 22003; (703) 425-2558. *Hours*: Mon-Thur, 8:30 am to 7 pm; Fri, 8:30 am to 2 pm.

• *Loudon Campus*   The store carries new and used textbooks, with a good selection of titles in horticulture, agriculture, art, interior design, veterinary medicine, computer science and data processing. There is also a small selection of general interest books. 1000 Harry F. Byrd Highway, Sterling, VA 22170; (703) 430-9639. *Hours*: Mon & Thurs, 9 am to 3 pm; Tues & Wed, 9 am to 7:30 pm; Fri, 9 am to 12 noon.

• *Manassas Campus*   The store carries new and used textbooks, with a good selection of titles in computers, computer science and business and some general interest books. 6900 Sudley Road, Manassas, VA 22110; (703) 368-8554. *Hours*: Mon-Fri, 9:30 am to 2:30 pm (also open Tues-Thurs, 5 pm to 7 pm).

Prince George's Community College Bookstore   PGCC's store has a large selection of textbooks (especially nursing) and a small general interest section (fiction, nonfiction, reference books and study aids). It also stocks school, art, engineering and office supplies, gifts and clothing.

301 Largo Road, Largo, MD 20772; (301) 336-6844. *Hours*: Mon & Tues, 9 am to 8 pm; Wed & Thurs, 9 am to 5:30 pm; Fri, 9 am to 5 pm.

Trinity College Bookstore   The store carries new and used textbooks for Trinity College classes, some general interest books, clothing, sundries and other items.

Trinity College, 125 Michigan Avenue NE, Washington, DC 20017; (202) 939-5117. *Hours*: Mon-Thurs, 9 am to 5 pm; Fri, 9 am to 6 pm; Sun, 10 am to 2 pm.

University Book Center The Center serves University of Maryland students and the general public with a large selection of textbooks and supplies and many trade books in all categories: history, politics, religion, women's studies, new age, psychology, sports, study guides, computers and computer science, reference books, math, engineering, sciences, the humanities, travel, media and film. The Center offers an out-of-print book search for technical and professional books, and will accept special orders.

Adele H. Stamp Union, University of Maryland, College Park, MD 20742; (301) 314-2665. *Hours*: Mon-Fri, 8:30 am to 7:30 pm; Sat, 9 am to 5 pm; Sun, 12 noon to 5 pm.

University of the District of Columbia Bookstore The store carries textbooks, supplies and a selection of trade books for students at the University of the District of Columbia. It also stocks clothing, gifts, sundries and other items.

UDC Campus, 4200 Connecticut Avenue NW, Washington, DC 20008; (202) 966-5947. *Hours*: Mon-Thurs, 9 am to 5 pm; Tues & Wed, 9 am to 7 pm; Fri, 9 am to 4 pm.

Universities Bookstore Serving the University of Virginia and Virginia Tech Extension Campuses, the store sells new, used and remaindered textbooks on business and management, computer science, economics, education, engineering, nursing, reference, public administration planning, family and child development and human nutrition. It also carries some general interest books, college supplies, gifts and greeting cards.

2990 Telestar Court, Suite 400, Falls Church, VA 22042; (703) 698-6899. *Hours*: Mon-Thurs, 9:30 am to 8:30 pm; Fri, 9:30 am to 5 pm; Sat, 9 am to 12 noon.

Used, Rare & Out-Of-Print
(Store & Mail Order)

Air, Land & Sea This store, formerly called *The Nostalgic Aviator*, specializes in used and out-of-print books about transportation, as well as models and collectibles. Subject areas include aviation, surface and submarine navy and modern armor and ships.

1215 King Street, Alexandria, VA 22314; (703) 684-5118. *Hours*: Mon-Fri, 10 am to 6 pm; Sat, 10 am to 5 pm; Sun, 1 pm to 5 pm.

Attic Books   Attic features general interest used books, everything from art to zoology. It has large sections of science fiction, fantasy and history, as well as literature, drama, poetry and the sciences.

100 Washington Boulevard, Laurel, MD 20707; (301) 725-3725. *Hours*: Wed-Sat, 10 am to 7 pm; Sun, 1 pm to 5 pm. Closed Mon & Tues.

Barcroft Books   This store specializes in military history worldwide, with an emphasis on Queen Victoria's "little wars" and WWII. It also offers a large selection of titles on American Indians and the American West, travel (classic travel literature and picture books) and oversized military picture books.

3621 Columbia Pike, Bailey's Crossroads, VA 22004; (703) 521-0743. *Hours*: Mon-Fri, 11 am to 7 pm; Sat, 10 am to 6 pm.

Ben Franklin Booksellers   This store carries books on history, science and technology, art and music, plus classical literature and children's classics. It also sells prints, sheet music, toys and classical records. Special and mail orders are accepted.

27 South King Street, Leesburg, VA 22075; (703) 777-3661. *Hours*: Mon-Sat, 9 am to 5 pm; Sun, 12 noon to 5 pm.

Leonard S. Blondes Used Law Books   This store carries a large selection of used and out-of-print law books, and specializes in larger sets of law books for Federal, Washington, DC and Maryland law practices.

7100 Crail Drive, Bethesda, MD 20817; (301) 229-7102.

Bonifant Books   Bonifant carries many general interest used books, everything from classics to comics. It also has a specialized selection of vintage paperbacks.

11240 Georgia Avenue, Wheaton, MD 20902; (301) 946-1526. *Hours*: Mon-Fri, 10 am to 8 pm; Sat, 10 am to 6 pm; Sun, 11 am to 6 pm.

The Book Alcoves These three stores carry general interest used books and remainders, including classics, mysteries, gardening, ecology, crafts, history, self-help, home repair and anthropology titles. There are a number of antique, rare and out-of-print books for sale, including an assortment of Heritage Press and Folio Society books. Custom bookcases are also on sale.

• *Gaithersburg* Shady Grove Shopping Center/Rear, 15976 Shady Grove Road, Gaithersburg, MD 20877; (301) 977-9166. *Hours*: Mon-Fri, 10 am to 8 pm; Sat, 10 am to 6 pm; Sun, 12 noon to 5 pm.

• *Reston* 23373 Hunters Woods Plaza, Reston, VA 22091; (703) 620-6611. *Hours*: Mon-Sat, 10 am to 9 pm.

• *Rockville* 5210 Randolph Road, Rockville, MD 20852; (301) 770-5590. *Hours*: Mon-Fri, 10 am to 9 pm; Sat, 9:30 am to 9 pm; Sun, 12 noon to 6 pm.

The Book Cellar You can find used, rare and out-of-print books on all subjects and in many languages for collectors, scholars and avid readers at the Cellar. The store's large, eclectic selection ranges from humanities to science, first editions to cookbooks. Prints, maps and shelf music are also on sale.

8227 Woodmont Avenue, Bethesda, MD 20814; (301) 654-1898. *Hours*: Mon-Fri, 11 am to 6 pm; Sat, 11 am to 5 pm; Sun, 11 am to 5 pm.

Book Ends This general interest used bookstore specializes in American history and military history (especially WWII).

2710 Washington Boulevard, Arlington, VA 22201; (703) 524-4976. *Hours*: Fri-Mon, 12 noon to 6 pm.

The Book Market This store features a sizable selection of used books in all categories, with an emphasis on economics, political science, psychology, sociology, science fiction, mysteries and general fiction.

2602 Connecticut Avenue NW, Washington, DC 20008; (202) 332-2310. *Hours*: Mon-Fri, 11 am to 10 pm; Fri-Sun, 11 am to 12 midnight.

The Book Nooks These two stores feature used and collectible books on all subjects, including a large selection of children's books and comic books. Puppets and toys are available for children to use while parents browse.

• *College Park* 8911 Rhode Island Avenue, College Park, MD 20740; (301) 474-4060. *Hours*: Mon-Sat, 10 am to 5 pm.

• *Glen Burnie* 143 Delaware Avenue NE, Glen Burnie, MD 21061; (301) 766-5758. *Hours*: Mon-Sat, 10 am to 5 pm.

The Book Stop This store features used books in all categories, with large sections on art and architecture, the Civil War, WWII, Virginia history, travel and railroading. Some first editions and rare books are available, along with collectible sheet music and memorabilia. A search service is available.

Bradlee Shopping Center/Rear, 3640A King Street, Alexandria, VA 22314; (703) 578-3292. *Hours*: Mon-Wed & Fri, 12 noon to 6 pm; Sat, 11 am to 6 pm; Sun, 1 pm to 5 pm. Closed on Thursday.

Books Plus Owned and operated by Martin Luther King, Jr. Public Library, Books Plus carries used books of all kinds, fiction and nonfiction ($1 each hardcover, 50 cents each paperback). It also carries a few new titles—Washingtoniana, African-American history and others. The store also stocks greeting cards, posters, mugs, jewelry and stationery.

901 G Street NW, Washington, DC 20001; (202) 727-6834. *Hours*: Mon-Sat, 11 am to 5 pm; Sun, 1:30 pm to 4:30 pm.

Booked Up This cozy Georgetown store carries a varied range of rare, out-of-print and antiquarian books, including many first editions. Booked Up is co-owned by Pulitzer Prize winner Larry McMurtry and partner Marcia McGhee Carter.

1209 31st Street NW, Washington, DC 20007; (202) 965-3244. *Hours*: Mon-Fri, 11 am to 3 pm; also by appointment.

BookHouse Here is one large house filled with hundreds of general interest used and rare books for sale. BookHouse carries a large selection of American history titles, with smaller collections of natural history, art, world history and literature titles. A search service is available.

805 North Emerson Street, Arlington, VA 22205; (703) 527-7797. *Hours*: Wed, Fri & Sat, 11 am to 5 pm; Tues & Thurs, 12 noon to 6 pm.

Burke Centre Used Books & Comics One-half of this store carries general interest used books, while the other half is filled with new and back-issue comic books. Categories include science fiction, westerns, romance, biography, historical fiction, war, arts and crafts, cooking, children's, classics, science, and comics. There are also role-playing games/modules and posters for sale.

5741 Burke Centre Parkway, Burke, VA 22015; (703) 250-5114. *Hours*: Mon-Fri, 11 am to 8 pm; Sat, 10 am to 6 pm; Sun, 12 noon to 5 pm.

Colusa Books Colusa carries general interest used books of all kinds, with an emphasis on history, the arts, philosophy, natural sciences, political science, business, economic and financial theory. A search service is available.

Brookfield Plaza, 7060 Spring Garden Road, Springfield, VA 22150; (703) 644-1707. *Hours*: Wed-Fri, 12 noon to 8 pm; Sat & Sun, 10 am to 6 pm.

Ellen's Book Rack Here you can find a large selection of recent used paperbacks in all categories, as well as a small selection of new books. Ellen's will also special order new titles.

8727D Cooper Road, Alexandria, VA 22309; (703) 780-2325. *Hours*: Mon-Thurs, 11 am to 7 pm; Fri & Sat, 10 am to 6 pm; Sun, 12 noon to 5 pm.

Ellie's Paperback Shack Ellie's has used books of all kinds for sale or trade.

Acton Square, Rte 301, Waldorf, MD 20601; (301) 843-3676. *Hours*: Mon-Fri, 10 am to 5 pm; Sat, 10 am to 4 pm.

Encore Book Store Encore carries general interest used, rare and out-of-print books, with an emphasis on mystery and detective, science fiction and fantasy, romance, political science and Victorian poetry. You can find a good selection of foreign language, UK imports, children's books, remainders and first edition titles in these categories. Encore also carries new books in some categories.

7335 Old Alexandria Ferry Road, Camp Springs, MD 20748; (301) 868-8990. *Hours*: Mon-Sat, 10 am to 9 pm; Sun, 9 am to 5 pm.

Estate Book Sales This store features a wide variety of general interest used books, with an emphasis on art,

art history and literature. It also carries titles in biography, classics, military and diplomatic history, poetry, general fiction, literary criticism, philosophy and psychology.

2914 M Street NW, Washington, DC 20007; (202) 965-4274. *Hours*: Mon-Sun, 11 am to 7 pm.

Flanagans' This store carries general interest used, rare and antique books, as well as a large selection of maps.

Antique Emporium, 7120 Little River Turnpike, Annandale, VA 22030; (703) 256-4188. *Hours*: Wed-Sun, 11 am to 6 pm. Closed Mon & Tues.

Franklin Farm Used Books & Comics Franklin Farm carries general interest used books, with an emphasis on science fiction, fantasy and romance. It also stocks new and back issue comic books.

13320I Franklin Farm Road, Herndon, VA 22070; (703) 437-9530. *Hours*: Mon-Fri, 11 am to 8 pm; Sat, 10 am to 6 pm; Sun, 12 noon to 5 pm.

From Out Of The Past Books You will find general interest used, old and rare books in most categories here, with large selections of Americana and military history and a lot of older fiction and smaller sections of regional material and African-American history. There is also a large collection of back-issue magazines (up to the 1970s), plus decorative advertisements, posters and paper memorabilia (including road maps).

6640 Richmond Highway, Alexandria, VA 22306; (703) 768-7827. *Hours*: Tues-Sat, 11 am to 6 pm.

Fullers & Saunders Books This store carries used, rare and out-of-print books on Americana and regional history. Its owners are interested in purchasing books and/or library collections.

3238 P Street NW, Washington, DC 20007; (202) 337-3235. *Hours*: Thurs-Tues, 11 am to 6:30 pm (closed Wednesdays).

Georgetown Book Shop Here is a general interest second-hand shop which specializes in history (especially military and Soviet history) and carries books on most other subjects, including literature, art, photography, cookbooks, illustrated children's books, architecture, baseball and philosophy. The Shop also stocks many old magazines, as well as bound volumes of *The New York Times*.

7770 Woodmont Avenue, Bethesda, MD 20814; (301) 907-6923. *Hours*: Daily, 10 am to 6 pm.

Ground Zero Books This store carries used books on war, peace and politics, with an emphasis on military affairs and conflict resolution.

946 Sligo Avenue, Silver Spring, MD 20910; (301) 589-2223. *Hours*: Mon-Sat, 11:30 am to 6:30 pm; Sun, 12 noon to 5 pm.

William F. Hale Books This store specializes in general antiquarian, first editions, illustrated books, art books and scholarly literature.

1222 31st Street NW, Washington, DC 20007; (202) 338-8272. *Hours*: Usually Mon-Sat, 12 noon to 6 pm. Call ahead.

Hearthstone Bookshop Hearthstone specializes in genealogy and related subjects, including Americana and local history. It also carries maps, genealogy software, preservation materials, family tree charts and forms, documents and photographs. Special orders are accepted for out-of-print books and even handpainted coats of arms. A search service is available, and the store will also undertake restoration of old photographs and/or repair and preservation of old documents.

Potomac Square, 8405H Richmond Highway, Alexandria, VA 22309; (703) 360-6900. *Hours*: Mon-Sat, 10 am to 5 pm (open Thurs until 8 pm).

Idle Time Books Idle Time carries current, used and out-of-print books on politics and current affairs, as well as memoirs, literature and a large selection of current periodicals.

2410 18th Street NW, Washington, DC 20009; (202) 232-4774. *Hours*: Daily, 11 am to 9 pm (or later).

Imagination Books This is an arcade of six used book shops which specialize in general interest, romance, works by and about African-Americans, science fiction, mysteries, war & peace, politics and more. You will find first and limited editions, illustrated books, and old, rare or out-of-print books. Search and library appraisal services are available.

946 Sligo Avenue, Silver Spring, MD 20910; (301)

589-2223. *Hours*: Mon-Sat, 11:30 am to 6:30 pm; Sun, 12 noon to 5 pm.

The Lantern (Bryn Mawr Bookstore)   The Lantern carries many used books on a wide range of subjects, including fiction, travel, literature, children's, biography, Washingtoniana, literary criticism, history, psychology, African-American studies, poetry, classics and reference books. It has an excellent section of 19th-century and rare books, and also carries antiques, including china, silver, oriental rugs and small furniture. Proceeds from the store support a nonprofit corporation.

3222 O Street NW, Washington, DC 20037; (202) 333-3222. *Hours*: Mon-Fri, 11 am to 4 pm; Sat, 11 am to 5 pm; Sun, 12 noon to 4 pm.

Richard McKay Used Books   Here you will find general interest used books, with large selections of children's books, reference, textbooks and fiction. The store also sells used audio books.

Newgate Shopping Center, Lee Highway & Sully Road, Centreville, VA 22020; (703) 830-4048. *Hours*: Mon-Sat, 10 am to 9 pm; Sun, 11 am to 7 pm.

The Old Forest Bookshops   Both of these stores, named after a well-known Peter Taylor short story, feature general interest used and remaindered books, with specialization in literature, history (concentrating on Americana) and art. Both locations also offer an extensive selection of titles on cooking, literary biography and criticism, philosophy, religion and other subjects.

• *Georgetown*   3145 Dumbarton Street NW, Washington, DC 20007; (202) 965-3842. *Hours*: Tues-Sat, 11 am to 7 pm; Sun, 12 noon to 6 pm.

• *Bethesda*   7921 Norfolk Avenue, Bethesda, MD 20814; (301) 656-2668. *Hours*: Tues-Sat, 11 am to 7 pm; Sun, 12 noon to 6 pm.

Old Soldier Books   Old Soldier carries new, used, rare and out-of-print Civil War books, autographs, letters, photographs and documents. It will also undertake publishing of reprints.

18779–B N. Frederick Avenue, Gaithersburg, MD 20879; (301) 963-2929. *Hours*: Mon-Fri, 9 am to 4 pm; Sat, 9 am to 3 pm.

Ptak Books   Ptak specializes in out-of-print, uncommon and rare science books in such subjects as the history of science, math, medicine, logic, technical and electrical engineering. The store also carries antiquarian maps, patent models and 19th-century technical drawings.

1531 33rd Street, NW, Washington, DC 20007; (202) 337-2878. *Hours*: Wed-Sat, 11 am to 6 pm. Call ahead.

R. Quick, Bookseller   Here you will find general interest rare and out-of-print books, mostly nonfiction titles. There is an emphasis on history, standard classics, cookbooks and children's books.

Montgomery Farm Women's Cooperative Market, 7155 Wisconsin Avenue, Bethesda, MD 20814; (301) 652-2291. *Hours*: Wed-Sat, 9 am to 3 pm. Additional hours by appointment.

Reston's Used Book Shop   This shop features a complete selection of used fiction and nonfiction books on all subjects.

Lake Anne Center, 1623 Washington Plaza, Reston, VA 22090; (703) 435-9772. *Hours*: Mon-Fri, 10 am to 7 pm; Sat, 10 am to 6 pm; Sun, 12 noon to 5 pm.

Rock Creek Bookshop   The shop carries many used books, with an emphasis on history, biography, military (especially the Civil War) and philosophy.

1214 Wisconsin Avenue, NW, Washington, DC 20007; (202) 342-8046. *Hours*: Mon-Sat, 1 pm to 7 pm.

Secondhand Prose   Located directly across the street from Politics & Prose, this is P&P's well-stocked secondhand outlet, featuring literature, fiction, biography, history, mystery, philosophy, poetry, psychology and records.

5010 Connecticut Avenue NW, Washington, DC 20008; (202) 364-8280. *Hours*: Tues-Fri, 11 am to 7 pm; Sat, 10 am to 6 pm; Sun, 12 noon to 6 pm.

Second Story Books   This local chain of two general interest bookstores features used, rare and out-of-print books on all subjects. Facsimile editions, fine binding, first and limited editions are all on sale. The store also stocks remainders and some half-price new books. Book appraising and search service are available.

- *Bethesda*   4836 Bethesda Avenue, Bethesda, MD 20814; (301) 656-0170. *Hours*: Daily, 10 am to 10 pm.

- *Dupont Circle*   2000 P Street NW, Washington, DC 20036; (202) 659-8884. *Hours*: Daily, 10 am to 10 pm.

Stewart's Stamp & Book Store   This store carries general interest used books, with an emphasis on history (especially military history). It also carries stamps and supplies for collectors, plus postcards and military board games.

6504 Old Branch Avenue, Camp Springs, MD 20748; (301) 449-6766. *Hours*: Tues-Fri, 11 am to 5:30 pm; Sat, 10 am to 4:30 pm.

Tales Retold   Tales Retold carries general interest used books, with an emphasis in biography, philosophy, religion and women's studies. It also carries literary T-shirts and postcards.

9399 Bonifant Street, Silver Spring, MD 20910. *Hours*: Mon-Sat, 10:30 am to 6 pm.

Waverly Auctions   Waverly holds public book auctions of fine and rare books on all subjects. Absentee and attending bidders are both welcome. The store also sells prints and autographs. Eight catalogues are available each year by subscription ($35).

4931 Cordell Avenue, Suite AA, Bethesda, MD 20814; (301) 951-8883. *Hours*: By appointment only.

Yesterday's Books   This store carries used and rare books on all subjects, including history, religion, Americana, ecology, mysteries, children's literature, fiction, poetry, art, science fiction, travel and more. There are large sections on literary criticism and *belles lettres*. A search service is available.

4702 Wisconsin Avenue NW, Washington, DC 20016; (202) 363-0581. *Hours*: Mon-Thurs, 11 am to 9 pm; Fri & Sat, 11 am to 10 pm; Sun, 1 pm to 7 pm.

U.S. Government

U.S. Government Printing Office Bookstores   All three of these bookstores carry hundreds of government publications on all subjects, including history, military history, outdoor leisure, the environment, foreign affairs, energy, environment, science and technology, transportation, aeronautics, space exploration, criminal justice, agriculture, employment, labor issues and business/finance.

• *Farragut West* 1510 H Street NW, Washington, DC 20005; (202) 653-5075. *Hours*: Mon-Fri, 9 am to 5 pm.

• *Laurel* 8660 Cherry Lane, Laurel, MD 20707; (301) 953-7974. *Hours*: Mon-Fri, 8 am to 3:45 pm.

• *U.S. Govt. Printing Office* 710 N. Capitol Street NW, Washington, DC 20401; (202) 275-2091. *Hours*: Mon-Fri, 8 am to 4 pm.

U.S. Pentagon Bookstore Within the world's largest office building one finds a store featuring a large selection of books on military studies, military reference, intelligence and technology. The store also carries Washingtoniana, children's books, mass market fiction, psychology, health, family, sports and cooking titles. A mail order service is available. The store's phone number for suggested reading is (703) 695-0868.

U.S. Pentagon, Arlington, VA 20301; (703) 295-0870. *Hours*: Mon-Fri, 8:30 am to 5 pm.

Women's

Lammas Bookstore This well-stocked feminist bookstore specializes in women's literature, feminist theory and non-sexist child rearing books. Lammas has large lesbian fiction and nonfiction sections, and also carries small press publications, records and cassettes by women artists, videos, gifts, games, newspapers, magazines and cards. The store, which is a ticket outlet for many community cultural events, also has a community bulletin board. Special orders are accepted.

1426 21st Street NW, Washington, DC 20036; (202) 775-8218. *Hours*: Mon-Sat, 11 am to 9 pm; Sun, 12 noon to 7 pm.

Favorite Hangouts
& Watering Holes

Many contemporary authors drink more than they write.

—MAXIM GORKY

As surely as they need air or water or especially food, writers need to break away from their word processors after the last paragraph is done. You can find them sometimes, huddled together in places buzzing with straight talk, friendly banter and a good story or two. In a comfortable watering hole, the loneliness of writing eases and falls away. It's a great way, as Hemingway said, to "refill the well."

The following 21 hangouts and watering holes, all located in the District of Columbia, come recommended by various authors who live and work here. As diverse as the writers they attract, these bars and restaurants represent a potpourri of atmospheres and personal styles. For this edition, the hands-down winner was The Tabard Inn, followed by the Brickskeller, Herb's, Quigley's & Quigley's II and the Round Robin Bar at the Willard Hotel.

The key word to remember in choosing any hangout is "character." Or maybe you'll just want to go to see some of the characters haunting the premises.

Au Pied de Cochon One of the few 24–hour bistros in town, the "foot of the pig" (as it translates from French) is a good place to rev up, wind down or grab a bite at any time of the day or night. Au Pied is the home of the "Original Yurchenko Shooter," so named because it is from this establishment that Soviet master spy Vitaly Yurchenko re-defected to the Soviet Union, leaving his young CIA escort waiting for his return. There's even a copper plaque on the north wall describing the incident.

Au Pied de Cochon, 1335 Wisconsin Avenue NW, Washington, DC; (202) 333-5440.

The Brickskeller   Forget that old ditty about "99 Bottles of Beer." This place has more than 500 kinds of beer in its refrigerators from every corner of the globe. The basement alcoves are cozy and just right for long sessions of studious imbibing. A unique resource for any writer who must absorb the local flavors of far-flung locales. Just call it "research," and maybe your accountant will let you write it off at the end of the year.

The Brickskeller, 1523 22nd Street NW, Washington, DC; (202) 293-1885.

Café La Ruche   Here's a charming Georgetown hideaway near the C&O Canal where the desserts are heavenly and the atmosphere is down-to-earth. Taking its name from the French word for "beehive," Café La Ruche continues to give its patrons hours of rich, satisfying pleasure in thousand-plus calorie servings. Please ignore the evil stares from runners, joggers and walkers who may happen along and covet what you are eating.

Café La Ruche, 1039 31st Street NW, Washington, DC; (202) 965-2684.

Café Lautrec   French in motif and fare, this comfortable place is actually more bistro than cafe. It is, in any case, refreshingly free of snobbery. You'll recognize the establishment's small namesake looming large on the outside facade. And, for entertainment, bar tap-dancer John Forges keeps things hopping when he's in town. At the right moment—sipping a coffee-and-liqueur drink, feeling the ratta-tat-tat atop the bar, listening to the whoops and delighted laughter of nighttime patrons—you may imagine yourself being transported back to Paris during the 1920s.

Café Lautrec, 2431 18th Street NW, Washington, DC; (202) 265-6436.

The Childe Harold   This loud, happy, crowded place proudly takes its name from Lord Byron's famous epic hero. You'll find lots of nooks and crannies to hide in, and an all-over-the-map jukebox to please every musical taste.

Childe Harold, 1610 20th Street NW, Washington, DC; (202) 483-6702.

Duke Zeibert's Wear your tie, fill your wallet and come otherwise well-heeled to this establishment, where one's table location signals one's place within the city's power circles. Here, well-known authors and journalists gather to bask in the glow of their successes and exchange lamentations over lazy agents and irascible editors. Duke's is a place where diners like to see each other and be seen.

Duke Zeibert's, 1050 Connecticut Avenue NW, Washington, DC; (202) 466-3730.

Food for Thought A comfortable, reasonably priced place that evokes memories of the mid–1960s. Not long ago, the all-vegetarian menu finally made concessions to carnivores. On stage, local musicians ply their trade seven days a week: folk, contemporary, jazz and blues. Don't be surprised to find the musician's hat passed your way, because that's how the performers get paid. Check out the crammed bulletin board near the front door to see all that's happening in D.C.—underground, above ground and floating somewhere through the mystical ether.

Food for Thought, 1738 Connecticut Avenue, NW, Washington, DC; (202) 797-1095.

Hawk and Dove An elbows-on-the table pub popular with journalists who cover Capitol Hill and their sources. Here, you'll find a lively mix of ages and professions seeking to mingle and swap business cards.

Hawk and Dove, 329 Pennsylvania Avenue SE, Washington, DC; (202) 543-3300.

Herb's Owner Herb White has long been a friend and patron of local authors, and one of his walls is even covered with their book jackets. He's also set aside a large round table for a group of successful authors and media stars who meet every so often; call it The Algonquin Roundtable South. Theater, art and writers' groups often hold parties, benefits and celebrations here. Explore the garden seating in comfortable weather.

Herb's, 1615 Rhode Island Avenue NW, Washington, DC; (202) 333-4372.

Hotel Washington's Sky Terrace Offering one of the better aerial views of downtown Washington, including the National Mall, the Sky Terrace in this famous hotel near the White House is a lovely place to get away from it all. In a city scaled scrupulously low, the Sky Terrace gives its patrons the unusual opportunity to sip iced drinks while gazing down on the bustle of Capital ambitions. It's nice to feel above all that, if just for a little while. The Sky Terrace opens in early spring, and closes in fall when it starts to get cold.

Hotel Washington, 15th Street & Pennsylvania Avenue NW, Washington, DC; (202) 638-5900.

Jenkins Hill Saloon Those who write lean, trendy copy will feel at home in the glow of the overhead Tiffany shades. That smart clacking sound is being made by heels crossing the hardwood floors. Hot days are tempered by ceiling fans. When you order soda, say Perrier.

Jenkins Hill Saloon, 223 Pennsylvania Avenue SE, Washington, DC; (202) 544-6600.

Kramerbooks & Afterwords Combining a cafe with its bookstore, Kramerbook's unique blend of food for thought and food for real has been attracting grateful patrons for awhile. One may peruse the tables and shelves of hardbound and paperback books for a book that looks intriguing, then retire to a seat at the espresso bar or one of the cafe tables to savor the purchase. In temperate months, Afterwords serves patrons at sidewalk tables facing 19th Street.

Kramerbooks & Afterwords, 1517 Connecticut Avenue NW, Washington, DC; (202) 387-1462.

National Press Club Getting in can be tricky if you're not with a card-carrying member of the National Press Club. Once inside, you'll find a colorful atmosphere of heavy wood furnishings, rows of pictures of distinguished journalists from the past and several excellent bars filled with local and international newshounds of the present. Keep your ears open, and perhaps someone will reveal the real identity of Deep Throat.

National Press Club, 529 14th Street NW, Washington, DC; (202) 662-7500.

Old Ebbitt Grill Replete with a massive mahogany bar and expensive drinks with clever names, the Old Ebbitt serves nouvelle cuisine, hearty fare and a swell Sunday brunch. The soft lights and potted plants serve to put patrons at ease and invite reverie. The only reminder of the "old" Old Ebbitt, which used to be around the corner, are some of the hunting trophies still hanging on the walls.

Old Ebbitt Grill, 675 15th Street NW, Washington, DC; (202) 347-4800.

One Step Down One of Washington's finest jazz bars, the One Step Down is affordable, unpretentious and committed to straight-ahead jazz music, right down to a superb jukebox. While it's best enjoyed at night, the One Step Down is also open during the afternoons. Expect to pay a cover charge at night to keep the musicians alive and in the groove.

One Step Down, 2517 Pennsylvania Avenue NW, Washington, DC; (202) 331-8863.

The Post Pub A classic journalist's hangout, this small bar is a hop, skip and a dodged-libel from the offices of *The Washington Post*. But don't look for ferns in the windows. This is a "joint" and damned proud of it. It's the conditions that keep 'em coming back: reasonably priced libations, loud chatter, cigarette smoke, enthusiastic drink orders and plenty of inside scoops.

The Post Pub, 1422 L Street NW, Washington, DC; (202) 628-2111.

Quigley's & Quigley's II These two fine eating and drinking establishments feature large wood-carved bars and lots of booths and small tables for serious palavering. At the original Quigley's in upper Northwest, a group of young publishers, agents and other literary types has started meeting regularly there to plot the transformation of book publishing in the nation's capital. Watch this space for further details.

Quigley's, 3201 New Mexico Avenue NW, Washington, DC; (202) 966-0500. Quigley's II, 1825 I Street NW, Washington, DC; (202) 331-0150.

Sherrill's Bakery Now immortalized in an award-winning documentary, Sherrill's pulls a first-time patron back into a genuine time warp, circa 1948. At that time, however, the delightfully cranky waitresses were all younger than retirement age. Many faithful clients, including writers and Congressmen, drop in for breakfast, a pastry or just a little coffee-shop theater from the hard working crew.

Sherrill's Bakery, 233 Pennsylvania Avenue SE, Washington, DC; (202) 544-2480.

The Tabard Inn   Romancing the writer's life: fresh flowers, intimate seating and a quiet garden patio. Once the home of noted author, critic and chaplain Edward Everett Hale, the Tabard will make you feel as if you've been transported back to Washington as it was during the late–1800's. The front drawing room has a number of comfortable Victorian couches and divans, the bar is small and friendly, the food from the restaurant is savory and the parlor upstairs near the garden is an ideal place to sip after-dinner coffee or drinks.

The Tabard Inn, Hotel Tabard, 1739 N Street NW, Washington, DC; (202) 785-1277.

The Tune Inn   In a word: funky. The "eclectic" decor includes the heads of stuffed animals mixed in with political memorabilia. There's actually one other word for The Tune Inn: crowded. Choose the hour of your visit wisely. During lunch and happy hour, you'll discover harried waitresses wriggling through the throng of drinkers and eaters waiting for a spot to open in the rows of booths or along the bar.

The Tune Inn, 331 ½ Pennsylvania Avenue SE, Washington, DC; (202) 543-2725.

Willard Hotel's Round Robin Bar   Festooned in green velvet around a setting of heavy wood tables, chairs and booths, this stylish, circular saloon is steeped in tradition. Paintings of famous writers and American figures hang on the walls. Successive generations of journalists and lobbyists have hung out here since its creation. In fact, it was in the Willard's spectacular lobby that the term "lobbyist" was coined, due to the large crowds of men who would wait to seek special favors of Lincoln, Johnson and especially Grant.

Round Robin Bar, Willard Hotel, 1401 Pennsylvania Avenue NW, Washington, DC; (202) 637-7440/628-9100.

Index